THE PAST WE SHARE

THE
PAST WE SHARE

THE NEAR EASTERN ANCESTRY OF
WESTERN FOLK LITERATURE

E. L. RANELAGH

QUARTET BOOKS
LONDON MELBOURNE NEW YORK

TO VANCE RANDOLPH

First published by Quartet Books Limited 1979
A member of the Namara Group
27 Goodge Street W1P 1FD

Copyright © 1979 by E. L. Ranelagh

ISBN 0 7043 2234 X

Printed and Bound by
The Garden City Press Limited
Letchworth, Hertfordshire SG6 1JS

'The Tale of the Father of Farts' from *The Arabian Nights, The Book of the Thousand Nights and One Night* by Dr J. C. Mardrus, translated by Powys Mathers is reproduced by permission of Routledge & Kegan Paul Ltd, London, and St Martin's Press, Inc., New York; the tale of Dame Sirith from *Medieval Comic Tales* by Derek Brewer is reproduced by permission of D. S. Brewer Ltd, Ipswich; sections of the *Disciplina Clericalis* from *The Scholar's Guide* by Joseph R. Jones and John E. Keller are reproduced by permission of the Pontifical Institute of Mediaeval Studies, Toronto; the extract from *The Romance of Alexander the Great by Pseudo-Callisthenes* by Albert M. Wolohojian is reprinted by permission of Columbia University Press.

Contents

Acknowledgements

I thank the following people for their help and advice during the preparation of this book: Dr Jacob Teicher, Professor Otto Robert Frisch, Professor Bryce Gallie, Dr Malcolm Lyons and Ursula Lyons of the University of Cambridge; Dr Daniel D. Patterson of the University of North Carolina; Dr Paul F. Watson of the University of Pennsylvania; Dr Albert M. Wolohojian of Rutgers University; Tom Kjäras, John T. Taft, George Cardona and Diana Richmond. Particular thanks go to my editor Janet Law for perception and dedication, to kind John Boothe of Quartet Books and to Wilfrid Lockwood of the University of Cambridge library for his meticulous checking of the typescript and many, many good offices.

For the privilege of using the Cambridge University Library I cannot express enough gratitude; this book would not have been possible without it.

Illustrations

Author's Note

A note about the transliteration of Oriental proper and common nouns. It is consistent here with that generally used in scholarly works, except that diacritical marks (*macra,* dotted s, h, etc.) have been omitted as unhelpful to the non-orientalist. However, the transliteration of extracts quoted from other works has been left unaltered, thus, e.g., in my text 'wazir' but 'wezeer' in quotations from Lane's translation of *The Arabian Nights*.

Between the chapters, short selections in boxes give first the western and then the eastern versions of familiar tales and jokes.

Introduction

Not news for scholars but startling to the rest of us is the concept of a threefold source of western culture of which one part is Arabian.

We were taught that our civilization stemmed from classical and Christian roots, Graeco–Roman and Judeo–Christian, and that the classical elements had been largely lost until their rediscovery, known as the Renaissance. But now that the world is smaller, communication easier, organized religion more relaxed and scholarly exchange more widespread, our common ground with Arabian tradition is being recognized. Medieval culture was in fact Greek, Latin and Arab.

Greek literature reached us through the Romans and was therefore in Latin, but the great part of Greek knowledge which included the sciences and philosophy was handed down by the Byzantines through translation from Greek into Arabic, was further developed by the Arabs, and in the Middle Ages was conveyed from Arabic into Latin. The massive translation projects in twelfth-century Spain and Sicily were major bridges over which scientific learning was carried from the Arabs into the then primitive western Europe.

The Latin component stands especially for western Europe, for Christendom and the surviving Roman Empire, with the vast number of places, dates, differences, changes, forces and interpenetrations that those words imply, in addition to what remained from pagan Rome. Thus despite its Hebrew origins and Greek translations, the Bible is classed as Latin because in Latin it was a possession of the Church.

What concerns us most because it is unfamiliar is our Arab heritage. It is not one simple thing. The people known in the Middle Ages as Saracens came from various ethnic groups, among them Greeks, Persians, Indians, Copts, Turks, Armenians and Jews. Their ancient rich civilizations had been assimilated into the Byzantine and Persian empires, but the lightning spread of Islam in the seventh century imposed on them a new culture, that of their conquerors, which expressed itself in a new *Arabian* way of life. Its central fact was Islam, the official religion, and its medium of expression was Arabic, the language of the Koran. Yet underlying these unifying factors was the complex intellectual history which Arabic literature in the Middle Ages reflects. Part of this was the great float of folk narrative, often first recorded in India or Persia and thus classified as literature as well as folklore, but none the less primarily oral, which Arabic-speaking peoples shared and which they brought with them in their expansion into Europe.

Although the medieval was the seminal period of Arab influence, cross-cultural traffic continued. The Renaissance occurred. Classical manuscripts brought Greek literature into the orbit of western learning, where the vernacular languages replaced Latin. The modern world occurred, with an infinity of modes of acculturation. Today the term European, comprehending as it does not only both Greek and Latin-Christian pasts but also modern nationalities, represents the Greek and Latin sections of the medieval tripartite division. During the Middle Ages there were three separate factors; it is only from the time of the Renaissance that we can instead speak of two: a Europe and an East.

In the case of this book which deals with written lore and folklore, our comparisons are for the most part between English and Arabic, western Europe and Near and Middle East. Here are some of the literary and folk traditions which we share with Arab culture, ones that we perhaps thought were uniquely ours.

I

JOSEPH AND POTIPHAR'S WIFE

John Murray, Lord Byron's publisher, expressed a doubt 'as to the propriety of putting the name of Cain into the mouth of a Mussel-man'. Byron replied with a nicety which was perhaps lost on Murray, 'Do you suppose that no one but the Galileans are acquainted with Adam and Eve and Cain and Noah – why I might have had Solomon and Abraham and David and even Moses . . . When you know that Zuleika is the Persian poetical name for Potiphar's wife, on whom and Joseph there is a long poem in the Persian, this will not surprise you.'

We have to be told this all over again, for it does surprise us to learn that we share with the Koran 'our' Bible figures. Joseph's story is there too, like the others, different in detail from the Old Testament but very much the same account. The Potiphar's Wife episode appears as part of it, and it changes further in post-Koranic tales expanded from the Koran, of which the long poem by Jami to which Byron refers is the classic Persian example. By the time of Muhammad, the brief bald reference to the wife in Genesis 39 had already developed in the Near East, through stages of Hebrew commentary and folklore and through the mingling of these with Hellenized Hippolytus-Phaedra legends, into a not unsympathetic characterization. In their turn, commentators on the Koran and later writers added to the narrative and to the sympathy, until Yusuf and Zulaikha became the most popular love story in Islam.

On the other hand, in Christian countries, in addition to recording extraordinary devotion to God, the history of Joseph has the perennial appeal, not of a love story, but of a success story. Joseph is the single centre of attention, the favourite son who is given a coat of many colours, who is abandoned by his jealous

1

brothers and sold into Egypt, but who interprets the dream of fat years and lean years, becomes second in command to Pharaoh, and ultimately is the forgiving benefactor of his brothers.

In such a success story, an incident with his master's wife is simply a brief setback on a hero's upward path. But, underplayed as it is, it is this primitive form of Joseph and Potiphar's Wife which has through the centuries remained stable in the West – simply because of its place in biblical canon. It is the encounter described in Genesis which has given its name to a widespread folk-motif, that of the chaste youth and the lustful stepmother, although it is not the oldest analogue of this theme nor even the most characteristic in Judeo-Christian tradition. But thanks to the authority of Holy Writ, it was fixed for ever more in its Old Testament form and with the key words, Potiphar's Wife.

From the long story in Genesis 39, verses 1 to 23 are the relevant ones.

And Joseph was brought down to Egypt; and Potiphar, an officer of Pharaoh, captain of the guard, an Egyptian, bought him of the hands of the Ishmelites, which had brought him down thither.

2 And the Lord was with Joseph, and he was a prosperous man; and he was in the house of his master the Egyptian.

3 And his master saw that the Lord was with him, and that the Lord made all that he did to prosper in his hand.

4 And Joseph found grace in his sight, and he served him: and he made him overseer over his house, and all that he had he put into his hand.

5 And it came to pass from the time that he had made him overseer in his house, and over all that he had, that the Lord blessed the Egyptian's house for Joseph's sake; and the blessing of the Lord was upon all that he had in the house, and in the field.

6 And he left all that he had in Joseph's hand, save the bread which he did eat. And Joseph was a goodly person, and well favoured.

7 And it came to pass after these things, that his master's wife cast her eyes upon Joseph; and she said, Lie with me.

8 But he refused, and said unto his master's wife, Behold, my master wotteth not what is with me in the house, and he hath committed all that he hath to my hand;

9 There is none greater in this house than I; neither hath he kept back any thing from me but thee, because thou art his wife: how then can I do this great wickedness, and sin against God?

10 And it came to pass, as she spake to Joseph day by day, that he hearkened not unto her, to lie by her, or to be with her.

11   And it came to pass about this time, that Joseph went into the house to do his business; and there was none of the men of the house there within.

12   And she caught him by his garment, saying, Lie with me: and he left his garment in her hand, and fled, and got him out.

13   And it came to pass, when she saw that he had left his garment in her hand, and was fled forth,

14   That she called unto the men of her house, and spake unto them, saying, See, he hath brought in an Hebrew unto us to mock us; he came in unto me to lie with me, and I cried with a loud voice:

15   And it came to pass, when he heard that I lifted up my voice and cried, that he left his garment with me, and fled, and got him out.

16   And she laid up his garment by her, until his lord came home.

17   And she spake unto him according to these words, saying, The Hebrew servant, which thou hast brought unto us, came in unto me to mock me:

18   And it came to pass, as I lifted up my voice and cried, that he left his garment with me, and fled out.

19   And it came to pass, when his master heard the words of his wife, which she spake unto him, saying, After this manner did thy servant to me; that his wrath was kindled.

20   And Joseph's master took him, and put him into the prison, a place where the king's prisoners were bound: and he was there in the prison.

21   But the Lord was with Joseph, and shewed him mercy, and gave him favour in the sight of the keeper of the prison.

22   And the keeper of the prison committed to Joseph's hand all the prisoners that were in the prison; and whatsoever they did there, he was the doer of it.

23   The keeper of the prison looked not to any thing that was under his hand; because the Lord was with him, and that which he did, the Lord made it to prosper.

Here we have the nucleus of our story: Joseph, brought to Egypt as a slave, is sold to Potiphar who is an officer of Pharaoh. God makes his dealings for his master prosper and thus he wins a position of trust. Joseph's master's wife brazenly solicits him. Although he rebuffs her because he cannot sin against God, she continues her suit, and once, when no one else is in the house, she catches him by his garment, which he leaves in her hand as he runs out. She accuses Joseph to her husband's men and to her husband, whereupon Potiphar has Joseph imprisoned. But thanks to God's continued mercy, the prison keeper soon reinstates Joseph as a manager, and ultimately he becomes Pharaoh's prime minister.

3

This reflects a very basic Hebrew idea that the godly man will triumph, that he who does good will also do well. Joseph is handsome, trustworthy and clever at business, as well as chaste. The woman, on the other hand, is boldly lustful. In the face of temptation, Joseph invokes God and, even in prison, God benefits him. Although some details are specified, such as the actual words, 'Lie with me', and the particulars of the garment, the episode of Potiphar's Wife is dealt with in general terms and swiftly, so that the story-line can move on to the main theme, which is Joseph's material success and his ascendancy over his brothers. Potiphar's Wife is an unimportant incident showing, first, Joseph's obedience to God, and secondly, woman as the vessel of evil. The woman-as-evil element is presented as a matter of flat fact without sensuality or eroticism; instead, the point of absorbing interest is the righteousness of the man who will in due course be rewarded.

But the oldest recorded version of the chaste youth and the lustful mother-figure is not this one from the book of Genesis, which as it appears in the Bible was compiled from earlier documents at about the fifth century B.C. The oldest written redaction appears in an Egyptian folktale from a papyrus of about 1250 B.C. The tale itself, known as 'Anup and Bata' or 'The Two Brothers', must in fact be far older than the papyrus, because as an oral folk narrative it would have been current for many generations before being put into writing. Its folk elements are familiar. They include: advice from talking cows, obstacle flight, separable soul, evil prophecy, love through the sight of a hair, life token (foaming beer), and repeated reincarnation, as well as the Potiphar's Wife motif. Here the characters are Anup the elder brother, Bata the younger, and Anup's wife. Bata lives with Anup, and Anup's wife, having tried in vain to seduce him, accuses him to Anup. Anup waits to kill him, but Bata is warned by a talking cow and escapes across a magic river. Anup cannot reach him, but from the far bank Bata tells Anup of his false wife, whom Anup duly kills. Bata departs for further adventures, including a false wife of his own from whom he is eventually rescued by Anup. Bata succeeds to the throne of Pharaoh and calls Anup to share the kingdom with him. The latter part of this ancient tale is strikingly similar to the modern fairytale, 'The Two Brothers'.

The points here are first, that Anup and Bata is truly a folktale and can claim a prior history of centuries of oral circulation before 1250 B.C., and secondly, that the whole story is more comparable to the Bible account of Joseph in its entirety than the chaste youth-lustful wife incident alone might indicate. Both Joseph and Bata invoke the help of God, go on to wives of their own, live prosperously under the patronage of Pharaoh, are further involved with a loving brother (in Joseph's case, Benjamin) and do good to that brother. These resemblances strengthen the argument for a common origin of the two stories. If, as is believed, the historical Joseph lived in Egypt in the seventeenth century B.C., there would have been opportunity for his legend to be influenced by the Egyptian tale then current or, conversely, for the oral Hebrew legend of Joseph to have been taken over and adapted by the Egyptians.

As far as the seduction motif is concerned, some initiating myth or legend may have been known in the Near East from very remote times. If we disregard the dates of written recensions and hypothesize oral ones, a period as early as 2000–1500 B.C. can be assigned to an archetypal narrative. On the other hand, since in early polygamous societies there would have been a plethora of stepmothers, stories such as this would have served both as warnings to wives and rationalizations for the patriarchal view of women as temptresses. Therefore it seems equally reasonable to suggest that this particular folk theme could have arisen independently among various ancient peoples.

That it was written down independently by various peoples is a matter of fact. Its first appearance in Greek literature was in the *Iliad* in the eighth or seventh century B.C., where there are two passing references to lustful stepmothers. The *Iliad* antedates both Genesis and the famous play from fifth-century Athens, the *Hippolytus* of Euripides, which was so formative of future treatments of the theme. The play was based on the Theseus-Phaedra-Hippolytus triangle which was itself drawn from older Greek mythology, Theseus for example figuring in Cretan minotaur tradition dated as before 1500 B.C. Since there are many Egyptian-Cretan connections, 'Anup and Bata' may have influenced both the Old Testament Potiphar's Wife episode and the parallel stories in Greek mythology. The simple motif, however, that is, of the lustful stepmother who accuses the son, also appeared in India in the Buddhist *Jatakas circa* the third century B.C., from which it descended via Persia into the *Book of Sindibad*. This book became one of the most influential in all literature when, in the eighth century, it was translated into Arabic. Its diffusion through the Arab world brought it into many languages and titles East and West: *Sindban, Syntipas, Libro de los Engannos, Mischle Sindbad, Sindibad-nameh, Seven Vezirs, Sept Sages de Rome, Seven Sages of*

Rome, Seven Wise Masters, Dolopathos, part of the *Tuti-Nameh,* part of *The Arabian Nights.* All of these are frame-stories in which the innocent prince is bound to silence, but his tutor, or seven tutors, defend him with accounts of the wiles of women until he can speak for himself. Sindibad is the name of the one, or chief, tutor. We will return to the *Book of Sindibad* frequently. At any rate, it is in these four diverse literatures, Egyptian, Indian, Greek and Hebraic, that the ancient versions of the motif are recorded. For the simple story of Joseph and Potiphar's Wife, (not the frame-story) since the papyrus containing 'Anup and Bata' was not discovered until the nineteenth century, the determining literary sources have been accepted as being the Bible and the Hippolytus materials.

But it was also from Islam and in the Middle Ages that the Joseph and Zulaikha story spread to continental Europe and England. The Arab sphere of influence extended from Persia to Spain, in both of which countries this narrative was possibly the single most popular subject of medieval redaction – eighteen separate literary versions have been noted from Persia, and as yet uncounted 'Josephina' poems, plays and stories from Spain.

The immediate source of the Islamic Joseph legend was of course the Koran. Islam regards the historic leaders of the Jewish and Christian religions including Jesus as, like Muhammad, prophets of the one God. As we have seen, in his preaching Muhammad recounted again some of the stories of the Old Prophets as they are called, Joseph's among them. Muhammad's revelations were collected twenty years after the date (630) of his death, and were written down and called the Koran, which means *recitations.* Many of its *suras* or chapters are allusive and disjointed; the *sura* of Yusuf is unique in that only one subject is treated throughout and that it is a consecutive and developed narrative. Obviously, the figure of Yusuf had great appeal outside as well as within the Jewish and Christian communities; the Koran calls his 'the most beautiful of stories'.

But in the centuries between the writing of Genesis 39 and the speaking of Muhammad, a wealth of additional material had accrued in the Near East around biblical characters. Thus there was not only the text of Genesis as a source of the Koranic Yusuf, but also Jewish midrashic and haggadic commentary on the Bible, besides apocryphal booklore and folklore, on some of which Graeco-Oriental traditions of the chaste youth and lustful step-mother had already had an influence.

The most important document of these is the pseudoepigraphical *Testaments of the Twelve Patriarchs*, committed to writing by Hebrew scholars in Palestine at about 100 B.C., which purports to give the autobiographies of the twelve sons of Jacob. Of these, the testament of Joseph is, again, unique. The other testaments continue in the stark admonishing style of the early books of the Bible, but Joseph's testament reminisces in detail about his experience with Potiphar's Wife. Although for him the erotic element is overlaid with the fear of God, it is none the less there – and is thus a new departure. He is as usual shown praying, weeping and fasting, but now also as possessing natural human emotions.

Other points in which the testament of Joseph elaborates on the Bible verses are the following: some texts describe the Potiphar figure as a 'eunuch of Pharaoh'; the wife's rather summary wooing of Joseph is lengthened to cover a period of time; she both threatens Joseph with death and promises that he will be her master; she praises his reputation for chastity as a screen for evil; she bares herself and adorns herself to seduce him; she offers to kill her husband; she offers to convert; she pretends to be sick; she threatens suicide; Joseph warns her that suicide would allow a rival wife to mistreat her children; when Joseph is imprisoned after her accusation she still sees him regularly.

The *Midrash Rabbah* (*Midrash* means legendary commentary on the Bible and *rabbah* means great), which is believed to have been started by Ezra in 444 B.C. and continued until around A.D. 270, makes its own additions. To the proposition that Potiphar was a eunuch, it supplies the explanation that this was God's punishment for his having bought Joseph for the purpose of sodomy. Because of her direct speech, 'Lie with me', the wife is regarded as a harlot. She is cruel as well – she is said to have taunted Joseph while he was in prison and to have put a fork under his chin to force him to look at her. Joseph is shown as susceptible to temptation, though steadfast in resisting it.

It is thought that a lost haggadic story introduced a banquet scene where the wife's women friends cut their fingers at the sight of Joseph. (*Haggadah* is the legendary element in the *Talmud*.)

Another early record, that of Josephus whose *Antiquities of the Jews* was written in A.D. 93, furnishes only one new emphasis, but an influential one – the remark that Joseph's beauty was the cause for the wife's passion.

In addition to Hebrew tradition, Greek tradition affected the Islamic Yusuf. This was chiefly through the Hippolytus-Phaedra legend. And, as well, Hippolytus-Phaedra analogues may have also influenced the Jewish traditions which influenced the Arab traditions. The Hellenization of the Joseph story in the Near East, and possibly of the Anup and Bata story, would have made mutual acculturation inevitable even before the advent of Islam. The Hippolytus story itself was known extensively in the Hellenized world both through folklore and written romances. That Euripides was very much admired in the Near and Middle East is clear from Plutarch's *Life of Crassus*. It happened that just after Crassus' assassination and beheading, the celebration of a noble betrothal took place in Parthia. The banquet tables had been removed, and a tragic actor was singing from the *Bacchae* the part where Agave is about to appear with Pentheus' head in her hand. At this moment, the head of Crassus was thrown into the centre of the company; the actor seized it and went into the role of Agave. This from Parthians during a war with the Romans, the Parthians showing themselves as alive to Greek tradition as were the Roman inheritors of the Greeks. Of all Euripides' plays, the *Hippolytus* appears to have been especially popular. Mosaics of the second century in Antioch show scenes of Phaedra and the nurse, indicating a widespread familiarity such as Shakespeare's most famous plays have with us.

The Hippolytus story is strikingly different from Genesis 39 in these ways: Phaedra's love is of long duration; it is inflamed by the gods and thus is not her responsibility; she wastes away; the women of Troezen are her friends; and she also has a devoted nurse who warns her that if she dies her stepson will take precedence over her children; on being rebuffed she commits suicide, but accuses Hippolytus in a letter; he cannot clear himself because of an oath to the gods; he is cursed by Theseus and is killed. The focus of the play is almost as much on Phaedra as on Hippolytus, and she is seen as a victim of the gods rather than as a villain. Here, deity acts against the chaste youth as well as against the woman, while in the Jewish versions God is exclusively on the male side.

Comparisons, then, of the traditions current in Muhammad's time show the humanizing elements of classic Greek and Hellenistic narrative as opposed to the didactic intention and the strict patriarchal concept of the Hebrew. But modification of the Potiphar's Wife story had occurred, as we have seen, as early as the *Testaments of the Twelve Patriarchs*, where the wife's suit of Joseph is shown to have been of some duration, where her pretence to be sick and her threat of suicide are introduced, and where Joseph warns her that suicide would leave her children at a disadvantage. All of these points have parallels if not sources in the *Hippolytus*. Her threatening Joseph with death and at the same time offering him mastery, her use of his chastity as a screen, and her proposal to kill her husband, have parallels in other variants and descendants of the Phaedra legend.

The description of Potiphar as a eunuch, the woman's undressing and adornment in order to seduce, her offer to convert, her visits to Joseph in gaol, and the addition from the *Midrash Rabbah*, Joseph's susceptibility – all these appear to be Semitic details which will occur again in Islamic redactions. Joseph's beauty as the cause of passion, first noted by Josephus, is another narrative element which will be much developed by later writers. Greek motifs from the *Hippolytus* will also appear: the exoneration of the wife because her love is decreed by God, her wasting away, her women friends who witness her condition, and her nurse. These are more than mere narrative elements; they are important humanizing factors in the story.

The Yusuf *sura* (XII) in the Koran, read in context with what has gone before it, already shows this softening attitude to women, ascribable to Hellenization or to Muhammad's own view, while it retains the God-Joseph axis and the normal exhortation of the Hebraic recensions.

And there passed by a caravan, who sent their waterman to the pit. And when he had let down his pail, he cried: 'Rejoice! A boy!'

They took Joseph and concealed him among their goods. But Allah knew of what they did. They sold him for a trifling price, for a few pieces of silver. They cared nothing for him.

The Egyptian who bought him said to his wife: 'Use him kindly. He may prove useful to us, or we may adopt him as our son.'

Thus We found a home for Joseph, and taught him to interpret mysteries. Allah has power over all things, though most men may not know it. And when he reached maturity We bestowed on him wisdom and knowledge. Thus We reward the righteous.

His master's wife sought to seduce him. She bolted the doors and said: 'Come!'

'Allah forbid!' he replied. 'My lord has treated me with kindness. Wrongdoers never prosper.'

She made for him, and he himself would have yielded to her had he not been shown a veritable sign by his Lord. Thus We warded off from him indecency and evil, for he was one of Our faithful servants.

He raced her to the door, but as she clung to him she tore his shirt from behind. And at the door they met her husband.

She cried: 'Shall not the man who sought to violate your wife be thrown into prison or sternly punished?'

Joseph said: 'It was she who sought to seduce me.'

'If his shirt is torn from the front,' said one of her people, 'she is speaking the truth and he is lying. If it is torn from behind, then he is speaking the truth and she is lying.'

And when her husband saw Joseph's shirt rent from behind, he said to her: 'This is one of your tricks. Your cunning is great indeed! Joseph, say no more about this. Woman, ask pardon for your sin. You have done wrong.'

In the city women were saying: 'The Prince's wife has sought to seduce her servant. She has conceived a passion for him. It is clear that she has gone astray.'

When she heard of their intrigues, she invited them to a banquet at her house. To each she gave a knife, and ordered Joseph to present himself before them. When they saw him, they were amazed at him and cut their hands, exclaiming: 'Allah preserve us! This is no mortal, but a gracious angel.'

'This is the man,' she said, 'on whose account you reproached me. I sought to seduce him, but he was unyielding. If he declines to do my bidding, he shall be thrown into prison and held in scorn.'

'Lord,' said Joseph, 'sooner would I go to prison than give in to their advances. Shield me from their cunning, or I shall yield to them and lapse into folly.'

His Lord heard his prayer and warded off their wiles from him. He hears all and knows all.

Yet though they were convinced of his innocence, the Egyptians thought it right to imprison him for a time.

The growth of the Joseph story is obvious here. Striking additions are that Yusuf responds to the attraction of the woman and only a sign from his Lord keeps him from sin; that his coat is torn from behind and a witness proves his innocence from this; that the women guests at a banquet are so dazzled by his beauty that they cut their fingers and absolve their hostess from blame; and that the wife eventually publicly admits her guilt. Other changes stem from the prior suggestions we have seen in midrashic and other Hebrew tradition, expanded and influenced by Greek and Hellenized romances of Hippolytus.

Sura XII was to set the pattern for future compositions in the Near East, which were in their turn expanded. In it, the woman does not yet have a name, but she is the centre of the banquet scene which became the great set-piece of later Islamic redactions, and she is the centre of the household trial as well as of the public recantation scene. Despite these, *Sura* XII is still primarily about Yusuf.

Again we see how the authority of Holy Writ, this time of Islam, gave the story an enduring form, along with the stories of the other Old Testament figures in the Koran. But unlike the western, the eastern canon was not exclusive – it accepted extracanonical exegesis. So if we look for the standard Arabic account of Joseph and Potiphar's Wife, we must go beyond *Sura* XII to the amplified versions of Koranic commentators, who explained, interpreted, filled in elliptical passages and enlarged concise ones, continuing to draw on the pre-Islamic folklore that Muhammad and his audiences had taken for granted. Of the commentators, the most important are the two tenth-century writers, al-Kisaʻi and al-Thaʻlabi, each of whom wrote *Stories of the Prophets*. In both, Yusuf and Zulaikha appear. The following extract (translated by Ursula Lyons) is from al-Kisaʻi with variations from al-Thaʻlabi shown in italics.

And a woman came to the slave owner, called Qariʻa daughter of Tariq ibn al-Rawwad . . . and said: 'Oh master, I will buy this youth from you for his weight in gold, silver and jewels,' whereupon he replied: 'I am seeking a price higher than that.' So Zulaikha sent to her husband Qutaifar, saying: 'Buy him at whatever price he reaches and don't let anything deter you from him.' So he bought Joseph for an immense sum of money . . .

Then Qutaifar took Joseph to the castle of Zulaikha, daughter of 'Akahira, and said to her: 'Treat him well. We may be able to make use of him or take him as a son.' Zulaikha marvelled at Joseph's beauty and fell deeply in love with him. She said to him: 'How beautifully you speak and how wonderful and delightful you are!' Light glowed between his eyes and from his skin and flesh like a lamp in clear glass. He replied: 'Oh Zulaikha, if you saw me when dead, you would have nothing to do with me. You would find nothing more repulsive than me.' She continued: 'Oh Joseph, I am deeply in love with you and am forced to try to seduce you.' He replied: 'Oh Zulaikha, even after you have seen the signs, do you still intend to ignore them and commit a sin?' Zulaikha replied: 'How beautiful is your language even if I cannot understand it.' Joseph said: 'It is the language of my grandfather Abraham, and if it were not forbidden to polytheists, I would teach it to you. But if you wish, I will speak to you in Qamari [?].' She answered: 'I like the Haurani language, the language of the people of Egypt.'

Zulaikha said: 'Oh Joseph, how beautiful is your hair.' Joseph replied: 'This will be the first thing to fall from my body when I die.' Zulaikha said: 'Oh Joseph, how beautiful are your eyes.' He replied: 'They will be the first things to melt and flow on to the ground from my body.' Zulaikha said: 'Oh Joseph, how beautiful is your face.' Joseph said: 'God fashioned me in the womb. The dust will eat it.'

Zulaikha was not deterred from trying to seduce him a second time. So she built for herself a splendid house, decorated with every kind of embellishment and which she named the House of Pleasure and Delight. Then, after decking herself out, she set herself on her couch and, inviting Joseph, seated him upon a chair, then locked the doors and lowered the curtains. She then said: 'Oh Joseph, come here – in other words, I am yours and have dressed (for you).' But he answered: 'Where is your husband Qutaifar?' She replied: 'What have I got to do with him when you are my beloved and I am yours?' Joseph said: 'Oh Zulaikha, I fear that this house will become the House of Sorrow and a place in Hell.' She said: 'Oh Joseph, my heart loves you. Lift up your head and look at me in my beauty and loveliness.' But he replied: 'Your lord has more right to that than I have.' She went on: 'Come nearer, Joseph.' He replied: 'I am afraid I will lose my share of Paradise.' She said: 'But I have concealed all this from people, so come close to me.' He replied: 'Who will conceal me from the Lord and master of us all?'

Zulaikha said: 'Oh Joseph, my body is quite limp at the sight of your face.' Joseph said: 'Satan has set his mark on you for this.' Zulaikha said: 'The garden is on fire. Come, extinguish it.' Joseph replied: 'If I extinguish it, it will burn me.' Zulaikha said: 'Oh Joseph, the garden is parched, come, give it to drink.' Joseph replied: 'He who carries the key to it has more right to do so.' Zulaikha said: 'Oh Joseph, the silken carpet is spread for you, come gratify my need.' Joseph said: 'Then I will lose my share in Paradise.' Zulaikha said: 'Come with me under the covering and I will cover you with it.' Joseph replied: 'Nothing will cover me from the Almighty if I rebel against Him.' Zulaikha said: 'Joseph, put your hand on my chest and so restore me.' Joseph said: 'My master has a greater right to it than I.' Zulaikha replied: 'As for your master, I will give him a cup to drink containing a golden lily and his flesh will disintegrate and his bones will break. Then I will wrap him in brocade and throw him into a small room none will know of . . . Oh Joseph, I have many pearls, sapphires and emeralds and I will give you all to expend in pleasing your Lord in Heaven.' But Joseph refused, and Satan came and, striking with one hand on Joseph's side and the other on Zulaikha's, drew them together . . . Zulaikha wanted Joseph to sleep with her and he also, that is, he wanted her as a wife.

She said: 'If you don't, I will kill myself this very instant and will kill you, too.'

Then she rose and reached for a knife in order to kill herself, but this was a ruse on her part to deceive Joseph. He promptly seized the knife from her hand and threw it away. She then threw herself upon him and unfastened the seven fastenings of his trousers, one after the other. They desired each other, but just then Gabriel descended, appearing before Joseph in the form of his father Jacob *and struck with his hand on Joseph's chest and his desire went out through his fingertips. Jacob said: 'Do not lie with her. For if you will not, you will be as the bird in the heavens, but if you do, you will be like it when it falls dead to the ground, unable to defend itself'* . . .

He undid his trousers and sat in the posture of a man with his woman, when lo, a hand without wrist or arm intervened between them, on which was written, 'Beware of a day when you will return to God'. . . .

The wife of the ruler went to the idol, stopping in front of it, keeping a garment on. Joseph said to her: 'Why do you do that?' She said: 'I am ashamed that it should see us.' He replied: 'Are you ashamed before something that can neither see nor understand? But I am not ashamed before Him who created and knows all things.'

When Joseph saw this vision, he hastened to the door, but Zulaikha followed him and seized his shirt from behind, pulling off a strip. Joseph went in this state to the ruler who asked: 'What is the matter, oh youth?' He replied: 'Oh ruler, I have seen an abomination in your castle and it shames me to tell you your wife tried to seduce me.' He told Joseph: 'Go back, or else I will kill you.' So they went back together. When they entered the castle, Zulaikha rushed up (to the ruler) crying and saying: 'Should not someone guilty of a crime against a member of your household be punished, either by having a severe punishment dealt him or being put into prison?' Joseph said: 'Oh ruler, she attempted to seduce me, and she has put me in a difficult position ever since I came to this house.' Qutaifar would have struck Joseph with a sword he had with him had not God come to Joseph's rescue in the form of a witness from among Zulaikha's household in the castle. This was a sleeping child belonging to her sister, aged six months, to whom God gave speech, saying: 'Oh Qutaifar, don't be hasty. I heard the garment being torn. If Joseph's shirt is torn in front, then Zulaikha is telling the truth and he is lying, but if it is torn from behind, then she is the liar and he is telling the truth.'

When Qutaifar saw that Joseph's shirt was torn from behind, his anger against Joseph was stilled. Going up to Zulaikha he said: 'This is very deceitful of you,' and to Joseph he said: 'Oh Joseph, don't mention this or let people hear of it, or they will abuse me.' To Zulaikha he said: 'Ask forgiveness for this sin of yours, for you have indeed sinned.'

But the news spread around the city that the wife of the ruler had attempted to seduce her slave, and the women blamed Zulaikha and rebuked her for it and said: 'We can see she was clearly in the wrong.' When Zulaikha heard of their deceitfulness, she sent for them and prepared couches for them, food and rugs, and decorated the room. She invited the wife of the scribe, of the wazir, the tax collector, the head of chancellery and other wives of the ruler's companions. When they were all come, they sat down and Zulaikha gave them bowls of citrons and honey (*citrons, melons, bananas and pomegranates*) as was the custom before eating, and each was given a knife. Then she decked out Joseph in the finest apparel and said: 'Go to them, smile and look cheerful so they can behold your beauty and loveliness.' Then she went back to them and gave each a knife and a bowl with a citron. The women began to eat the citrons, and then she sent for Joseph, saying: 'Come to them.' So Joseph went in as ordered, and when he smiled his teeth were like a string of pearls and his face was like the full moon. When the women looked upon him, instantly all became infatuated with him, cutting their hands as they were cutting the citrons. They said to Zulaikha: 'Oh Zulaikha, never has there been a youth like this, for he captivates all who set eyes upon him.' Zulaikha replied: 'This is he about whom you blamed me. I tried to seduce him but he resisted my tempting. If he does not do what I will now order him, then he will be put in prison and be despised.' But Joseph replied: 'By God, I prefer prison to what you are asking of me.' Then Zulaikha asked the ruler's permission to imprison Joseph and this was granted, and she had him put in a narrow cell, alone, away from others . . .

[While in prison Joseph interprets the dreams of two fellow prisoners, servants of the king. One of these returns to the king's service; when the king has a dream, he recommends Joseph, who interprets it, foretelling the seven full years and the seven lean.]

A cupbearer informed Joseph: 'The king has ordered your release.' But Joseph answered: 'Go back to your lord and ask about the women who cut their hands with knives the day they looked on me.' So the cupbearer returned to the king and told him of Joseph's question. The king replied: 'He is right. Bring the women here.' But not all could come as some had (meanwhile) died. When they came before him, Zulaikha being among them, the king asked: 'What if I say that you tried to seduce Joseph?' But they remained silent with embarrassment before him. He repeated the question and they replied: 'God forbid. We know nothing evil about him.' Then Zulaikha spoke: 'Oh king, now the truth is revealed. It was I who tried to seduce him and he spoke the truth.' The king said: 'Bring him here and treat him well.' Then he summoned his wazir, giving him his crown, his sword and the horse he rode only on ceremonial occasions, and the wazir then went to Joseph and set him upon the king's horse and took him to the king who embraced him and seated him on the throne right under the dome . . .

When Joseph came out of the prison, he wrote on its door: 'This is the grave of the living and the house of sorrows, the trial of friends, the malice of enemies' . . .

[The prophesied famine has taken place. It is now in the seventh year. Qutaifar has died.]

But Zulaikha had undergone the same trials and famine as the rest of the people; she had sold all she possessed for food and had become Joseph's slave. One day she went to him, saying: 'Oh Joseph, praise be to him who made slaves kings, exalting them for their obedience, and who humbled the mighty in their rebellion (against Him). There is no God but God and

JOSEPH AND POTIPHAR'S WIFE

He has no companion.' Joseph asked her: 'Who are you, woman?' She replied: 'I am Zulaikha, the wife of the ruler,' and she told him of her need for food. Joseph wept and said: 'I will send you all you need and return to you all your possessions and slaves, and you will be a lady as before.' Then he married her in the presence of the king and princes of Egypt. And God restored to her her beauty and loveliness and youth. When Joseph consummated the marriage, he found she was a virgin, and she told him: 'No man has ever slept with me. My husband Qutaifar was not capable of doing so because he was impotent.' She later gave to Joseph two sons, one called Ephraim, the other Manassa.

Since the *Stories of the Prophets*, there have been many, many eastern rewritings of *Yusuf wa Zulaikha*. A recently discovered Muslim manuscript of the thirteenth or fourteenth century demonstrates how, although always within the tradition, new touches were possible for generations of redactors – even touches of humour. In this poem, Zulaikha chides her friends when they cut their fingers: ' "Gently with yourselves! Do not cut your hands, but cast down your eyes! . . . If you intercede for me with him, he may relent . . ." So they came to him, every one inviting his attention for herself, not for any other. He said, "I swear by God; they were one; now they have become many. How can I escape from them?" ' As a result, when Zulaikha 'in full finery' personally asks the King to punish him, Yusuf goes thankfully to gaol.[1]

In the fifteenth-century Persian poem to which Byron referred, Jami embroiders on more of these strands of pre-Koranic folklore that had gathered early on. His *Yusuf wa Zulaikha* opens with Adam's vision of his glorious descendants, of whom Yusuf is to be the most lovely of all men ever: 'beauty faded at the sight of him'. Zulaikha is a sheltered young princess who dreams three times of an ineffably beautiful man who tells her that she must preserve her love for him. When at last he says he is the Grand Wazir of Egypt, she insists on her father arranging a marriage with this unknown person. Too late, actually at her wedding in Egypt, she discovers that her husband is not he of the dreams. But she is reassured by the angel Gabriel that through him she will find her true love. And she does immediately, in fact en route from the wedding. She sees Yusuf for sale at the slave market, and she persuades her husband to buy him. Pharaoh himself also wants this attractive slave, but because the Wazir is a eunuch he is allowed to have Yusuf as a son. The narrative continues along the lines of the *Stories of the Prophets*, but is elaborated at length in every detail:

Zulaikha's nurse who aids and abets her, the palace of love, the banquet, Yusuf's imprisonment and release, his replacing Zulaikha's husband as Grand Wazir, the husband's subsequent death, Zulaikha's repentance, her abject poverty in a hut near Yusuf's path, her reunion with Yusuf, their marriage. On the other hand, the nurse confidante who instigates action and the fact that God pre-plans Zulaikha's fate recall the Hippolytus legends. But perhaps of most interest, we see that like the western literary tradition of Phaedra, the eastern tale is here centred on the woman.

It is now Zulaikha's story rather than Yusuf's. Far from being a lustful matron, she has been an innocent virgin steadfast to a God-inspired dream. After repentance and conversion, her dream comes true; she is restored to youth and beauty and exonerated of all blame.

Thus the Joseph narrative has come full circle: from Byron's ironic 'Galileans' whose version of it in the western Bible does indeed preserve the harshness of the land and the time of its writing, to its Islamic form which instead passes on the humanizing influences of eastern romance and realism.

The Emperor's New Clothes

Many years ago there was an emperor who was so fond of beautiful clothes that he spent all his money on his attire. In the town where his palace was, life was happy; and every day new visitors arrived. One day two swindlers came. They told everybody that they were weavers and could weave the most marvellous cloth. Not only were the colours and patterns beautiful, but the cloth had the quality of being invisible to anyone who was unfit for his office or unforgivably stupid.

'This is marvellous,' thought the emperor. 'Now if I had robes cut from that material, I should know which of my councillors was unfit for his office. They must weave some material for me!' And he gave the swindlers a lot of money to start work at once.

'I shall send my faithful prime minister to see how the weavers are getting along,' thought the emperor. 'He will know how to judge the material.' The good-natured old man stepped into the room where the weavers were working and saw the empty loom. 'God preserve me!' he thought, 'I cannot see a thing!'

'Tell us what you think of it,' they demanded.

'It is beautiful,' he mumbled, adjusting his glasses.

At last the emperor himself decided to see the cloth. Attended by the most important people in the empire, he entered the room where the weavers were working furiously on their empty loom.

'Isn't it *magnifique*?' asked the prime minister.

'I can't see a thing,' thought the emperor. 'Why, this is a disaster!' Aloud he said, 'It is very lovely, it has my approval.'

All the councillors advised him to have clothes cut and sewn to wear in the procession at the next great celebration. The night before the procession, the two swindlers didn't sleep at all. Everyone could see how busy they were. At last they announced: 'The emperor's new clothes are ready!'

The emperor came and the swindlers acted as if they were dressing him. Then he walked in the procession and all the people of the town said that his new clothes were beautiful. None of them were willing to admit that they hadn't seen a thing; never before had the emperor's clothes been such a success.

'But he doesn't have anything on!' cried a little child. And the people whispered among each other and repeated what the child had said. 'He has nothing on!' shouted all the people at last.

The emperor shivered, for he was certain that they were right; but he thought, 'I must bear it until the procession is over.' And he walked even more proudly.[1]

The Invisible Cloth

Three impostors came to a King and told him they were cloth-weavers, and could fabricate a cloth of so peculiar a nature that a legitimate son of his father could see the cloth; but if he were illegitimate, though believed to be legitimate, he could not see it.

Now the King was much pleased at this, thinking that by this means he would be able to distinguish the men in his kingdom who were legitimate sons of their supposed fathers from those who were not, and so be enabled to increase his treasures, for among the Moors only legitimate children inherit their father's property; and for this end he ordered a palace to be appropriated to the manufacture of this cloth. And these men, in order to convince him that they had no intention of deceiving him, agreed to be shut up in this palace until the cloth was manufactured.

The King, wishing to have the opinion of someone first, sent the Lord Chamberlain to see it, in order to know if they were deceiving him. When the Lord Chamberlain saw the workmen, he dared not admit he could not see the cloth, and when he returned to the King he stated that he had seen it; the King then determined to go himself.

On entering the palace and seeing the men at work, he began to feel very uneasy, fearing he might not be the son of the King, who was supposed to be his father, and that if he acknowledged he could not see the cloth he might lose his kingdom; under this impression he commenced praising the fabric. Things went on thus until there came a great feast, when all requested the King to be dressed in some of the cloth.

When the clothes were made and the feast day had arrived the weavers brought them to the King. When the King had professed to dress himself in this suit he mounted on horseback and rode into the city; but fortunately for him it was summer time. The people seeing his Majesty come in this manner were much surprised; but kept their surprise to themselves, fearing dishonour. Not so, however, with a negro, who, having nothing to lose, said, 'Sire, to me it matters not whose son I am, therefore I tell you that you are riding without any clothes.' On this the King commenced beating him, saying that he was not the legitimate son of his supposed father, and therefore it was that he could not see the cloth. But no sooner had the negro said this, than others were convinced of its truth, and said the same; until, at last, the King and all with him lost their fear of declaring the truth, and saw through the trick. When the weavers were sought for they were found to have fled, taking with them all they had received from the King.[2]

II

SOLOMON AND
THE QUEEN OF SHEBA

We do not need to argue the point that the Bible has been unique in shaping the education and the categorical structure of the West. For Protestants it is the exclusive religious authority. And while on the other hand the Catholic Church has allowed a place for legends and traditions even though they are not part of Scripture, its primary interest has of course been the New Testament. In modern times, the extra-biblical legends of the Old have been forgotten in the Christian world, so that the Old Testament remains for both Catholics and Protestants a closed canon. We have seen an example of this in the story of Joseph, which in the West is preserved today as it is in Genesis. Its addenda from Hebrew and Greek elaboration, being outside the Bible, have been forgotten.

But not so with Solomon, who comes to us attired in all the glory of extracanonical lore. Why this difference? Because in the case of Solomon, it was *Christian* extracanonical lore and was therefore preserved. Joseph, although mentioned in passing in the New Testament, has weight only in the Old, but Solomon, in addition to the accounts of his reign in I Kings and II Chronicles, is given significant importance in the New Testament. As Pritchard points out,[1] it is in one verse only, but that is enough: Matthew 12.42, which is repeated in Luke 11.31. In this, Jesus, angry at the Pharisees, says: 'The queen of the south shall rise up in the judgment with this generation, and shall condemn it: for she came from the uttermost parts of the earth to hear the wisdom of Solomon; and, behold, a greater than Solomon is here.'

These words of Jesus, which singled out the Queen of the South or of Sheba on her visit to Solomon, are what admitted Solomon as a subject of patristic exegesis, and what fixed the attention of the Christian world on Solomon and Sheba as a joint concern. Although Solomon alone is a familiar character in medieval wisdom literature and exempla, and as Sulaiman is a fabulous magus in eastern narratives, it is the dual theme that primarily interests us here, not Solomon alone nor Sheba alone, but their meeting. Their partnership as we shall see takes all the turns from bi-national diplomacy to demonism, religious conversion, royal union, even to saintliness.

But we begin with the account of the golden days of King Solomon in Jerusalem in the tenth century B.C. as written in the fourth or third century B.C. in I Kings 10.

And when the queen of Sheba heard of the fame of Solomon concerning the name of the Lord, she came to prove him with hard questions.

2   And she came to Jerusalem with a very great train, with camels that bare spices, and very much gold, and precious stones: and when she was come to Solomon, she communed with him of all that was in her heart.

3   And Solomon told her all her questions: there was not any thing hid from the king, which he told her not.

4   And when the queen of Sheba had seen all Solomon's wisdom and the house that he had built,

5   And the meat of his table, and the sitting of his servants, and the attendance of his ministers, and their apparel, and his cupbearers, and his ascent by which he went up unto the house of the Lord; there was no more spirit in her.

6   And she said to the king, It was a true report that I heard in mine own land of thy acts and of thy wisdom.

7   Howbeit I believed not the words, until I came, and mine eyes had seen it: and behold, the half was not told me: thy wisdom and prosperity exceedeth the fame which I heard.

8   Happy are thy men, happy are these thy servants, which stand continually before thee, and that hear thy wisdom.

9   Blessed be the Lord thy God, which delighted in thee, to set thee on the throne of Israel: because the Lord loved Israel for ever, therefore made he thee king, to do judgment and justice.

10   And she gave the king an hundred and twenty talents of gold, and of spices very great store, and precious stones: there came no more such abundance of spices as these which the queen of Sheba gave to king Solomon.

11   And the navy also of Hiram, that brought gold from Ophir, brought in from Ophir great plenty of almug trees, and precious stones.

12   And the king made of the almug trees pillars for the house of the Lord,

and for the king's house, harps also and psalteries for singers: there came no such almug trees, nor were seen unto this day.

13 And the king Solomon gave unto the queen of Sheba all her desire, whatsoever she asked, beside that which Solomon gave her of his royal bounty. So she turned and went to her own country, she and her servants.

As we have seen in the case of Joseph, rabbinical annotations to the Old Testament included the legendary and the marvellous, and secular writers, too, added to what came to be an extensive body of apocryphal literature. For the Solomon and Sheba story, the most important of these sources is the Second Targum, *Targum Sheni*, on the Book of Esther, written between the third and sixth centuries A.D. The material in it would of course be much older. While a targum properly speaking is an Aramaic translation of a scripture, this targum departs from the text altogether. The relevant part, which may be summarized as follows, is related to the Book of Esther only by an analogy between Ahasuerus' banquet and a feast given by Solomon.

Solomon gave a great feast to which he invited all the kings of the East and the West, the beasts, birds, reptiles, devils, demons and spirits. All came except the hoopoe. Angry, Solomon summoned the bird on pain of death. The hoopoe's excuse was that he had flown to a country famed for its incense and so wealthy that silver lay about in its streets, which was ruled by a woman. He offered to bring her back to Solomon. Solomon gave him a letter demanding the presence of the queen. In response she sent him a fleet loaded with pearls and precious stones, six hundred boys and girls of identical birth and appearance, and the promise to travel to him in less than half the normal time required for the journey – three years instead of seven – as she had questions to ask him.

At length she arrived in Solomon's kingdom and was conducted to a room paved with glass in which he was seated. Thinking he was surrounded by water, she raised the hem of her garments. Solomon saw that her feet were hairy and commented on hairiness that 'to a woman, it is a shame'. The queen asked her hard questions, three riddles. The first was 'Wooden well and iron pail that draws up stones and watery flow. What is it?' The answer was, 'A tube of kohl'. Next, 'Dust comes out of the earth and its foot is dust, it pours like water and it looks homeward.' The answer, 'Naphtha'. The third, 'Wind rushes through their tops, it cries, its head is like a rush, it is the praise of princes, the reproach of the poor, glory for the dead, grief for the living, joy for the birds, sorrow for the fish.' The answer was 'Flax'. Since Solomon had answered correctly, the queen acknowledged him as the wisest of men.

The *Midrash Mishle* on the Book of Proverbs gives different riddles, and there are still other Hebrew writings which vary the details of this tale and expand it. Although it is not clear how much of what accrued in *Targum Sheni* came before Arab influence and how much is a result of that influence, it is clear that this story is the basis of the Koranic version.

The queen is shown as completely virtuous. But introduced here is her abnormal hairiness. Because in the Near East hairiness was already associated with demons, this led to her subsequent identification in Jewish folklore with Lilith, the cloven-footed queen of demons. And there is as early as *Targum Sheni*, a sensual overtone in Solomon's remark which fits in with this, since Lilith symbolizes promiscuity and perversion.

Between these two extremes – virtue and evil – a mystery arose about Sheba which in subsequent development of the legend became a second narrative element, a theme of its own: Solomon's doubt as to whether she is an evil spirit or not. The trick of a pool of glass is probably an ancient folk motif, as it is found also in the *Mahabharata*,[2] but in Solomon narratives the pool was later explained as his device to see whether her feet were those of a human or a demon.

Another motif with a future is found in a variant version of the riddles: she asks which end of a sawn log was the root. Solomon has the log put in water; the end which sinks was the root. Thus a log of wood in water is brought into the story as a second association of the visit of the queen with a pool or stream.

A fourth element found in some of the Jewish legends is the marriage of Solomon and Sheba. Outside our scope here, this union was of course to be much expanded on in the Ethiopian national genealogy.

Pre-Islamic Arabic-Aramaic-Judaic interchange in the Near East therefore supplied the Sheba story with several concrete narrative motifs far removed from the Old Testament. And from this same cross-cultural milieu, affected also by Christians, came the sources of the Koranic version of the tale. For while Muhammad's religious message was original, his stories were drawn from oral tradition already familiar to his hearers. Folk tradition was especially rich in Arabia, which had assimilated not only Jewish and Christian Bible stories, but also the influences of the great civilizations of the past – Sumerian, Egyptian, Syrian, Greek and Persian. Thus, the narratives in the Koran may be taken as synthesizing many strands of both literary and oral lore. The Koranic account of the meeting of Sulaiman and the queen shows this: its core is still the biblical visit, but it is a different story from I Kings 10 and also from targum and midrash. In this extract from *Sura* XXVII the hoopoe is called the lapwing.[3]

And he reviewed the birds, and said, 'How is it that I see not the lapwing? Is it one of the absent?

Surely, with a severe chastisement will I chastise it, or I will certainly slaughter it, unless it bring me a clear excuse.'

Nor tarried it long ere it came and said, 'I have gained the knowledge that thou knowest not, and with sure tidings have I come to thee from Saba:

I found a woman reigning over them, gifted with everything, and she hath a splendid throne;

And I found her and her people worshipping the sun instead of God; and Satan hath made their works fair seeming to them, so that he hath turned them from the Way: wherefore they are not guided,

To the worship of God, who bringeth to light the secret things of heaven and earth, and knowest what *men* conceal and what they manifest:

God! there is no god but He! the lord of the glorious throne!'

He said, 'We shall see whether thou hast spoken truth, or whether thou art of them that lie.

Go with this my letter and throw it down to them: then turn away from them and await their answer.'

She said, 'O my nobles! an honourable letter hath been thrown down to me:

It is from Solomon; and it is *this*: "In the name of God, the Compassionate, the Merciful!

"Set not up yourselves against me, but come to me submitting (Muslims)." '

She said, 'O my nobles, advise me in mine affair: I decide it not without your concurrence.'

They said, 'We are endued with strength and are endued with mighty valour. – But to command is thine: See therefore what thou wilt command us.'

She said, 'Kings when they enter a city spoil it, and abase the mightiest of its people: and in like manner will these also do.

But I will send to them with a gift, and await what my envoys bring back.'

And when *the messenger* came to Solomon, he said, 'Aid ye me with riches? But what God hath given to me is better than what he hath given you: yet ye glory in your gifts:

Return to them: for we will surely come to them with forces which they cannot withstand, and we will drive them from *their land* humbled and contemptible.'

Said he, 'O nobles, which of you will bring me her throne before they come to me, submitting? (Muslims).'

An Efreet of the Djinn said: 'I will bring it thee ere thou risest from thy place: I have power for this and am trusty.'

And one who had the knowledge of Scripture said, 'I will bring it to thee in the twinkling of an eye.' And when he saw it set before him, he said, 'This is of the favour of my Lord, to try me whether I will be thankful or unthankful. And he who is thankful is thankful to his own behoof; and as for him who is unthankful – truly my Lord is self-sufficient, bounteous!'

Said he, 'Make her throne so that she know it not: we shall see whether she hath or hath not guidance.'

And when she came he said, 'Is thy throne like this?' She said, 'As though it were the same.' 'And we,' said he, 'have had knowledge given us before her, and have been Muslims.'

But the gods she had worshipped instead of God had led her astray: for she was of a people who believe not.

It was said to her, 'Enter the Palace': and when she saw it, she thought it a lake of water, and bared her legs. He said, 'It is a palace paved with glass.'

She said, 'O my Lord! I have sinned against my own soul, and I resign myself, with Solomon, to God the Lord of the Worlds.'

The essential point of the Koranic account is that it is a summons to sun-worshippers to belief in the one God. The queen (still unnamed) submits to Solomon not to give him personal homage, but because he represents the true faith. In this, it is different from *Targum Sheni* and from I Kings 10. The incident of the throne is also new – it is a miracle produced as evidence of the power of God and a test of the queen's confidence in her own judgment. She sees that she has been wrong and acknowledges God as Lord of the Worlds.

But, as we have noted, the accepted forms of the Koranic tales go beyond the Koran. They include details filled out by Arab storytellers who drew on that rich common lore from its diverse sources in the dim past as well as from a hodge-podge knowledge of the monotheistic religions around them. The tenth-century *Stories of the Prophets* are systematic collections of these detailed accounts. Together with the Koran, they make up what are in effect the standard Arabic versions. We have seen this in Joseph and Zulaikha; it occurs again with Solomon and Sheba. In them, the queen now has her Arab name, Bilqis; so has the hoopoe a name, so have various other people and places. Solomon's majestic entourage is paraded and described minutely, as are richness of clothing and setting. Motifs from *Targum Sheni* left out of the Koran are brought back, such as the identical boys and girls. Bilqis' demonic inheritance is explained. But her conversion and the removal of the symbolic demonic element, hair, are given a spiritual value, presaging a new birth or baptism, which occurs with her marriage to Solomon.

For a biography of Bilqis, al-Kisa'i in his *Stories of the Prophets* summarizes the tenth-century folk versions of her origins. A summary of his summary follows: additions from al-Tha'labi are shown in italic. The translation is by Ursula Lyons.

The city Saba was named after the first king of Yemen, who was the first to *saba*, capture, the Arabs. He built a hundred castles of marble and stone, with roofs of ivory and ebony, and had seven sons to each of whom he gave a kingdom. But all his works were destroyed by the bursting of the Ma'rib Dam. His descendants returned to the area, and the wazir of one of the descendants, Dhu Sharakh b. Haddal, a fine and handsome man, given to the chase, one day came to a place where there were many trees and he heard voices reciting and singing. He realized he was in the valley of the jinn. So he cried at the top of his voice, 'All you jinn, I have come to you tonight, so let me hear your songs.' So they sang him a line of poetry, and then there appeared before him 'Umaira, daughter of the king of the jinn.

Bilqis' father was a great king who ruled over all Yemen. He married a daughter of the jinn called Raihana 'for people at that time could see and mix with the jinn'.

When he saw her he became infatuated with her. He swooned, and was filled with love of her. He then asked the jinn, 'Who is this girl?' They replied, 'She is the daughter of our king.' He asked them, 'I would like you to bring the king so I can behold him.' So they brought the king and the wazir said, 'Greetings and honour to you, oh mighty king,' to which the king replied, 'And likewise to you. Who are you?' 'I am the wazir of the lord of the city of Saba. Will you allow me to marry your daughter?' And the king was interested in him because of his beauty, and married him to her, and she bore him Bilqis . . . When the months of her pregnancy ended, she gave birth to a girl, radiant as the sun, the peak of perfection. The girl was named Bilqis. Then her mother died and she was brought up by the daughters of the jinn, and she grew in beauty until she became known as the flower of the Yemen. When she grew up, she said to her father, 'Oh father, I don't like staying with the jinn. Take me to the land of men.' He replied, 'But men have a tyrannical king who takes by force all the virgins among his people, and I fear for you.' She said, 'Oh father, build me a castle outside his city and bring me to it, and you will see that nothing can happen to me there.' So he built her a castle and gave her a throne of ivory there, and she lived in it. Eventually the news of her reached the king.

Bilqis was ambitious for the throne on the death of her father. Some rebels chose a king but he proves a bad one and needs to be removed.

The king rode and came to the castle. He sent in his steward who beheld Bilqis in all her beauty and loveliness and then hurried back to tell the king. The king, summoning his wazir, said to him, 'You built this castle without telling me about it.' The wazir replied, 'I built this castle recently when blessed with this girl by a daughter of the king of the jinn, but her mother died and . . . I brought her to this castle.' The king said to the wazir, 'I want you to marry me to her.' The wazir replied, 'Willingly, with great pleasure, but I need her permission.' Whereupon her father returned to her and said, 'My dear daughter, what I feared for you has happened. The king has asked me for your hand in marriage.' She replied, 'Oh father, marry me to him, for I will kill him before he comes in unto me.' Her father returned to the king and told him (of her acceptance). He was delighted at the news and wrote her a letter in which he said, 'I have courted you without seeing you. When you have read my letter, make haste and come to me.'

Bilqis offers herself to the king and he accepts. 'It was only despair that prevented me from asking you in marriage first.' 'It is you alone I want, so collect the men of my people and ask for my hand in marriage from them.' They said, 'We do not think she will do this.' He said, 'No, it was she who asked me first.' They sought for evidence

28

from her and she confirmed it all to them – 'I would like a child . . .'

Bilqis wrote a reply. 'I long to see your face, but this castle of mine is built by the jinn: in it I have prepared high mattresses such as befit the like of you.' When he received her reply, he rose and put on his most magnificent clothes and set off accompanied by his nobles. But when he drew near the castle, Bilqis ordered her father to go out to the king and tell him to come to the castle alone, which he did. The king dismissed his soldiers and came into the castle unaccompanied. Now the castle had seven gates and at each gate there was a girl from the daughters of the jinn, all like the rising sun and bearing in their hands trays of gold containing coins, dirhams and dinars which they had been commanded to display to the king as soon as they saw him. This they did when he entered. He began to say to each one of them, 'You are my mistress,' but each would reply, 'No, I am a servant of hers, she is ahead of you.' Thus it continued till he reached the last of the gates. When Bilqis came out to him, her beauty and loveliness was such that he was nearly deprived of his sense. She brought up to him a table of gold on which were all kinds of foods, but he said, 'I have no need of these.' So she brought him to drink and began to pour out for him and he drank and moaned. Then she brought him wine and he became drunk and fell to the ground like a log of wood, motionless. So she went and cut off his head and told her servants, 'Take this infidel and conceal him in the sea, weighing him down with stones lest he appear on the water.' They carried out her request. Next she sent a letter asking that all the money and treasure in the king's storehouse be brought to her . . . She next summoned the wazirs and gave them to drink and told them, 'The king says you must bring him your women and your daughters.' They flew into a passion and cried, 'Isn't what has happened enough for him?' When she realized they were overcome with anger, she said, 'I'll go back and tell him of your anger.' She absented herself for an hour and then returned and said, 'I have told him what you said and he said, "I must have this".' Whereupon their anger increased and she said to them, 'Would you like me to kill him, so you will all find rest from his wickedness, and then I will rule over you?' They agreed to this and swore loyalty to her. Then she went away for an hour, then returned with the head of the king, and they rejoiced exceedingly and appointed her to rule over them, and she reigned for seventeen years . . .

29

Bilqis has the slain king's head set up on the door of his house. The people say, 'You are more deserving of the kingship than anyone else.' Bilqis replies, 'But for the disgrace and hellfire, I would not have killed him, but I saw how general his depravity had become, and I was overcome by scorn so I did what I did.' And they appointed her to rule over them.

Now the narrative proceeds with the syncretic standard story of Solomon and Bilqis.[4]

When Solomon, the son of David, had finished building Jerusalem, he decided to go to the holy land, Mecca. He made his preparations for the trip and brought with him men, jinn, demons, birds and wild animals; his army occupied a hundred parasangs – he ordered the wind to blow and it carried them there. When they arrived at the sanctuary, he stayed there for the time it pleased God, offered sacrifices, performed all the ceremonies, and announced to his people the coming of our prophet Muhammad. He told them that he would be the lord of the prophets and the seal of the apostles and that this would be established in their psalms.

Then he wished to go to Yemen. One morning he left Mecca, took the road there in the direction of the star Canopus, and arrived at Sanca at the time of sunset; this was normally a month's journey. He saw a beautiful country, green and rich, and wished to go into it to pray and eat, but no water could be found. The hoopoe used to be his guide because she saw water under the earth as easily as one would see a glass in his hand; she would pick the earth with her beak, recognizing the place and the depth of water. Then the demons would come and draw aside the earth as one scrapes skins and make water spring forth. Solomon demanded the hoopoe, did not find her, and threatened her. This is what had happened:

When Solomon wanted to stop, the hoopoe said to herself, 'He will be busy getting down', and she flew up into the sky, looking at the world long and wide, right and left, and saw the garden of Bilqis. She went towards its greenness and slowed down. The hoopoe of Yemen was there, near whom she descended. The hoopoe of Solomon was named Yafur and the one of Yemen, Afir. This one asked, 'Where do you come from and where are you going?' 'I come from Syria with my master, Solomon, son of David.' 'Who is this Solomon son of David?' 'The king of the jinn, of men, demons, animals and winds. And you, from where do you come?' 'I am of this country.' 'Who reigns here?' 'A woman.' 'What is her name?' 'She is called Bilqis. Your king Solomon is a powerful king, but Bilqis does not rule under his authority, because she governs over all Yemen; she has under her order twelve thousand kings each of whom commands a hundred thousand warriors. Would you like to come with me to see this queen?' 'I am afraid,' said the hoopoe, 'that Solomon may be searching for me at the time of prayer if he needs water.' The Yemen hoopoe said, 'Your master will be happy if you bring him word of this queen.' They went off together and went to Bilqis; she saw her and did not return to Solomon until the time of the prayer of 'asr (in the middle of the afternoon). When he got down, it was at this time; he asked the men for water. They said to him, 'We do not know these parts.' He asked the jinn and the demons; they made the same response. The hoopoe was absent; he did not find her and threatened her. [According to the account of Ibn 'Abbas a ray from the sun fell on Solomon's head; he looked and saw that the place of the hoopoe was empty.] He called 'Arif al-Tair – he was the vulture, and asked after the hoopoe. 'May God favour the king,' he replied, 'I do not know where she is; I have not sent her anywhere.'

Solomon was angry and said, 'I will inflict a terrible punishment on her or I will kill her.' Then he called the eagle, the lord of the birds, and said to him 'Bring me the hoopoe immediately.' The eagle lifted his flight to beneath the vault of the sky, and the world appeared to him like a plate before someone; he looked right and left and saw the hoopoe who was coming from Yemen. He swooped down on her. When she saw him coming with evil intentions, she enjoined him by God and said, 'By him who gave you your strength and power, have pity on me and do me no harm.' So the eagle stood aside from her and said, 'Wretch, would that your mother had had no children! The prophet Solomon has sworn that he will punish you or kill you.' Then they flew together towards the king. When they arrived at the camp, the vulture and all the birds came before them and said, 'Where have you been today? The prophet of God has threatened you,' and they told her what he had said. The hoopoe asked, 'Did he not make some condition?' 'Yes, he said, "Unless she brings me a convincing reason".' The hoopoe and the eagle flew and came to Solomon who was on his throne. 'Prophet of God,' said the eagle, 'I have brought you the hoopoe.' As she approached, she raised her head, lowered her tail and her wings and dragged them on the gound in humility. Solomon stretched his hand towards her head, seized her and said, 'Where were you? I shall inflict a hard punishment on you.' 'Prophet of God,' said she, 'think of your appearance at the court of God.' Hearing these words, the king trembled and said, 'Who kept you away far from me?' She replied, 'I have learned something you do not know and I bring you news of Sheba. I found a woman reigning over men; people provide her with all sorts of things. She is called Bilqis, daughter of al-Bashrakh, the same as al-Hadhhadh.'

When the hoopoe had recounted all this to Solomon, he said to her, 'We shall see if you are speaking the truth or if you are one of the liars.' Afterwards she showed them where the water was; they dug pits and the people and the beasts of burden drank because they were thirsty. Then Solomon wrote this letter to Bilqis: 'From the servant of God, Solomon son of David, to Bilqis queen of Sheba. In the name of God, the kind and merciful, greetings to him who follows the straight path. Next, do not rise up against me, and come to me as Muslims.'

When he had written this letter, he sealed it with musk, stamped it with his seal, gave it to the hoopoe and said to her, 'Bring this letter and bring back theirs, then turn away from them but stay near them to see what response they make.' The hoopoe took the letter and brought it to Bilqis who was three days from there, at Ma'rib, in the country of Sanca. The hoopoe arrived at the palace where all the doors were closed, because while the queen slept she closed the doors, took the keys and put them under her head after she had gone to bed. The hoopoe came to her while she was sleeping stretched on her back and threw the letter on her breast. Bilqis took it, because she knew how to read and write, being an Arab of the people of Tubba b. Sharahil the Himyarite. When she saw the seal, she trembled and cringed, because the power of Solomon was on his seal, and she recognized that the one who had sent her this letter was greater than she. 'Certainly,' she said, 'a king who has birds for messengers is a great king.' She read the letter. The hoopoe stayed a little to the rear. Then the queen went to sit on her royal throne, called her principal leaders. They were twelve thousand kings, each commanding a hundred thousand warriors; she spoke to them from behind a veil. When some matter troubled her, she uncovered her face. When they had gathered and were in place, she said to them, 'I have received an august letter which concludes thus: "In the name of God, the kind and merciful, do not rise up against me, and come to me as Muslims".' Then she added, 'O chiefs, clarify this for me and advise me on what is happening; I will decide nothing without your agreement.' They replied, 'We are powerful and brave in war; it is to you that authority belongs seeing that you command us. You will find us obedient to your orders.' When she saw that they were willing for war, she said to them, 'When kings enter a city they devastate it; they make the most noble of its inhabitants the most miserable. I will send to Solomon and his people gifts in accord with my position and by this I will test whether he is a king or a prophet. If he is a king, he will accept the gifts and go away; if he is a prophet, he will not agree to them and will be satisfied only if we follow him in his religion.'

She sent him boys and girls, all·dressed in the same way, and she added sheets of gold. When Solomon learned of it, he ordered the jinn to gild the bricks which he had placed along the route. When the ambassadors arrived, seeing the road thus garnished everywhere, they said to themselves, 'We have come bringing something which we see thrown about everywhere and to which no one pays attention.' Their gifts from then on had little value in their eyes. Wahb b. Munabbih and some others say that Bilqis sent five hundred young girls and five hundred young men; the girls were dressed in the clothes of men, caftans and belts, and the boys in the clothes of women: gold bracelets on their arms, collars of gold at their necks, buckles and pendants inlaid with all sorts of jewels on their ears.

The girls were carried by five hundred horses, on each of which there was a gold saddle encrusted with precious stones and covered in brocade of many colours. She sent to him also five hundred bricks of gold and five hundred of silver, a crown ornamented with pearls and rubies of great price, as well as musk, amber, aloes and fragrant wood. She sent him also a box in which she had placed an unpierced pearl and a cowrie shell with a hole across it. She sent one of the most noble of her people, called al-Mundhir b. 'Amr, and added to him others endowed with judgment and intelligence. She wrote a letter with the list of the gifts, in which she said to him, 'If you are a prophet, distinguish between the girls and the boys, tell us what is in the box before opening it, pierce the pearl with an equal opening and introduce a thread into the shell.' Then she gave advice to the young men and said to them, 'When Solomon speaks to you, use feminine language and gestures', and to the girls, 'Speak with hard words, like those of men'. She then said to the ambassador, 'When you go to him, if he gives you an angry look, you will know that he is a king and do not be afraid of his glance, because I am more powerful than he. But if you see something gracious and affable about him, you will know that he is a prophet, a messenger of God. Understand his language and bring back his response.' He departed with the gifts. When the hoopoe saw this, she hastened to return to Solomon and tell him the whole affair.

The king ordered the jinn to make bricks of gold and silver; they obeyed. Then he had them put them about nine parasangs away in the form of a plaza around which he had walls erected, covered with gold and silver, which was done. Then he asked them, 'What are the most beautiful animals which you have seen on earth or in the sea?' 'Prophet of God,' they replied, 'we have seen in the sea animals of many colours with wings, a mane and crests.' 'Bring them to me immediately.' They obeyed. 'Attach them to the right and the left of the salon and give them their food.' Then he said to the jinn, 'Bring me all your children.' He assembled around himself a vast crowd whom he put in lines to the right and the left; he ordered the demons to put themselves in ranks over several parasangs, and the same for the men, the savage animals, the wild animals, the domestic animals and the birds. They took up many parasangs to his right and his left. When the ambassadors approached, they arrived near the plaza; when they saw King Solomon, and animals of which they had never seen the equal befouling the bricks of gold and silver, they esteemed their gifts of no account and threw away the presents they had with them.

Viewing the plaza and the demons, they saw an extraordinary spectacle and trembled, but they were told, 'Pass, you have nothing to fear.' They advanced between the ranks of jinn, men, birds, savage animals, wild animals, until they came before Solomon. He gave them an amiable look with an open face and said to them, 'What do you wish?' The chief of the embassy told him what they had brought and gave him the letter from the queen. When he had read it, the king asked, 'Where is the box?' They gave

33

it to him. He shook it and Gabriel came to reveal to him what it contained. Solomon said to them, 'Within this there is an intact precious pearl and a shell pierced crossways.' 'You have said the truth,' replied the chief ambassador. 'Now pierce the pearl and pass a thread through the shell.' Solomon asked, 'Who will pierce it for me?' He asked the men, no one was capable of doing it, the same for the jinn. He asked the demons; they said to him, 'Send for the termite'. He had him searched for and when he arrived, the termite took a hair in his mouth and crossed the pearl from one end to the other. Solomon asked him, 'What do you wish in return?' 'To find my food in trees.' 'That is granted you.' Then he asked, 'Who will pass a thread through the shell?' The white ant said, 'I will, prophet of God.' He took the thread in his mouth, went into the hole and came out the other side. Solomon asked him, 'What do you wish?' 'To find my food in fruits.' 'That is granted you.' Then he distinguished between the girls and the boys by ordering them to wash their faces and hands. The girls poured water from a jug into one hand and then into the other, then they washed their faces with it, while the boys took the water into both hands and washed their faces. The girls took the water in the cup of their hands; the boys on the back; the girls splashed the water when they poured, the boys were careful. Thus he told them apart.

Next he refused all the gifts and said, 'Do you assist me with riches? What God has given me is worth more than what he has given you. You please yourselves with your gifts because you are people of rivalry and emulation in the world and you know nothing except that, but the world is not my concern, because most high God has put it in my power and has given me what he has given to no one in the universe. God has honoured me with the gift of prophecy and of wisdom.' Then, addressing al-Mundhir b. 'Amr, the head of the embassy, he added, 'Return with the gifts to your own people; we will go to find them with an army against which they cannot hold; we will expel wicked men if they do not come to us as Muslims.'

When Bilqis' embassy left Solomon, returned to her and told her what had happened, she said, 'This is not a king and we cannot resist him.' She sent to Solomon to say, 'I myself will go to find you with the kings of my people to see your authority and the religion you preach.' Then she ordered her throne to be built; it was placed within seven chambers entered one from another and their doors were closed and guards were stationed. Then she said to the one she left to govern in her absence, 'Protect what is trusted to you and especially the throne of my royalty; let no one approach it nor see it until I have returned.' Then she ordered the public crier to proclaim her departure for Solomon with twelve thousand kings, each commanding a hundred thousand warriors.

Solomon, Ibn 'Abbas says, was a redoubtable man, beginning nothing that he did not accomplish. He went out one day, seated on his royal throne and saw a cloud of dust. He asked, 'What's that?' They said,

'Prophet of God, it is Bilqis.' 'Has she got down at such and such a place?' 'Yes.' He advanced at the head of his army and asked, 'Who of you will bring me her throne before they come to us as Muslims?' An 'afrit said to him, 'I will bring it before you rise from your place.' Solomon said, 'I want someone quicker.' One who had knowledge of the Book said to him, 'I will bring it to you before you can blink.' Solomon looked in the direction of Yemen. God sent angels who transported the throne swiftly under the earth in such a way that it split to let it pass and it rose before Solomon. When he saw it standing before him, brought from Mareb to Syria in the space of a glance of the eye, he said, 'This comes by the favour of God to prove if I am grateful or ungrateful. Whoever is grateful profits by it and whoever is ungrateful, his Lord can do without his gratitude because he is generous and does good to the exclusion of who is ungrateful.' Then he said, 'Show her unknowing this throne, to see if she recognizes it or if she is of those ignorant people who cannot be guided.'

The demons feared that Solomon would marry her and have a child with her, so that the secrets of the jinn would be revealed to him, and they would not be delivered from the domination of Solomon and of his posterity after him. They wished that he would stay away from her, and they spread malicious tales about her, saying, 'There is something lacking in her wit and her feet are like donkey's hooves.' Solomon wished to test her intelligence by making her throne unrecognizable and to see her feet by building a room. When Bilqis arrived, she was asked, 'Is this your throne?' She replied, 'One would say that it was; it is like it.' Now she had left it behind, in a house, behind seven closed doors for which she had the keys. She wished neither to affirm nor deny it. Solomon recognized the perfection of her intelligence. When the salutations were ended, she was told, 'Enter this room.' Solomon had ordered the demons to construct a salon of glass, as if it were water; below it they made water run and they had put fish in it. Then in the front they placed a throne on which he sat and around him ranged the birds, the jinn, and the men. When Bilqis arrived and saw the salon, she believed it was a pool of water and uncovered her legs to cross it to approach Solomon. He looked and saw that she had beautiful legs, but they were hairy. At this sight, Solomon turned his eyes away and said, 'This is a salon covered with crystal.'

When she was seated, she said to him, 'Solomon, I would like to ask you something.' 'Ask.' 'What is the abundant water that comes from neither the earth or the sky?' When Solomon was asked anything he did not know, he addressed the men to know if they knew, if not, the jinn, if not, the demons. These last said to him, 'That's a very easy one; order the horses to run, then a vase can be filled with their sweat.' He replied to her, 'It is the sweat of horses.' 'You have spoken the truth; inform me of the existence of your Lord.' Then Solomon got up from his throne, prostrated himself and swooned. The queen rose and the entourage dispersed.

Then Gabriel came to him and said, 'Solomon, your master asks what is your state.' 'God knows best what she has said.' 'Your Lord orders you to go back to your throne, and that you send for her as well as for all your troops and hers and that you question her as well as her troops about what you were asked.' He did it. When they were entered and in place, he said to her, 'About what did you question me?' 'About an abundant water which comes neither from earth or heaven, and you replied.' 'And after that?' 'I did not question you except on that.' Then he asked the troops; they replied the same thing. God had made them forget everything. God made this response sufficient for Solomon. Then he preached Islam to her. She had seen the affair of the hoopoe, the gifts, the throne, the salon, and replied to him in these terms: 'Lord, I have acted unjustly towards myself, but I submit, like Solomon, to the will of God, the master of the worlds.' When she had submitted, Solomon wished to marry her, but in thinking of it he had some reluctance because he had seen the abundance of hair on her legs. 'How ugly that is!' he said. He asked the men how to get rid of it. 'The razor,' they said. She replied, 'Iron has never touched me.' Use of the razor was repugnant to Solomon and he said, 'She will cover her legs.' He asked the jinn who said to him, 'We do not know.' Then he asked the demons who made the same response. When he insisted, they said to him, 'We will employ a means which will make her white as snow.' Then they made use of a depilatory powder and a bath. Then Solomon married her. He loved her with a strong love, established her on her throne, and ordered the jinn to build three castles in the Yemen, of which the equal in height or beauty were never seen; they are Salhin, Ghumdan and Banyun. After he had sent her back to her realm, he visited her once a month and stayed three days with her.

We have seen that the account of a diplomatic visit of the Queen of the South to the court of King Solomon gave rise to Jewish and Muslim tales extra to the Bible and the Koran. In both these traditions, the queen has a touch of the demonic, since the *Stories of the Prophets* drew on the Jewish lore of the queen after she had been associated with evil spirits. Thus here, the jinn fear her marriage to Solomon, because of the belief that she was the daughter of a jinn or half-jinn. Therefore she and her children would know the secrets of the jinn, and their subjugation to the line of Solomon would continue. But in the legend, the marriage takes place none the less, and Arab stories emphasized in the union the conversion of Bilqis to the true faith. Later, Islamic religious writers saw a mystical interpretation, in which Solomon stood for the Perfect Man and Bilqis for the Soul turning away from the material world to seek for God.

The story of Bilqis is indeed complex. As W. M. Watt summarizes it, her encounter with Solomon can be seen as the 'encounter of two rival magics . . . Because the story was mentioned in the Koran it had *droit de cité* in Islam. It had already been developed somewhat in extra-biblical Jewish literature; and now in an Islamic context and with various specifically Islamic features it gathered to itself many themes from popular imaginative thinking'.[5]

Because of Jesus' words in Matthew 12, a Christian legend on the Queen of Sheba was also developing, in which visual art played a great part. Jesus, as recorded by Matthew, cited the queen as a prophetic witness to the Last Judgment because of her correct recognition of the wisdom of Solomon. The Old Testament references had told of her coming to his court with questions which Solomon answered, and bringing him gifts of gold and spices to which he responded with even greater gifts. This story was used by Hebrew commentators as an illustration of the glory and wisdom of the king and the submission of the Gentiles to Israel. Now, early Christian interpreters found it equally useful. Metaphorically, Jesus' statement authorized Solomon as a type of the Messiah and Sheba as a type of the Gentiles who converted to Christianity. Thus the two personages fell neatly into the biblical exegesis established by the Church Fathers, in which specific people and actions in the Old Testament were held to foretell specific ones in the New. The study of Christian symbolism in these pairs became known as typology. From about 1480, collections of types and anti-types were known from printed books, in particular from editions of works called the *Biblia Pauperum,* which were guides for priests, but were also indispensable to painters and others concerned with sacred art and iconography.

The queen's long journey from an exotic land became a prefiguration of the Adoration of the Magi: the Queen of the South was shown on the one hand, and the Three Kings of Orient on the other, the occasions linked by the fact that gifts were brought in devotion to the true God. Representations of these associated scenes are fairly widespread. Paul Watson[6] gives examples from a manuscript of the *Speculum Humanae Salvationis* from Alsace, manuscripts and printed copies of a South German *Biblia Pauperum,* a triptych painted in Madrid by a Flemish master, an illuminated Bible from Paris by the Boucicaut Master, stained glass in England at Canterbury Cathedral and in King's College Chapel, Cambridge, and preliminary oil sketches for Rubens' now lost paintings in the Jesuitenkirche, Antwerp.

As early as the seventh century, Isidore of Seville, followed 'almost word for word'[7] by his contemporary Bede in England, interpreted the queen as an allegory of the Church itself, 'which assembles from the utmost limits of the world to hear the voice of God'. Thus, she also developed into a type of the Christian community rather than merely of the converted Gentiles. She came to Solomon as the Church comes to Christ. Typology of this sort is found in medieval Europe in statues of Solomon and Sheba at the Baptistery in Parma, at the cathedrals of Chartres and Amiens and the coronation church at Rheims. Then, in the late Middle Ages, another aspect was given to the queen by including her in the legend of the True Cross. This first circulated in the thirteenth century in Byzantine and eastern folklore, and was then popularized in Europe by the bishop Jacobus da Voragine as one of the stories in his *Legenda Aurea*, a compilation of saints' legends that became the standard sourcebook of Renaissance religious painters.

According to this legend, when Adam was dying, the archangel Michael gave Adam's son, Seth, a branch (or three seeds, in some versions) from Paradise, of the Tree of the Knowledge of Good and Evil, telling him that when this would bear fruit, Adam would be made whole. Seth planted the branch on his father's grave and it grew prodigiously. With one of its boughs, Moses performed his miracles in Egypt and brought water out of the rock. Under this tree David sat when he bewailed his sins. By the time of Solomon, it surpassed all the trees of Lebanon. At his order it was cut down to use in building the Temple, but the resulting beam defied the workmen by being at times too short and at times too long. Angrily, Solomon had it thrown over the stream Cedron, so that all might trample on it as they crossed. When the Queen of Sheba approached his court with her retinue, there it was, a footbridge. But the Queen perceived the holiness of this piece of wood and refused to walk on it, preferring to wade through the stream instead.

The incident makes a scene of Solomon and Sheba much pictured in Tuscany, where the myth was especially popular because various churches there possessed relics of the True Cross. Agnolo Gaddi's frescoes (*c.* 1390) are in Santa Croce itself in Florence; there were also frescoes, now lost, in Volterra and Empoli. The most famous are possibly the cycle of the True Cross in Santo Francesco in Arezzo, painted by Piero della Francesca in 1464. In these Tuscan paintings, the queen is shown kneeling in reverence of the wood.

The story continues that Solomon then buried it, and later dug the pool of Bethesda on the same spot. The pond at once healed the sick, drawing its miraculous properties from the beam beneath it. When the time came for the crucifixion, the wood rose to the surface, and was thus discovered and used.

It had a subsequent history too. As Baring-Gould says, 'such is the Legend of the Cross, one of the wildest of medieval fantasies'. [8]

A development which started with the glass or watery floor is evident in the True Cross narrative. In some variants, Sheba is said to have had a deformed foot which was made normal as she waded through the brook – a rather tidy reverse of the demonic into a minor miracle, influenced doubtless by the later cures of the water of Bethesda. A connection with the riddle of the sawn log which Solomon put in water seems probable as well. It would be typical of oral transmission that various associations, perhaps dimly recalled, would be rationalized and re-used.

The attention throughout our story to the queen's feet doubtless led to another phase of folklore about her – the legend that she had a goose-foot. As Paul Watson describes her, she became 'the reine pedauque, a slightly sinister figure with one webbed foot . . . the European version of Talmudic and Islamic legend, and therefore sub-Christian'. The deformed foot of the True Cross story probably was a Christian western interpretation of the hairy-legged queen. Watson cites one, datable between 1154 and 1159, in which the queen is termed 'lady of Sheba and also of Ethiopia, and a Sybil, with goose-like feet and eyes shining like a star'. He points out that this motif had limited circulation, being found only in a few medieval German references, and that the goose-footed queens recorded as sculptured figures, now lost, which once adorned churches in Burgundy, probably derived from the same German scources. But Rabelais referred, if only indirectly, to an image of the reine pedauque, and of course so did Anatole France, much more recently. And, Watson tells us, her picture is still to be found on the label of 'a fine Beaujolais produced in Aloxe-Corton in upper Burgundy, not far from where the Romanesque statues were'. [9]

In direct contrast to a goose-footed Sheba are the representations of the courtly marriage of Solomon and the queen as types of Christ and the Church, as in Ghiberti's Solomon panel from the bronze Gates of Paradise installed at the Baptistery in Florence in 1452, and more secularly on various marriage chests decorated for wealthy Tuscan families.

From this exuberant western tradition of Sheba, what is left for us today? Because the Christian emphasis on the visit of the prophetic queen to the wise king preserved their meeting for western culture, the mainstream western image of Solomon was in connection with her, not of himself alone. But in the modern world, the influence of the religious past is now fading. In the West, we are left at best with a confused impression of the superlative ascendancy of a personage named Sheba. In Shaw's *Pygmalion*, Higgins says of Eliza: 'In three months, I could pass you off as the Queen of Sheba.' 'Who do you think you are, the Queen of Sheba?' is common folk-speech, a reaction to arrogant behaviour, uttered without any biblical knowledge whatsoever. Similarly, 'Oh, you Sheba!' is a comic-strip cat-call at a pretty girl. All we know is that this queen, whoever she was, was the most prestigious ever, and she was beautiful; perhaps nothing else remains. Her historic life is of interest only to archeologists; her demonic attributes are isolated in Jewish folklore which did not enter western tradition; her saintly days are confined to art of the past.

And if Solomon does even now have a place without Sheba in western culture, it is a minor one, consisting of the catch-phrase of his proverbial wisdom which is all that is left of a body of wisdom literature widely known in the Middle Ages. The story of his decision between the two women claiming the one baby is also still fresh, perpetuated in imitations such as *The Caucasian Chalk Circle* as well as in traditions. The legend of his temple continues too, if only because of its connection with the Masonic Order. But as a pair, Solomon and Sheba have gone out of the Christian West.

In the Near East on the other hand, in addition to the Koranic stories about both Solomon and the queen, Solomon occupies a place of enormous fame distinct from Bilqis. Down to the present century, Arab storytellers could still hold audiences night after night with variations of tales about him: the building of the temple by the master mason from Tyre; the blocks of stone hewn for it by the miraculous pebble Samur which the demon Sakhr procured from the sea-eagle; the canopy of all the birds flying together which protected Solomon from the sun; his magic carpet of green silk on which he travelled in a day from Syria to Afghanistan; his untold wealth; his thousand glass-roofed houses which contained three hundred couches and seven hundred wives; his throne of pure gold; his table of green beryls; the sun which stood still so that he could say his evening prayers; his imprisonment of evil jinn in vessels of lead; his signet-ring which was his chief instrument of magic and contained four jewels, each given by an angel, which brought to his aid angels, birds, powers over land and sea, powers over spirits; his wanderings when a devil tricked his ring from him and usurped his place; the ring found again inside a fish; and his judgments which, in contrast to all these marvels, were usually psychological common sense applied to detection of crime. After his death, he was buried in a cavern beyond the seven seas, seated on his throne, wearing his ring, surrounded by enormous treasure, and guarded by a serpent who killed those who approached. Thus Solomon the magus and the magician survives in Arab folklore even more vigorously than Solomon the prophet, consort of Bilqis.

So: in the Near East over the centuries, Solomon has been the important figure; the queen less important. But in the West, the meeting with Sheba, and Sheba herself, have made the impact. The situation is the reverse of the Joseph cycle, where the western view is of Joseph alone, while the eastern is the love story of Yusuf and Zulaikha. For although Christian tradition took for its own the one lady, and Muslim tradition took the other, in both cases popular imagination was caught by a figure of minor importance in Scripture whom exegesis built up to a major legend.

She Floated Upstream

They used to tell about the time old Dunk Hargrove's wife fell in the river, and everybody come out to help find the corpse. They was dragging the blue holes and shooting off dynamite down below the bridge. Pretty soon somebody seen old Dunk poking around brushpiles, away up above the place where she fell in. They thought he was just drunker than common, and turned around, but that wasn't it. He figured that Elsie was so contrary she wouldn't float downstream, no matter if she *was* dead.

The Contrary Wife

A man had a wife so contrary that she always did the reverse of what he commanded, and received in a surly manner the guests whom he often asked to dinner. One day he invited several to dine with him, and had the table set in the garden near a stream. His wife sat with her back to the water, at some distance from the table, and regarded the guests with an unfriendly face. Her husband said: 'Be cheerful to our guests, and draw nearer the table.' She, on the contrary, pushed her chair farther from the table and nearer the edge of the stream at her back. Her husband, noticing this, said angrily: 'Draw near the table.' She pushed her chair violently back and fell into the river and was drowned. Her husband, feigning great grief, entered a boat and began to seek his wife up the stream with a long pole. When his neighbours asked him why he looked for his wife up the stream instead of below as he should do, he answered: 'Do you not know that my wife always did what was contrary and never walked in the straight way? I verily believe that she has gone up against the current and not down with it like other people.'[1]

III

ALEXANDER THE GREAT

Chaucer could say, but we cannot:

> The storie of Alisaundre is so commune,
> That every wight that hath discrecioun
> Hath herd somewhat or al of his fortune.

Two thousand, three hundred years after his death and six hundred years after Chaucer's, it is difficult to give even a faint idea of the unique impact of Alexander the Great on mankind, since knowledge of him is now sealed up in books rather than freely available in folklore. The nearest comparison is Napoleon, whose image after less than two hundred years is also fading, but who is still the one name in modern history of whom every western wight has heard. Ask any teacher of a polycultural group, such as the Americans; or witness the proverbial delusion of the insane who 'thinks he is Napoleon'. Both Bonaparte and the historical Alexander embodied military genius, charisma, generosity, and the ability to organize empires and to plan and build on that grand scale, and the intellectual curiosity which so greatly furthered science and the arts. But Alexander also was the first of the world explorers, informed – as Pliny the Elder recounts – about the lands, people, flora, fauna and minerals of the known earth, and unsparing of himself in his search for the unknown. He founded eighteen new cities. He was the first westernizer of the East. By the time his legend coalesced in the Middle Ages, West and East shared the belief that Alexander the Great was in fact the greatest, ever, of men.

But the basic point about the European tradition of Alexander is that the accomplishments of his historical life, unsurpassed as they were and are, had little to do with his fame. The historical life of this phenomenal king of course started the original legends about him, doubtless even while he was still alive, but only his legendary life was popularly known in medieval times. Contemporary records had existed – the journal of his official historian, a nephew of Aristotle named Callisthenes, was one – but very little survived.

By the time Roman historical accounts of him were first written, about three hundred years after his death, even these had been influenced by legend, and in the general lapse of classical learning during the Dark Ages, his real career was forgotten. Thus it was that his fame grew not out of the facts, but out of the fascinating adventures known today as the Alexander Romance.

Most of the tales of Alexander in the Romance were in oral tradition in the Near East, where they were put together in a Greek manuscript probably in Alexandria and probably before A.D. 300. The manuscript was wrongly ascribed to Callisthenes and is therefore called the Pseudo-Callisthenes. The importance of the Pseudo-Callisthenes lies in its being the oldest extant source of Alexander's legendary life, and that through it, especially through one branch which stemmed from a lost Greek version translated in the tenth century into Latin by Archpriest Leo of Naples, the medieval West received most of the stories about him. A redaction of Leo known as the *Historia de Proeliis* was exceptionally widely diffused, not only in Latin but in the budding national languages as well; it was the source of some forty Alexander-books in nearly every European vernacular from England to Russia. Thus it is thanks to the Pseudo-Callisthenes that the Alexander Romance became the earliest and best-known of medieval epics, and Alexander the foremost hero in the medieval world.

This status is borne out by the frequency of Alexander stories in the medieval anecdotes called *exempla*, which flourished from the early twelfth century on. Exempla were literally examples, brief narratives told for and by clerics throughout Europe to illustrate Christian morality; their contents may be taken as an accurate measure of the knowledge then expected of the semi-educated or illiterate common man. Exempla were collected in books which tended to repeat from previous books the same allegories and warnings. The preachers who used them in sermons, pardons, pilgrimages, and other devotional occasions tried to interest as well as to edify their audiences, and like modern professional speakers – of whom they are the equivalent – knew the advantage of linking a story to a familiar name. In a comprehensive survey of exempla,[1] whose name is the most used? Alexander's. An index of exempla by numbered story type (disregarding the vast number of variants of each story) shows that he outplaces everyone else. Fifty-nine different types cite him as main subject. The Blessed Virgin is represented by only forty-eight; Charlemagne, the nearest man, has only eleven; our old friend Solomon a mere nine. Aristotle has seven, two

46

of which involve Alexander. Even Christ has fewer! Only fifty-seven. (The one figure who is more employed than Alexander is the devil, with one hundred and thirty-three exempla types.)

The references in exempla serve as a Gallup poll of the range of medieval knowledge, and of Alexander's pre-eminent place. In addition, exempla added in their turn to the popular concept of Alexander. But they themselves very often came from eastern sources, and for centuries before entering Europe had circulated in Near Eastern folklore, while the western image of Alexander, as we have mentioned, was established long before the time of European exempla, by the Alexander Romance in its dozens of titles and languages – descendants of the Pseudo-Callisthenes.

But long before that work, in fact soon after the death in Babylon in 323 B.C. of the historical Alexander, the legend of Alexander had come into being, gathering unto itself in the usual way the familiar local themes from religion, beliefs, earlier legends and folktales. However, in this case, the local area was unconfined; it was as wide and as multinational as Alexander's empire of over two million square miles. Greek, Hebrew, Palestinian, Syrian, Arabian, Cilician, Armenian, Babylonian, Egyptian, Median, Parthian, Persian, Afghan, Indian, et al. elements are therefore implied. These early traditions – which do not include the later dominating contributions of Christianity and Islam – are often still traceable in the basic 'package' of the Pseudo-Callisthenes. Indeed, if we question how the tales of the Near East became the tales of the West, few illustrations are more useful than the Pseudo-Callisthenes, which from the third century in Greek and the fourth century in Latin was available to the literate in the West in writing. But before, during, and after its diffusion in manuscripts, the material in the Alexander legend was passed along orally in the various local dialects of the folk. This would have occurred in the Europe of the Dark Ages when Graeco-Roman tradition and culture in general were in eclipse, the arts were non-representational and crude, and recreational literature and lore were subordinated to the Church. To the simple listeners of the time, our barbarian ancestors, this exciting story must have seemed like an enchantment, since the Pseudo-Callisthenes mixes the marvellous and the historic, the sensual and the ideal, in a way that is compelling even today – as we shall see.

The original Graeco-Egyptian fourth-century manuscript of the Pseudo-Callisthenes is lost, but a copy made in the thirteenth century has preserved a fifth-century translation from the Greek into Armenian that very closely follows it. Because the thirteenth-century Armenian copy has recently been translated into English, we have the happy circumstance of being able to read, as if just received from fifth-century Egypt, this Near Eastern progenitor of the western Alexander epics. In language and psychology it is strangely modern.

A History of the Great World Conqueror, Alexander of Macedon

A Life of Bravery and Heroic Deeds and, too, a Death Marked with Marvels

After they had determined the size of the earth and the sea and counted the stars of the sky, the wise men of the Egyptians imparted to the whole world power, the discovery and disposition of words, and the knowledge of practical skills. For it is said that the last king of Egypt, Nectanebos, after whom the kingdom fell from glory, conquered all men by magic sorcery; even the natural elements obeyed him. For if ever a marauding horde rose against him, he did not work at machines of warfare, stockpile arms, prepare man-killing iron weapons, nor did he proffer any ingenious devices. Rather, he went to his palace alone, took a basin, and, isolating himself, worked this sorcery of the basin. He poured spring water into his basin, and with his hands created ships and men from wax, and set the men upon the ships and put them into the basin: and the men came to life. And he, Nectanebos, took an ebony staff in his hand and by incantation invoked the gods of the earth and the spirits of the sky; and in this fashion, he baptized the ships which were in the basin. As they were being baptized, the ships which were coming against them by sea from their enemies were destroyed. And because of the masterful magic power of the man, his kingdom was at peace.

After much time had passed, certain men, who are called 'exploratores' by the Romans and scouts by the Armenians, came to Nectanebos and reported that a horde of soldiers had arrived. For the commander came to him and said: 'Great king, set aside the festivities of peace and turn to war, for there is a great assemblage at hand. For not one nation comes upon us but many; the Indians, Kauanians, Koumenians, Oxydarkians, Eberians, Konians, Lelapians, the Bomtyrians, Argives, Azanians, and the Loukhalians, and all the numberless nations that live in the East have reached Egypt with great armies. Recall the two Homeric verses: "It is not fit nor proper that the wise man, to whom the people and so many cares have been entrusted, remain at sleep the whole night." '

And after the commander said this, Nectanebos smiled awhile and he said: 'You spoke as was proper, which is fine; you are faithfully keeping your trust. However, you have spoken timorously and not as a soldier. For strength lies not in numbers but in the compulsion of desire; for one lion has caught many deer, and one wolf has harassed many flocks of sheep. So then, go with the soldiers assembled under your command and stand at your assigned watch; for with one word, I shall sink the barbarous hordes of countless nations in the waves of the sea.'

Having said this, he dismissed the commander, and got up and went into the palace; and he ordered all those within to leave. When he had isolated himself, he brought in the basin and set it down; and once again he performed the same act. Staring into the basin, he saw the gods of the Egyptians and they were leading the ships of the oncoming enemies from the barbarous nations – he was a man who was accustomed to being among and speaking with the gods magically through his sorcerer's skill. And upon learning that the kingdom of the Egyptians had come to an end, he filled his belt with much gold and silver and shaved his hair and his beard. Having disguised himself, he fled away, without anyone's knowing, through Pellousion; and after travelling through many lands, came to the Macedonian city of Pella. And clad in flaxen cloth, he sat there practising astrology as an Egyptian prophet, for he was really so skilled.

And when he was found not to be in the city, the Egyptians beseeched their god and asked him what had become of the king. And he who was god in the underworld of Sinopos delivered an oracle, speaking in this fashion: 'That king of yours who fled will come again into Egypt, not having aged but rejuvenated. He will subdue your enemies the Persians.' And when they had been given such an oracle by their gods, they sought to learn what these utterances could in fact mean. And they wrote them upon the pedestal beneath the statue of Nectanebos.

And in Macedon, Nectanebos became so famous to all by examining the natural order, that even the queen, Olympias, was to come and question him. For it happened in the time when Philip had left and gone to war. She ordered that the man be brought in to her for the examination of her affairs. And gladly coming in to see Olympias at her expressed wish, he stood stiffly before the queen without bowing; for he was pleasure-mad for women. He extended his hand and said, 'Rejoice and be glad, Thou queen of the Macedonians' – he who was formerly the 'Lord' did not think it fit to say 'Lady'. And Olympias replied, 'My joyful greetings upon you too, brave one; come, be seated.' And when he had gone and sat down, she said to him: 'Are you the learned astrologer, Nectanebos, renowned in every city? Supposedly those who have interrogated you have learned every truth from you. By doing what kind of scientific study do you recount the truth?' And he said: 'Queen, many are the researchers' ways of examining; for there are dream tellers, omen solvers, dream judgers, the seers of Ammon, basin gazers, birth readers, fortune tellers, fate tellers, who are called magi, and in their power rest all scientific matters.' And having said this, he looked sharply at Olympias for he was smitten with lustful desire. Olympias, the queen, said, 'Why did you stand stiffly upon seeing me?' He answered: 'Royal lady, I remembered the oracle once made by my gods that I am to consult with a queen and investigate her affairs; and what I learned from their responses is true. So now, say what you wish.'

And taking his hand out from beneath (his garment), he showed a table which no word nor effort can describe; for it was made of gold and ivory and showed seven stars: the ethereal astrologer, Aramazd, a sun of icy crystal, a moon of amaranthine, an Ares of hematite, an emerald Hermes, an Aphrodite of sapphire, and a Kronos of serpentine. And the horoscope was made of white marble. Olympias was amazed at the complex object and at the beautiful appearance of the stars. She came close to him and sat down and ordered all who were within to go out. She said to him: 'Examine my birth and Philip's; for it is rumoured that when he comes back from war, he is going to put me aside and take another wife.' And he told her, 'Set down your and Philip's birth sign.' And she asked, 'What is this you are doing?' Nectanebos set down also his own birth sign next to Olympias' and making his examination, said: 'The rumour you have heard is not false. Yes, that is in fact destined for you. But as an Egyptian prophet, I am able to help you, so that you will not be put aside by him; and, even if you are, you shall find the one who shall avenge you.' And Olympias said, 'Is that true?' And he replied: 'According to what you have presented me, you are destined to mate with an earthly god and to conceive from him; and after conceiving, to give birth and to nurse, and to have this (child) as your avenger of the wrongs which will come to you from Philip.' 'With which god?' asked Olympias, and he replied, 'With the god of the Lybians, Ammon.' Olympias went on, 'How tall is he, is he young or middle-aged, and what is his physical appearance?' And he said: 'He is white haired and has the horns of a ram above his jaws. Now then prepare yourself as a queen and a woman, for you shall see a dream concerning this and the god mated with you.' And Olympias replied, 'If I see the dream, I shall revere you not as a man but as a god.'

Nectanebos went forth from the palace and quickly picked and gathered a plant which he knew suitable for provoking dreams. And having rapidly done this, he made a female body of wax and wrote on the figure Olympias' name. Then he made a bed of wax and put on it the statue he had made of Olympias. He lit a fire and poured thereon the broth of the plant, saying over it the vows suited for these doings, until the spirits appeared to Olympias; for he saw, from the signs there, Ammon united with her. And he rose and said, 'My lady, you have conceived from me a boy child who shall be your avenger.'

And when Olympias awoke from her sleep, she was amazed at the learned diviner, and she said: 'I saw the dream and the god that you told me about, and now I wish to be united with him. Now let this be your concern; you should notify me at whatever hour he would mate with me, so that I might be found most ready for the bridegroom.' And he said: 'First of all, my lady, what you saw was a dream; but that very one who was the god in the dream is coming to unite with you. Allow me to sleep near you in the room, so that you be not afraid when the god is upon you.'

And she said: 'You have spoken wisely, Prophet. I shall give you access to my room; and if I experience the mating and conceive, I shall greatly honour you as an infallible seer, and I shall receive you as though you were father of the child.' Nectanebos said: 'The first harbinger of the god who is coming to you is this: when you go inside and sit in your room, you shall see a serpent come slithering to you. You are to order those who are there to leave. Do not extinguish the light of the lamps, go and recline on your couch and cover your face. Once again you shall see the god whom you saw come to you in your dreams.' Having thus spoken, he left.

And immediately she gave him another room there close to her chamber. And he prepared the softest fleece of a ram together with the horns from its head, and a staff and a white robe. And he made a serpent, and he made it soft and limp; and it slithered out of his hands. All of a sudden he set the serpent loose and it entered Olympias' bedroom. And when she saw it, she was not afraid, for she had been expecting it. And she bid those who were there to go away, each to his own place. And she reclined on the bed and covered her face; only out of the corner of her eye did she see him assuming the appearance which she saw in the dream. And he put aside the date-tree wood staff, got up onto the bed and turned Olympias toward him and mated with her. Then he put his right hand upon her side and said: 'Invincible and indomitable child. Long may you live, my lady, for you are pregnant with a boy child who shall be your avenger and become world conquering king of the whole civilized universe.' And having said this, he took his staff and left the room; and he hid the things he had.

And when it was morning, Olympias arose and came to Nectanebos' room. Awakening, he asked: 'My lady, what is it? Tell me; did your dream come true?' Olympias replied, 'Your words came true.' And he said, 'I rejoice with you, my lady.' And Olympias asked: 'Now is he not again to come to me? I await as a wife his coming and mating with me; for I received him with loving desire, Prophet. But I am surprised if this happened without your knowing, and you were not aware of it.' And he rejoiced for he was loved by the queen. He said: 'Listen, Olympias, I am the prophet of this god. If you will let me sleep here so that no one is disturbed or upset, I shall do the customary ablution for him and he will come to you.' And Olympias said, 'Let your will be done hereafter.' And she said to her doorkeepers, 'Give him the key to that room.' And when he acted, he did so secretly; and indeed he came to her as many times as Olympias desired that he come to her. Ahead of time, she let her wishes be known through the prophet, and he, as was his custom, mated with Olympias, giving the illusion that he was Ammon.

Her stomach was swelling, and she asked, 'Prophet, what shall I do if Philip comes and finds me pregnant?' And he said: 'Be not afraid, my lady, for the god Ammon is helping you in this matter; he will come to him in a dream, and inform him of what was destined to happen. And you are to be unreproached and unpunished by him.' Now depraved Olympias carried on in this fashion, revealing her true nature through the force of magic.

And Nectanebos made a sea falcon and bewitched it. And as quickly as he wished, he saw Philip in his dreams. And exercising his magic on the falcon, he spoke, and caused the falcon to fly. And having flown over land and sea, in two days and two nights it reached the place where Philip was (and spoke to him in a) dream (as he had been taught by Nectanebos. Upon seeing the dream), Philip woke up troubled, and he summoned Babylonios, the reader of dreams, and said to him: 'I saw, in a dream, a handsome white-haired god with the horns of a ram in his beard above his jaws. And he came in the night to my wife Olympias and lay with her. And upon rising, he said to her, "You have conceived from me a boy child who shall fructify you and shall avenge his father's death." And I seemed to patch up the womb of my wife with papyrus and to seal it with my seal. And the ring was of gold and the insignia, sunlike, with the head of a lion and a lance. And this is what I thought I had done when the falcon came to me and awoke me from my sleep with his wings and gave no sign.' The dream reader said to him: 'The dream that you saw is true, since your sealing the womb of your wife is a proof-laden oracle. For the seal is proof, indicating that your wife has become pregnant, for no one seals an empty vessel but rather a full and loaded one; and this, with papyrus. Since papyrus is found nowhere else but in Egypt, the man is Egyptian. And the seed is not vile but distinguished and glorious and radiant, especially because of the gold; for what is more glorious than gold, with which the gods are honoured. And as the seal showed the sun and had a head of a lion and lances, he who is begotten shall reach as far as the East, and act in every matter just as he pleases according to his desires, like a lion. And he shall spear down peoples and cities on account of the spear that is in the dream. As for your seeing the horned hoary god, he was the god of the Libyans, Ammon.'

When the interpreter of dreams had finished this explanation, Philip did not docilely hear of the pregnancy of his wife, even though he knew it was by the gods. And having won the war, he rushed back to Macedon. Meanwhile, Olympias was afraid, and Nectanebos comforted her.

And when Philip returned and went to the queen, Olympias came to him, but, on account of the above happenings, not confidently. Upon seeing her troubled, Philip said: 'My lady, you are not the cause of these things, for others are to blame; and what happened was pointed out to me in a dream so that you might be innocent and blameless. For we kings are able to do all things, but we can do nothing against the gods. For you were not smitten by any common vulgar man; nor was anyone cheaply covetous of your beauteous form; rather, it was the gods, who are all powerful.' By having said this, he sent Olympias away in a happy frame of mind. And she was grateful to the forewarning prophet. And thereafter Philip was with Olympias.

Meanwhile Nectanebos was there in the palace, but did not appear to anyone since he did not wish to. But he heard Philip saying, 'You were not made pregnant by the gods, but, in fact, were smitten by someone else whom I shall send forth from this life with pitiless tortures if he falls into my hands.' And Nectanebos heard what was being said.

And while they were celebrating the king's return, only the king was sad, because of his wife's becoming pregnant. And while the crowd was in merriment, Nectanebos transformed himself into the form of a serpent much bigger than the first. He passed through the palace breathing so fiercely that even the foundations quivered. And those who saw him fled away, startled and shaken by fear. Olympias recognizing her bridegroom was stunned and raised her right hand from her lap and extended it. And he circled the room, and then came to Olympias' knees, and flicked out his double-forked tongue and kissed her. The serpent thus, with positive proof, showed the spectators his loving embrace. But Philip was both frightened and amazed, and revealed his unawareness of its coming. And since Nectanebos did not wish to be seen too much by the audience, he transformed himself from the serpent into an eagle and flew away from there. As to where he went, it is unnecessary for me to say.

But Philip had been terribly frightened. When he regained his composure, he said: 'My lady, as sure proof, I saw the god come to help you in your peril. But, as to who the god was, I did not know, for he showed us the forms of Aramazd and of Ammon.' Olympias said, 'As he revealed himself to me at the time of mating with me, he is Ammon, the god of all the Libyans.' And when the king heard this, he considered himself blessed for 'I am destined,' he said, 'to be the father of a child of a god.'

And a few days later, Philip had gone and sat in a grove in the palace where there were many birds feeding. Suddenly, while he was busy with important affairs, a bird came and laid an egg on his lap and flew away. And the egg rolled from his lap to the ground and broke open. From it a little serpent came forth and circled it many times. Then, wanting to go back into the egg from which it emerged, it struck its head on the way in and died instantly.

And since Philip was much troubled, he sent for Antiphonta, who was a celebrated omen teller of that time. And he told him the omen that had occurred: the bird, the egg, the serpent, its circling, its death. And Antiphonta, because special information had been inspired in him by the will of the god, said: 'O King, you will have a son who, having traversed the whole world, shall subdue everyone by his strength and shall be subdued by no one; and while returning to his country, he shall die, having lived but for a short time. For the serpent is a royal animal, and the egg from which the serpent emerged, like the whole world. And when it had encircled the world and wanted to enter again the place from which it had emerged, it failed to do so and died.' The man interpreted the omen in this fashion and related it to him; and upon receiving presents from Philip, he departed.

And when the fixed birth span of nine months for the completion of the pregnancy had come to an end, Olympias went and sat on the child-bearing throne to give birth. And Nectanebos stood close by, measuring the heavenly position of the stars. And by directing the disturbed natural elements by his own power, he learned that the time was not right and he said: 'Control and restrain yourself, my lady, for the present time and be like the person who gave you birth. For if you give birth now, your offspring will be born in servitude or as a slave to others.'

When the woman was again impatient about having the child, for her many pains were unbearable, Nectanebos said, 'Be patient a little longer, Queen, for if you give birth now, your offspring will be castrated or deformed.' And Nectanebos comforted the woman with consoling words; and he put his hand on her natural passageways and learned what was needed. And Nectanebos, with his power, prevented the birth. He looked again into the heavenly stars at the position of the natural elements, and he recognized that the whole universe was in harmony and that Kronos had come into the middle of the sky. He saw a bolt of lightning in the sky at noon, caused by the power of the sun; and he said to Olympias, 'Give forth the cry of childbirth.' And he himself delivered her child and said, 'If you give birth now, O Queen, the one you bear is a world conqueror.' And Olympias cried out louder than a bull and gave birth to a boy child.

And when the boy fell to earth, there was an earthquake and thundering; and frequent lightning flashes appeared on the earth, while nearly the whole world trembled. And Philip said: 'I do not wish to rear that one, my lady, for he is not my offspring. But since I see that your seed is from the gods and that your birthgiving was accompanied by the omen of elemental occurrences, I shall rear him in the memory of my child who died, the one who had been born to me from my first wife; and he shall be called Alexander.' Because Philip spoke in this fashion, the child received proper care; and there were crowning festivities throughout Macedon, Pella, Thrace, and throughout the nations. And so as not to linger very long on the matters which concern the rearing of Alexander, I shall start from the beginning to tell of the attentions he received. For when he was weaned and developed in size and shape, he did not resemble in the least Philip and Olympias, and not even his father; but rather, he developed features of a singular type. For he had the hair of a lion and one eye was blue; the right one was heavy lidded and black, and the left one was blue; and his teeth were as sharp as fangs, and he looked upon a defensive attack the same as a lion would. And his personality very clearly indicated what the boy would be like. And in time he grew up and tried his wings at learning and at ruling.

His governess was Lakrine, the Celt, sister of Melanos; and his pedagogue and tutor was Leuonides, the Lakonian. The teacher of songs, Polinicos; and of music, Leucippos, the Lemnian; of geometry, Menechmos, the Peloponnesian; of rhetoric, Anaximenos Aristocles, the Lamphsakenian; and of philosophy, Aristotle of Nicomitachos, the Stagirite from the city of Meliteos. But Paphovranos mentioned these matters in the fourth book of his all-encompassing learned histories.

And Alexander became learned in every matter and trained himself so well, as I said before, that it became clearly evident that he was being taught by some divinity. When he was free from tutorial counselling, from time to time he umpired his fellow students. And when he saw a team being defeated, he joined in the battle, and then, in turn, it was victorious. Thus it was clear that the victory was of his doing.

And at that time, the stablers came and brought to Philip from his stables a huge, powerful horse. And they brought it and stood it before him and addressed him in this fashion. 'Lord King, we found this (creature), who is more beautiful and faster than Pegasus or than Arion, born in your stables, and we have brought him from Lamomentios and we offer him to you.' He was very surprised at seeing such great beauty and size, and said, 'I swear by my salvation that he is beautiful.' 'However, Lord,' they said, 'he is a man-eater.' And he observed: 'It is true that such things have happened among the Hellenes. For he received a nature that was disposed to good and evil. Now since he has become evil, take him away and shut him up in a cell; bridle him and imprison him so that we may throw before him anyone who, captured for a crime or a murder, falls under the laws of punishment.' Once the king had spoken, the action was faster than the words.

Meanwhile, Alexander was growing and maturing. When he was twelve years old, he began to work with his father. He armed himself and went forth with the troops, and he liked to ride on horseback. And he saw that Philip was not on good terms with Olympias. Olympias had called Nectanebos to her and said, 'Find out what Philip is thinking about me.' When he had investigated, he came and sat down with her. And Alexander asked, 'Father, are those heavenly stars which you are now talking about visible?' 'Surely, son,' he replied. 'Can I, too, see them?' and he said, 'You may, son.'

And when it was night, he took the child out of the city, and looked up into the sky and showed Alexander the stars. And Alexander seized him and took and threw him down into a pit. And he suffered severe blows on the neck in falling, and he said, 'Alexander, my child, why did you want to do that?' And he replied, 'Blame yourself, Astrologer.' And he asked, 'Why?' 'For,' he replied, 'while not knowing the earth, you seek to study the affairs of the heavens.' And he said: 'I am dying, Alexander, for I suffered grievous harm in falling. But nothing and no mortal person can conquer fate.' And the child asked, 'Why?' And he replied: 'I know how they had apportioned my life, for it was written that I was to be slain by my son. And I was not able to escape this lot, but have been slain by you.' And Alexander asked, 'Am I then your child?' And he replied, 'Indeed.' 'Really?' asked Alexander. 'That is true,' replied Nectanebos; and thus he told him of the flight from Egypt, the coming to Olympias, the inquiry into the stars, his desire, and how 'I went to her as my god and I mated with her.' Saying this, Nectanebos spat forth his spirit.

And upon learning that it was his father who had died, Alexander was afraid to leave him in the pit lest he be eaten by wild beasts, for it was night and the place was desolate. Moved by compassion and pity for his sire, he lifted him tenderly and bore him nobly on his shoulders within the gates. And coming before his mother, he told her everything that he had heard from the astrologer-magician. And Olympias was astonished and amazed; and she reproached herself, for, misled by deceptive and ingenious magic, she had committed adultery. Then she buried him, that very Nectanebos, as befitted the father of her child. She prepared a grave, and put him there.

It is astonishing to consider the destiny of Nectanebos. For the Egyptian came to Macedon and was shrouded and buried in the Greek fashion. While Alexander, who was Macedonian, came to Egypt and had a native burial befitting a god.

Meanwhile, after Philip had returned to his land and entered his palace, he sent to Delphi to get an oracle as to who would rule after him. And the oracle of Delphi, after drinking from the Castelian river of the underworld, spoke to him thus: 'Philip, he who mounts the bullheaded horse and rides through Hellas shall rule over the whole world and subdue all men with his spear.' And that horse was called bullheaded because he had on his thigh an unusual scar which had the shape of a steer. And when the king heard the oracle, he was ever watching for a new Heracles.

And Alexander educated himself only with Aristotle, the Stagirite. And as there were many children at Aristotle's for their education, and of these many were the sons of kings, the philosopher said to one of them, 'If you inherit your father's kingdom, what will you give your teacher?' And he replied, 'You shall live with me; and I shall appoint you co-ruler of my glorious kingdom.' And he asked another, 'And you, son, what will you do?' And he said, 'I shall make you my administrator, and I shall appoint you adviser of matters to be judged by me.' Questioning Alexander, he said, 'If you rule the fatherland of the Macedonians, what will you do?' And he was silent a long while; then he looked at his teacher and said: 'When you have no assurance of tomorrow, do you really seek to learn what is to be? Then shall I give what I shall pick and choose when Providence above decrees the time, hour and promise to be given.' And when Aristotle heard this, he said to Alexander, 'Hail, world conqueror, for you are destined to be a great emperor.'

And now Alexander was loved by all as a keen-witted, intelligent, and gifted warrior. But Philip was of two minds. For he rejoiced in seeing such a warring spirit in his son, but was saddened at seeing that he did not look like him. Meanwhile Alexander distributed as gifts to others many things which he had been sent by his father . . .

And when Alexander reached fourteen years of age, he happened to pass the place where the bullheaded horse was put away in a cell. He heard terrible neighing, and turning aside, Philip's son said: 'What is this noise? Is it the neighing of a horse or the cry of a lion?' Ptlomeos, who was afterwards called the Saviour, was following him and he said, 'Lord, this is the bullheaded horse which your father locked up and shut away for it is a man-eater.' When the horse heard Alexander's voice, he neighed a second time, not a terrible and frightening outcry, but sweet, pleasant, and gentle. It seems to me the bullheaded horse was commanded by a god to act thus with Alexander. His whole mien was calm and clear as he started forward; and how gentle was the suppliant manner he showed his master.

And when Alexander saw his new mien, and noticed the traces of the many men who had been put to death, he, as a man, felt pity. And he elbowed aside the guards and opened the grated doors of the cage. Trusting in his ancestry, he grabbed the halter of the horse and subdued him by physical strength rather than by luck, and he mounted him without a bridle. And immediately, someone ran off and recounted this to Philip. And he, recalling and remembering what had happened concerning this, went forth to meet his son. And he greeted him, saying, 'Hail, Alexander, conqueror of the world.' And Philip remained cheerful and happy in the secret and hidden hope for his son.

And one day when Alexander was fifteen years old, he found his father at leisure, and he embraced him and said, 'Father, I beg you to permit me to go by boat to Pisa.' Philip asked, 'Do you wish to see the Olympic contest?' The youth replied, 'No, father; I want to take part in the contest.' He questioned: 'And in what sport have you been trained so that you would try to do it? For I know that as the son of a king, you know nothing more than to take part in the war-horse exercises. You do not know how to fight nor wrestle, nor any other discipline.' Alexander replied, 'I wish to drive a chariot, father.' He said: 'I shall see; let horses from my stables be prepared for you and let them be brought immediately to you, and you concern yourself in a praiseworthy fashion with the care of training them.' He replied: 'Just give me permission to go. I have my own horse which I have trained from the time he was young and I have raised him for myself.' And he embraced him and was amazed at his eagerness; and he said, 'Son, if you so wish, go.'

And when he heard that he was going, he took the responsibility upon himself of ordering that a brand new ship be prepared and that the horses and chariots be put aboard. And sailing with Hephestion, his friend, he easily reached Pisa. And he went out and took lodgings after ordering the servants to exercise the horses frequently and to work them hard. And he went off to stroll with Hephestion. And he happened upon a man whose name was Nikolaos. He was a man of perfect stature, the king of the Akarnanians; and he was inflamed with the greatness of his possessions and with his good luck, two wavering gods; and he put his trust in bodily strength. He approached Alexander and greeted him at once, saying, 'Greetings and welcome, young man.' And he replied, 'Greetings to you, too, whoever you are and from wherever you may be.' And he asked: 'To whom indeed do you think you are talking? My name is Nikolaos, king of the Akarnanians.' And Alexander said: 'Don't be so arrogant, Nikolaos, about the glory of your kingship, nor deem ephemeral things sufficient. For good luck does not come and stand firm in one place; but the tides of change shift always, and we have to accept strange things.' And the other said to him: 'You said that very nicely. But why have you come here? For I recognize that you are the son of Philip of Macedon.' And he replied, 'I have not come here to participate in the horse-riding contest, for I am still a boy; and not in the two-horsed chariots and in no other such contest.' 'Then,' asked Nikolaos, 'what do you want?' 'I wish to drive a chariot.' Nikolaos, bilious with rage, scorned his size not knowing the mettle of his spirit. He spat at him and said, 'May no good come to you, nasty little boy.' And since he was well counselled and disciplined, he patiently refrained from an instinctive act and wiped off the saliva he had received from the enemy. And giving him a deadly smile, he said: 'Nikolaos, I swear to you by my foolish father and the wonderful womb of the mother who bore me that I shall conquer you here with the chariot and, in the land of the Akarnanians, I shall devastate you with my spear.' And they parted from one another, with spirits heated for battle.

And a few days later came the time set for the contest. Nine charioteers entered, of whom four were sons of kings: that very same Nikolaos, Xanthias the Boeotian, Kimon the Corinthian, and Alexander himself. The others were sons of generals and of satraps. The urn was placed; the trumpeters present apportioned the lots. First came Nikolaos; second, Xanthias; third, Kimon the Corinthian; fourth, Klitomachos, the Balkan; fifth, Aristippos, the Olynthian; sixth, Pieros, the Phokoean; seventh, Kimon the Laconian; eighth, Alexander, the Macedonian; ninth, Nicomachos, the Lokrian. They took their positions on the race track, each upon his chariot.

The trumpet sounded the call to contest. The gate was opened. They all rushed forth, and with a fearful charge sped through the first lap, the second, the third, and the fourth. And when the horses had been readied and had taken their positions, Alexander was the fourth charioteer. Behind him was Nikolaos, who was not thinking so much of winning as of slaying Alexander, for the father of Nikolaos had been killed in war by Philip.

Since keen-witted Alexander knew this, when those riding ahead fell to the ground, Alexander let Nikolaos pass ahead; and, not realizing the cunning trap, he gladly passed in front thinking he was to be crowned victor. And he stayed ahead for two laps at which point Nikolaos' right horse stumbled and the whole chariot, together with the charioteer, collapsed in a heap. And Alexander savagely attacked him with the charge of his horses, and Nikolaos perished. Alexander continued on. And there was a saying about his dying that goes thus: He who plots evil for another does it to himself; and a bad thought is very bad for the thinker.

And after Alexander had triumphed, he went to Olympian Aramazd to be crowned with a crown made of a wild olive bough. And the guardian of the shrine of Aramazd said to him: 'Olympian Aramazd first of all tells you this, Alexander: that just as you conquered Nikolaos, so shall you conquer many people by war.'

And thus, after Alexander had slain Nikolaos and had received a crown and superb honours worthy of a god, the conqueror went on to Macedon. He found his mother cast out by Philip; for he had taken in marriage as his wife his sister, Cleopatra, the daughter of Attanos.

And on the very same day that the wedding celebrations were taking place, he entered the dining hall with the Olympian crown on his head and said: 'Father, accept my first crown of victory. And when I give my mother as bride to some king, I shall call you to Olympias' wedding.' Having said this, he went and sat before the king. But Philip was disturbed over the words that had been spoken. And a certain man named Lysius, who was a parasite of Philip's, a dinner clown, a jester, was sitting there, and he said to Philip: 'Now that your and Cleopatra your wife's wedding is taking place, may you who are mighty in all cities have from her truly legitimate sons similar to you in appearance.'

And when Alexander heard this, he became angry; and he threw the goblet that he was holding and struck the buffoon's head and slew him. Seeing this, Philip stood up armed with a sword, and leaped at Alexander. But he struck his foot and stumbled upon the couch. When Alexander saw this, he remarked that he who had sped to take Asia and had captured all of Europe was not able to jump over the couch. Saying this, he snatched the sword away from his father and almost mortally wounded all those sitting there.

And before you, were to be seen the battles of the Lapiths and the Centaurs, and the things that happened because of the wedding of Perithias. For some of them crawled under the throne; and some danced with tables as though they were weapons; and others headed into dark places and fell. And there was a new Odysseus to be seen there as he went forth slaying Penelope's lovers; and he took his mother, whom he had avenged for the wedding festivities, inside; and his soldiers lifted Philip and lay him on the royal couch, performing their final duties.

And days later, Alexander went in to him and sitting near him said: 'Philip, I shall call you by your name lest it seem hard for you to be called father by me; for I have come to you not as your son, but as a friend to intercede in these things you have done. Now tell me this: Did Alexander do right in slaying Lysius for his unseemly words? And did you act rightly in attacking your own son, Alexander, and wanting to kill him? And also, in wanting to take another to wife, even though you were denied nothing by your former wife, Olympias? Now stand up and behave like yourself; for I know why you are feigning sickness. You are suffering not physically but spiritually for your sins. Now I beseech you to reconcile Olympias with you. I know that she will be persuaded for her son Alexander's sake, although you do not wish to be called his father.' He said this and left.

And he came to his mother, Olympias, and said: 'Mother, do not be angry about what your husband has done to you; for your own faults are hidden to him, and I am the son of an Egyptian father. Now go to him and entreat him to be reconciled with you, for it is proper that the wife obey the husband.' Having said this, he raised his mother to her feet, took her by the hand, and led her to Philip, and said: 'Turn this way; now I shall call you father, for you conceded to your son, Alexander. Now I have come here; and you have accepted my many entreaties to come to you and to forget faults. Now embrace one another. Nothing is shameful for you in front of me, for I am your offspring.' Speaking thus, he reconciled his parents, while all the Macedonians marvelled over him.

And people who want to get married invoke Lysius' name; and they do not remember that by naming him they, whose marriage is taking place, may be separated because of the slaying of Lysius.

Concerning the Subjugation of Mothone to His Father

There was a city named Mothone that had revolted from King Philip. Alexander's father sent him with his armies to make war upon them. And when he arrived at that place, he persuaded them, with the wisdom of his words, to heed and to submit, rather than be enslaved by the force of arms.

When he returned from the city of Mothone to his father and saw before him men in barbarian clothing, he inquired, 'Who are these men?' And they said, 'They are the satraps of Darius.' Alexander asked, 'Why have they come here?' And they replied, 'They are demanding the customary tribute from your father.' 'From whom were they sent here?' asked Alexander; and they replied, 'From the king of the Persians, Darius.' Alexander continued, 'Why do they demand tribute?' They answered and said, 'For the lands of Darius.' And Alexander said: 'The gods grant mankind these things as gifts to provide them food; and he is putting the gifts of the gods under tribute; it is not right that Philip give tribute to the barbarians.'

And since he himself wished to make the Hellenes subservient to his command, he called the barbarians and said: 'Go tell Darius that Alexander, the son of Philip, says this: that when my father was childless, he paid you tribute. But now that he has his son Alexander, he no longer gives you tribute. And furthermore, I shall not leave you the tribute which you have

taken from him, but am coming to demand it from you and bring it back.'
So speaking, he dismissed the messengers. And he did not deem him who
sent them worthy of a letter. And his father rejoiced upon seeing Alexander acting so boldly.

And when once again another Thracian city became disorderly and
revolted, Philip sent Alexander with great forces to make war upon
it.

And there was a Thessalonian nobleman by the name of Pausianos,
who had a large personal army and huge wealth. This man lusted for
Olympias, and secretly sent men who could gain her trust so that he might
persuade Olympias to leave Philip and become his wife. But Olympias did
not agree to do this. And Pausianos made the following plan upon learning
that Alexander was going to war and that there was a concert of perfor-
mers of all kinds of artistic songs taking place and that Philip was at the
concert. Pausianos, bared sword in hand, entered the theatre with other
brave men, intent on killing Philip so that he might abduct Olympias. And
with his sword he struck at Philip's side, and he struck him hard, but he did
not die. There was a huge crowd in the theatre, and Pausianos rushed to the
palace with the intention of abducting Olympias.

Meanwhile, on the same day, Alexander, having won the war, came
and entered the city and saw a big commotion. He asked the reason for it,
and they recounted what had happened and that Pausianos was in the
palace with Olympias. He had the soldiers force back the doors, and he
saw Olympias being embraced. He had Pausianos trapped and wanted to
hurl his iron lance at him, but was afraid that he might strike his mother.
And Olympias said, 'Throw your lance, my son, for Ammon sustains me,'
and Alexander threw it and struck and mortally wounded Pausianos. And
when he found out that there was still life in his father, he asked, 'What do
you desire?' And he said, 'Bring him to me.' And he took his sword and
put it in his father's hand; and he took the sword and slew Pausianos.

And Philip said: 'Son, I do not grieve that I am dying, for I have been
avenged; and I myself slew my enemy. Truthfully, then, did Ammon say
to your mother, "You have in your womb a male child who shall fructify
you and shall avenge his father's death." ' And saying this, Philip immediately gave up the ghost. But he had slain his enemy too. Philip was left
with his crown, and Olympias took him and buried him. And all Macedon
shared in her sorrow and mourned him.

And, after the slaying of Pausianos, when peace ruled the city, Alexander climbed up on the statue of his father Philip, and proclaimed loudly:
'Sons of the Pellians and of the Macedonians; of the Thetalians, and of the
Thracians; of the Hellenes, and of the Amphiktionians; of the Lacedemonians, and of the other Hellenic cities: Come with me; entrust yourselves
to Alexander. Let us invade the barbarian nations and free ourselves from
servitude to the Persians, for we Hellenes are not going to serve the
Persians.' Since this was his intention, he sent a written decree to the cities.

And all men in the flower of youth assembled together, and came to Macedon of their own will, as if invited by a god-sent voice. And Alexander opened his father's storerooms and gave weapons to the youths. And he summoned to battle the men who had fought with Philip. Since they were old, they said to Alexander: 'We are feeble with age, and have borne arms under your father. There is no more strength left in our bodies to withstand enemy attacks. For this reason, we give you our resignation from the army.'

Alexander answered this by saying: 'Indeed, I shall make you soldiers all the more, even though you are old men. For it is in the nature of things that old age is very much more powerful than youth. For youth trusts in and vaunts the strength of the body, and many times misses what it wishes to attain, and is cruelly betrayed into danger. But an old man first of all carefully considers what he wishes to attain and, victorious through his good counsel, is freed from danger. Thus you shall soldier with us not by opposing the enemy but rather by encouraging the youth to fight bravely, for encouragement benefits both parties. Now then, go, fortify and strengthen that army with your advice. For in battle it is very clear that you know that the victory you bring the city is your salvation too. In the event of defeat, the attacking enemy would come upon good-for-nothing youth; while upon the triumph of the victors, recognition for glory would be given the advisers.' Alexander spoke thus and persuaded even those who were greatly over age to follow him.

And, having collected the original forces of Philip, Alexander counted and found 25,000 men in the Macedonian infantry, 2,700 mounted Macedonians, and also an auxiliary of 800. And counting these together with the men he had with him, he found 74,600 altogether, including these 25,000 and an auxiliary of 8,700; and 7,600 Thracians, Plinthians, and Scythians, with whom he filled the need for scouts. And taking all the soldiers there, of which he had 71,600, including these and the soldiers which he had from his father, he went to Macedonia. And he took 41,860 talents of gold and outfitted ships and galleys for war.

And having traversed Macedon and Lake Magon and the upper region of Thrace, which was completely submissive to him because of his father Philip's strength, he collected choice men there and 500 silver talents. He passed on to Likauonia and offered sacrifices with the generals there. Then he went on to Sicily and subdued some people who were rebelling against him. He then went on to the land of Italy.

And the generals of the Romans sent their representative, Marcus Emmelius, with the crown of Capitoline Aramazd, made of gold and pearls, to say to him: 'We, too, following Alexander's custom, crown you with this golden crown worth 100 liters.' And when he had received their favours, he promised that, with his power, he would make them great men. And he took 1,000 soldiers from them and 400 talents. And they said that they would give him even more soldiers, if they were not presently engaged in waging war with the Karchedonians.

And from there, he crossed the sea in between and arrived in Africa. And the generals of the Africans came to meet him, and begged him to remove the rule of the Romans from the city. And he censured their fatuity and said, 'Either be noble men or pay tribute to those that are.'

And then, departing from there with a few soldiers, he left all of Libya above him and went and reached the temple of Ammon. And he ordered the army to sail to that place called the island of Pharos, and to stay there. And when he had bowed before Ammon and had offered sacrifices he recalled the words of his mother who had said that he was the son of Ammon. He stood at prayer and said, 'Father, if my mother speaks the truth in saying that I am your son, give me an oracle.' And Alexander saw, in a vision, Ammon locked in intercourse with Olympias. And having truly experienced the power of the god, he adorned the temple with this inscription from him: 'To father, the god Ammon, from his son, Alexander.' And he begged to have an oracle from him as to where he might build a city in eternal memory of his name. And again in a vision he saw Ammon, who said to him: 'O King, I, the taintless, perfect ram's horns say to you: If you wish to remain eternally ageless, fresh for time without end, build a noteworthy city a little above the island of Proteus over which perpetually presides Plutonios, personally ruling over the endless world girt with five crested peaks.'

When Alexander had received this oracle, he beseeched the god and asked which was the island that in fact Proteus influenced and over which the god presided. And when he had asked his questions and had offered sacrifices to his paternal god Ammon, he received directions to a village of the Libyans, where he gave his armies rest. And while Alexander was walking about, a big deer hid itself in a cave. And Alexander called a bowman to him and ordered him to fire arrows at the stag. And he drew his bow and made his shot, but did not hit the stag. And Alexander said, 'Fellow, you missed your mark.' From this, that place was called Paratonion because of Alexander's exclamation.

And from there, he went to Taposiris and upon inquiring, learned from the local people that the shrine was the grave of Osiris. And he sacrificed to the god and hastened on his way. He came to an open plain, and saw that it was a huge and immeasurable place which had spread out and encompassed the property of twelve villages. And these were Steramphis, Phronetek and Edmitos, Akonis, Epyrgos, Tetrakotis, Edios, Aponis, Skambetkh, Nepheletkh, Memnes, Tiatkh, and Pelasos. And Hrakotis was more famous than the others for it was the capital. And the twelve cities used to have twelve rivers, which poured forth to the sea; and until now, the blocked-up passageways remain. The sealed-off rivers were both the little streets of the city and its broad avenues. And there remain only two which flow to the sea. The river of Hrakotis, which still flows, is dedicated to the great god Sarapis. Then there is the canal which is supplied by the avenues, and the big river called Khouleras, which is now the

Aspetia. Then there is its canal, which is a shrine of fortune; and the big river of Kauponios. And there is the big canal and the river Nephrotes which are now out-of-the-way places, and whose shrine of Isis Nephrotes was built before Alexandria. And the biggest of all is the river which is called Argeos, where the column of Argeos is. Then there is the canal of Ares; the pillars and the canals belonging to the Kanopian river, which goes in the direction of Zephyros; and the great river of Heracles is the harbour, for it extends from the place named Pandita to the place called the Herakleotion harbour, the length of the city.

Then Alexander plotted the area; and its breadth extended from Mendidos to the little city of Hermes. But they do not call it Hermoupolis, but Hermapolis, for whatever went to and from Egypt headed for that place. Alexander laid out the city as far as that point; for this reason it is called the land of the Alexandrians. But Kleomenes, the Naukratian, and Dimocrates, the Rhodian, gave Alexander this advice: 'Don't make such a large city for you will never find it filled with people. And if you should fill it, then the lands will not be able to cater to their essential food needs. Those who will be living there will war upon one another when they are so vast and numberless. For small-town people are prompt with advice and help; but, being unfamiliar and unacquainted with one another, a huge crowd of people, such as the inhabitants of so large a city, rebel and fight amongst themselves, having become enemies because of their endless numbers.'

And Alexander was persuaded; and he ordered the architects to make the city of whatever size they pleased. And they plotted the length of the city from Dracontis beyond the grave of Taposiris to Agathemon, which is near Kanoron; and its width extended from Mendidos to Eleurechos and Melanthios. And he ordered the people living there to withdraw to a village about thirty miles outside of the city; and he granted them land and he called them Alexandrians.

Eleurechos and Melanthios were the creators of the thoroughfares from which their names came and have remained. And he thought of finding other architects for the city. Among them were Kleomenes, the Naukratian, and Krateron, the Olynthian, and an old man by the name of Eroa, a Libyan by nationality. This man had a brother by the name of Hiponemos, who advised that before making an excavation for the city's foundation, Alexander make aqueducts which would flow to the sea. And the king was persuaded, and he ordered made what no other city has. And they are called Hiponoses because he who invented them was the Libyan named Hiponemos.

And, there is no city greater than Alexandria, for all charted cities have been measured. The great city in Assyria is Antioch, which is 8 stadia and 72 feet; while in Africa, Carthaginia measures 21 stadia and 305 feet.

And when he arrived at unparalleled Alexandria, he found the rivers, the canals, and the towns built on the land there. And seeing an island on the sea, he asked, 'What island is that?' And the local inhabitants said: 'It is called Pharos. Proteus lived on it; and the tomb of Proteus, which is worthy of worship, is in our land.' And they brought him to the top of a high mountain, the one which is now called Herod's Grave, and showed him the coffin. And he offered sacrifices there to the hero Proteus. And when he saw that in the long course of time the tomb had fallen into decay, he ordered that it be immediately restored.

And he ordered that the circumference of the city be plotted. They took meal and outlined the area; and birds of various species picked up the meal and flew off in all directions. And Alexander, anxious about the meaning of this, hastened to summon soothsayers and told them what had happened. And they said: 'This city which has been built shall feed the entire world, and the men born in it shall be everywhere; like birds they shall travel through the entire world.'

And they began to build the city of Alexandria in the middle of the plain. First the place was given a name so as to begin from there the building of the city. And a serpent used to come to those who were busy working, and it frightened the workers and put a stop to the work. Because of the serpent's raids, Alexander came and said, 'Let it be captured by the workmen wherever it is found tomorrow.' And upon receiving the order, they subdued and slew the beast when it came to that place which is now called Yark. And Alexander asked that a shrine be built for it there, and they buried the serpent in it. And he asked that all kinds of garlands be made in memory of the serpent's appearing. And he declared that the excavation for the foundations be made nowhere else but on that same spot, where to this day the high mountain called the Albiwrk' appears.

And when he had laid the foundation for most of the city, he wrote upon it the five letters: A, B, C, D, E; A, Alexander; B, the greatest king; C, of the greatest nations; D, in the place of Aramazd; E, descended and built a unique city. And there were donkeys and mules at work there. And when the shrine had been built for this divinity, he set it upon the pillar. And many serpents came out of it and slithered into the houses that were now there. For Alexander was still there on the twenty-fifth of Tubi, building the city and that very shrine for the serpent. Thus, when these snakes come into the houses, the gatekeepers worship them as kindly spirits, for they are not poisonous, like wild animals, but rather, drive out poisonous beasts. And sacrifices are made to him as being of the family of serpents. And they wreathed all the beasts of burden and let them rest on that day; for, by bearing burdens, they had done their share in the building of the splendid city. And the king ordered that grain be given the guards. And when they had ground the grain and made bread, this was given the inhabitants as in time of great rejoicing. On account of this, to this day these customs are kept among the Alexandrians on the twenty-fifth of Tubi. They garland all beasts of burden, and offer sacrifices to the god, and render homage to the serpents who safeguard the home, and make a distribution of bread.

And when he had found atop five prominent peaks the land where the pillars of the sun and of Helion are (located) and also the temple of that god, he looked for the shrine of Sarapis, in compliance with the oracle given him by Ammon; and he sought the one who is the greatest god of all. For the oracle of the gods had spoken thus: 'O King, I, Phoegos, the ram, say to you that if you wish to remain forever ageless, build a noteworthy city on the island of Proteus, over which Plutonios presides, encompassing the boundless realm with five crested peaks.' And he invoked the god who sees everything.

And there, opposite the shrine of the god, he set up a great altar which from that time on they call the altar of Alexander. He offered elaborate sacrifices upon it and stood at prayer and said, 'Whatever god you are, who have the divine responsibility for this land and watch over the endless earth, accept my sacrifices and be my help in war.' And having said this, he placed the sacrifice upon the altar. Suddenly a great eagle swooped down, seized the entrails of the sacrifice, and flew off into the air. It circled around and released them upon a different altar. The learned examiners pointed out the place to the king. And when he got there, he immediately saw the entrails on top of the altar. It was an altar which had been built a long time ago, and seated within there was a copper image whose nature mortal man cannot relate. And, there was, with the inviolate image, a large statue of a maiden.

And he inquired of the inhabitants there as to which god it was. And they said that they did not know; but according to the story of their forefathers, it was said to be the shrine of Aramazd and Anahit. And in it he saw the obelisks which remain to this day in the shrine of Sarapis outside the city wall, which at that time was at the shrine of Sarapis. And divine dedicatory writings were marked on the shrine, and the city was marvell-ous. And Alexander asked what the obelisks were. They said, 'They belong to the world-conquering king, Sesonchousis.' And in letters, on the shrine, there is this dedicatory inscription which was translated for the king as follows: 'I, Sesonchousis, king of Egypt and conqueror of the world, built and dedicated this to Sarapis the first god revealed to this land.'

And looking at the god, Alexander said, 'Great Sarapis, give me a sign that you are the god of this land.' And Sarapis appeared most clearly to him in his sleep, and said: 'Alexander, have you forgotten what happened while you stood at prayer, making sacrifices? Didn't you say: "Whoever you are, guardian-protector of this land, who watch over the boundless earth, accept my sacrifices, and be my help in battle"? And suddenly an eagle swooped down and put the entrails on the altar. Was it not evident to you that I am the guardian and protecting god of all?'

And in his dream, he entreated the god and asked: 'Will this city remain true to the name Alexandria in which it was built? Or will my name be changed to that of another king? Advise me.' And he saw the god, who took him by the hand and led him to a high mountain and spoke in this fashion: 'Alexander, can you move this mountain to another place?' He thought about it and said, 'How can I, O Lord?' And the god said to him. 'And so too can your name never be changed to that of a king of other peoples. But rather, Alexandria shall flourish and overflow with bounty; and it shall help and deliver from evil the cities which existed before it.'

To this, Alexander replied, 'Lord, disclose this to me too; how am I destined to die?' And he said: 'It is griefless and good and honourable that mortal man not know in advance what the time of the end of his life will be. For men do not understand that this life seems endless and infinitely varied when they are ignorant of its evils. And so it should seem good to you too not to know your destiny, dear one. But if you ask and wish to learn about your fate, I shall tell you forthwith: with my help, you, a callow young man, shall subdue all the races of barbarian nations; and then, by dying and yet not dying, you shall come to me. Then the city of Alexandria, which you are building in the middle of the land, is to be coveted by the world; a land where gods shall dwell for long days and time to come. And it shall be surpassing in good things, since it shall have been adorned with many temples and diverse shrines, and shall abound in beauty, in magnitude, and in its enormous crowds of men. And all who settle there shall stay on and forget their former fatherlands. And I shall be its protecting deity for all time to come; and forever fresh and ageless, I shall preside over it, and strengthen the land. And the city that has been built shall remain strong forever. It shall cast light upon the fire and illuminate the infernal regions. And it shall make the south wind quail when it breathes its harmful breath, so that the terrible doings of the evil spirits shall be of no avail against this city. For earthquake is to grip it but a short while, and likewise, plague and famine; so, too, shall there be war, but it shall not present great danger; rather, like a dream, it shall quickly pass through the city. And many kings shall forever revere you as one who has become a god according to the customs of this land. And when you die, you shall be revered as having become a god. And they shall have a great crowd of people on the public square and all the more because of the temperate weather. And I shall be its protector and defence, so that no hardship shall remain permanently, either earthquake or deadly plague, but shall pass through the city like a dream. And many kings shall come to it, not to make war, but to make reverence to you as one who has been apotheosized and revered. And when you have died, you shall receive gifts from kings, forever. For you shall dwell there both when you are dead and when not yet dead; for this city you are building is to be your grave. And I shall quickly prove to you where you were meant to be. Take two hundred and add one; then one hundred and one; and four times twenty, and ten;

and take the first number and make it the last; and learn for all time what god I am.' And having given the oracle, the god departed from there.

And when Alexander awoke and recalled the oracle which had been delivered to him by the gods, he recognized the great Sarapis, lord of all. And he built a great altar and ordered that fitting sacrifices be brought for the gods. And he had them slaughtered and put upon the altar. And he had huge quantities of aromatic gum burnt and piles of varied incenses put upon the altar. And he ordered all men to rejoice. And he had Parmenion, the architect, make this copper statue, and build this shrine, which brought to mind Homeric verses, as that wondrous bard, Homer, said: 'And the son of Zrowan made a sign with his azure brows, and his marvellous godly locks moved on the king's immortal head. And Olympus, soundly shaken, trembled.' In this way, Parmenion built a shrine called that of Sarapis. Now the preparation for the building of the city was as we have related.

And Alexander took his troops and hastened to reach Egypt. And he sent his warships to wait for him in Tripolis. He was troubled for the army's sake, for the journey was difficult. There were, waiting for Alexander outside every city, prophets who brought forward their particular gods; and they offered sacrifices, naming him a new world-conquering Sesonchousis. For, when he reached Memphis, they sat him on the throne of Hephestos and they dressed him in a robe, like an Egyptian king.

And Alexander saw a statue of this king; it was made of black stone and had this writing on the base: 'This king who fled shall return to Egypt, not having grown old, but rejuvenated. And he shall make your enemies, the Persians, subject to you.' And he asked, 'Whose statue is this?' And they said: 'This is the last king Nectanebos. When the Persians were coming to make war upon the Egyptians, he, through the sorcery of his magic power, saw the gods of the Egyptians in the enemy armies at the time of their entry into Egypt. And having thus learned of their betrayal, he secretly fled. And when we sought him and entreated the gods as to where the king might have fled, the one who is god in the Sarapean temple in the underworld gave this oracle: "Your king who has fled shall return to Egypt, not old, as he was, but as a tender youth." '

And when Alexander heard this, he ran and climbed up onto the statue and embraced it and said: 'This is my father, and I am his son. The oracle of your god did not lie to you. But, still, I am amazed that you were really completely vanquished by the barbarian nation; for you have walls not made by human hands that could not be taken by the enemy. For there are surrounding rivers which protect your city, and winding paths so narrow and hard to pass that it is impossible for a large army to attack you. For I, even with a small force, had to struggle to reach you because of the hard going. This is rather the justice of Providence above and of God. For why did you who have fertile land and rivers obey those who did not have such dominion? For if you had also ruled well with these things which you had received as gifts, the barbarians who had not been granted these things would have perished. Since they do not have resources for war and you have agricultural skill, why should you serve those who have not? And why should those who have not take from those who have?'

And having said this, Alexander sought the same tribute from them as they were paying Darius. And he said, 'I shall not hoard it in my storeroom, but rather shall spend it on your city Alexandria, which is in Egypt, and is the capital of the whole world.' And when he had thus spoken, they gladly gave him their possessions; and they directed the king with honours through Pellousion. And Alexander took his army, and journeyed directly to Assyria. And he made the neighbouring cities obedient and docile.

To go on with the Alexander Romance, at this point a conflation of the Pseudo-Callisthenes with its European derivatives and with material from other sources, seems most useful, as their added incidents give the story best known in the West. The order of events varies in the varying versions, but the following summary is fairly representative.

Alexander next lays siege to the island city of Tyre, which he conquers only after building a bridge from the nearby mainland and using catapult towers and a fleet as well. He razes the city, but goes on to Jerusalem peaceably, and there shows appropriate respect for the High Priest. After a threatening letter from Darius, he marches against the Persians. In spite of their fearful scythe-armed chariot-wheels, the Persians lose, and lose vast numbers of men. Darius himself escapes, but his mother, wife and children are captured. Alexander treats them with honour.

He comes to Troy and is disappointed in the size of the river Scamander, scene of a great battle in the *Iliad*. When his minstrels say they will praise him better than Homer, Alexander replies, 'I would rather be Thersites in Homer's story than Achilles in yours'. Some time later, food runs out. He orders that the horses be slain, saying that they can be replaced while the Macedonians cannot be. Because the famed city of Thebes sends troops against him, he devastates it. On to Corinth next, where he is asked to conduct the Isthmian games, which a Theban wins. As a gift to the winner, Alexander rebuilds Thebes.

After debates by the great Athenian orators of whom Demosthenes is chief, Athens decides to give him tribute. Later the Lacedemonians fight him and are defeated. Alexander pushes on towards Darius but becomes ill in Cilicia. His physician Philip prepares to cure him, but another courtier writes to Alexander that Philip plans to poison him. With his eyes on Philip, Alexander takes his medicine, and only afterwards shows him the letter. At Philip's request, the writer is killed.

In Great Armenia Alexander bridges a river with arches and bars. His men refuse to cross until he leads the way. When all are on the other shore, he has the bridge demolished and explains that they must fight with the idea of conquering, not of fleeing. At first afraid, the men now cheer him. Next a Persian spy tries to kill Alexander because Darius has promised him his daughter as reward. Praising his single-mindedness, Alexander sets the man free. Another Persian asks for troops to capture Darius and hand him over, but Alexander says, 'Help your own king – I would not trust my people to you who have betrayed yours'.

As the Macedonians approach Darius' city, Alexander ties boughs to the sheep grazing on the plains and drives them behind his army. A mountain of dust is raised which makes the Persians think the army is immense. Alexander is advised by a dream to go himself to Darius as his own messenger. He comes to the river Stranga which has a way of freezing and unfreezing. Since it is now frozen, he rides over it and as Alexander's messenger is brought by guards to Darius. Darius invites him to dinner, where Alexander pockets the gold goblet he drank from. Darius asks him why. He replies that this is the custom at Alexander's court, and the Persian courtiers are impressed. However, one of them recognizes Alexander and tells Darius. Alexander rushes out, seizes the only torch, jumps on his horse and rides off. The Persians stumble after him in darkness. He crosses the Stranga just as the ice breaks – his horse is carried away. The Persians cannot follow him, and he rejoins his army.

Darius attacks. Since the river has frozen again, the Persians are able to cross it. But they are routed, and again the scythes on their wheels cut their own men. More Persians are drowned as they flee across the Stranga, where the ice has now melted. Darius offers tribute but is refused. Alexander spares the palace and grave of Xerxes, who had conquered Greece. He awards Persian land and money to those of his troops who have been maimed. Then he pursues Darius, who has meanwhile been treacherously stabbed by two of his own men. He dies in Alexander's arms, having asked Alexander to marry his daughter Roxiane.

Alexander buries Darius with all honour. He tricks the killers into revealing themselves and crucifies them, and then arranges for his marriage to Roxiane to take place with due ceremony.

He writes to his mother and to Aristotle telling them of strange sights met on his journeys: lion-faced men, dog-like men, trees that alternately grow and shrink, huge lobsters. He describes his ascent to the skies in a cage tied to four griffins, and his descent underwater in a glass bowl.

He then leads his army to India to attack Poros, an ally of Darius. His strategy is to heat bronze statues which burn Poros' famous fighting elephants and disperse them. He challenges Poros to single combat and overcomes him. Alexander goes on to meet the gymnosophists or brahmans and to ask them philosophical questions which express his own fatalism. He writes to Aristotle about seeing the trees of the sun and moon, talking trees which tell Alexander that he will soon be killed. He walls in the brutish tribes of Gog and Magog.

On to Samiram, which is ruled by a beautiful queen, Candace, who sends him gifts and orders one of her messengers secretly to paint a likeness of Alexander. It happens that one of Candace's sons, Candaules, comes to the Macedonian camp for help in rescuing his wife from a local king who has just seized her. Alexander has his friend Ptlomeas pretend to be himself while he poses as his deputy. On Alexander's advice, the Macedonians attack at night, kill the local king, and return Candaules' wife to him. Candaules brings Alexander back to Candace's court, which is very splendid. She recognizes Alexander from the portrait but does not reveal his identity as one of her sons is married to Poros' daughter.

Alexander next exacts tribute from the Amazons and the Parasangians. In a letter to his mother he describes visits to the Pillars of Hercules, the Atlas river, and the City of Bronze.

On his way to Babylon he assists two young knights whose city, Defur, he has besieged. He gives each of them a princess and her territories. Then he has an adventure seeking the water of life, which his vizier or servant finds. Thus he becomes immortal instead of Alexander. Alexander takes the road to the Earthly Paradise, but is not allowed to enter. The old man who guards it gives him a wonderstone which is in the form of an eye. It outweighs any amount of gold, but once dust is sprinkled on it, a feather outweighs it. Aristotle explains the value of the eye while it is part of a living man and its worthlessness once the man is dead. *

*Similarities between the *Iter ad Paradisium* episode and the wasteland of the Grail legend have been noted, including the old man and the lonely castle often surrounded by water. The wonderstone itself is equated with the Philosopher's Stone in alchemy. Joseph Campbell points out that it is this very stone, called 'The Wish of Paradise', which instead of a vessel is the Grail itself in Wolfram von Eschenbach's *Parzival*. ²

Before Alexander can reach Babylon, Antipater, whom he had left in charge of Macedonia, arranges to have Alexander poisoned by his own cupbearer. Dying in great pain, Alexander writes a will dividing his empire. His grief-stricken troops demand to see him, and he orders that the men be let file through his room. This is done. He then dies.

His body is brought first to Memphis but is buried in Alexandria in a golden sarcophagus.

In addition to this extended account, there are other legendary incidents in the life of Alexander which are also part of western tradition, but they are associated less with the Romance than with sources outside it. Always allowing for borrowings to and from, three other fonts of material remain distinct: anecdotes from the historic life which were written down in Latin at least three or four hundred years after his death, but which provide the first documentation, since the Roman writers were repeating what had previously circulated; secondly, separate anecdotes which accrued around his name but which came largely from earlier Levantine folklore; and thirdly, Christian legends.

In the first class, that is, based on history and from Latin sources, is the single best-known story about him, that of the famous Gordian knot which bound the ancient chariot of King Midas to its yoke. The Macedonians came upon it at Gordium when they marched through Phrygia. It was made of cherry-bark, so intricately tied that no one had been able to loose it in the four hundred years since Midas. According to current belief he who could, would rule Asia. At a great assembly, Alexander loosed it by cutting it with his sword.

The horse Bucephalus was also historical; about him there are several tales. The one most told is how Alexander as a mere boy tamed him when no one else could – by noticing that he went wild on seeing his own shadow. By facing him to the sun, Alexander was able to mount and train him. Bucephalus was Alexander's constant companion for twenty years. Once the royal saddle was placed on him, he would refuse any other rider; even when he was wounded at the siege of Tyre, he would not let Alexander change to another horse. As he grew old and feeble, Alexander would parade him before battle in front of the troops; then he was led off and a new mount brought on for the actual fighting. When Bucephalus died in India in the campaign against Poros, Alexander founded a city at his grave and named it after him.

The story about Thais may also be based on fact. Urged on by this lovely courtesan from Athens, and flushed with their victory over the Persians, Alexander and his companions leaped up from their banqueting and drinking to fling torches at the magnificent Palace of Persepolis, which burned down – to Alexander's later great regret. This episode was used by John Dryden in his poem, 'Alexander's Feast'. And then there was his magnanimous treatment of the defeated Poros, who was asked how he wished to be dealt with. 'Like a king', he said. Alexander, pleased with his answer, left him his kingdom intact and made him an ally. There was the wit of the courtier condemned to death one night, who appealed the next morning 'from Alexander drunk to Alexander sober' and was spared – which survives, cheapened, in modern western 'speakers' treasuries' as from Alexander the Small to Alexander the Great. There was the tradition that his expert knowledge of natural history resulted from thousands of reports sent regularly by hunters, fishermen and the like, which Aristotle compiled for him.

But the stories of Alexander's wit and liberality were perhaps the most numerous; in many cases they came from early records, suggesting that they were in keeping with his known nature. Of course praise of anyone's liberality is a popular motif in which the folk have a vested interest, and wit is relished at all levels; these however are compatible with facts. The most famous, recorded by Seneca, is Alexander's answer to the amazed veteran to whom he had given a city – that he was not concerned with what it was right for a soldier to receive, but with what was right for himself to give. Akin to this is his retort to envoys from Asia who offered half their city to him: 'It is not a question of your giving me your city, but of your keeping what I choose to give you back.' He liked the plain truth and spoke it, but equally, out of generosity and forbearance, would reward an honest answer directed against himself. Cicero tells of the notorious pirate Dionides, who when captured by Alexander commented: 'You take the whole world, while I out of necessity take only a ship; I am called thief, but you in the grand class are called emperor!' Far from punishing the man for impudence, Alexander liberated him and gave him a new start in his army. This anecdote is retold by St Augustine, by the *Gesta Romanorum*, and by Chaucer in 'The Manciple's Tale'. Another example is his rebuke to a soldier also named Alexander who fled from a skirmish: 'Either change your name or live up to it.'

Because Alexander's reputation, as transmitted by the Church Fathers from writers such as Cicero, Seneca, Valerius Maximus and

Pliny the Elder, was now white, now black, his literary image was not constant. Pliny, for example, who refers to him repeatedly, credits him with the discovery of the East and even with the first importations of paper and perfume, while Seneca chooses to dwell on his rashness and pride, as did the Christian moralists after him. But since material about him written in Latin was confined in the Dark Ages to learned, that is, clerical circles, the bad press or good press of his literary image had little effect on his growing legend.

On the other hand, the Alexander of the folk was consistent. The crowds of the Middle Ages are in a sense the successors of his soldiers, whose memories of their adored leader set the future pattern. In folklore he is more intelligent than anyone else, fearless, foremost in danger, devoted to his men, approachable, eager for knowledge, magnanimous, liberal, spirited and responsive to spirit, forgiving and forbearing. These qualities are illustrated not only by the Romance, but also in the historic stories, and in narratives from the second source, the tradition of the Near East, where familiar tidbits, used to entertain, circulated by word of mouth before and concurrent with Greek manuscripts in the East and Latin–written versions in the West. Many of these free-floating anecdotes were originally not associated with him – those that remained attached to his name were those that were in character. It was through them that the popular, versus the priestly or the later courtly, concept of Alexander took shape. His encounter with Diogenes is an instance. Seneca had heard this story too, and moralized from it that Alexander's vaunted liberality was a cloak for vanity. Alexander offers Diogenes, who lives in a tub, any boon he wishes. The only thing that Diogenes asks is that Alexander should stand out of his light. Alexander accepts this rebuff and respects the view of life it expresses, as he does in other similar eastern stories told about him and various pauper philosophers. An example of these is the tale of Iskandar Dhu al-Qarnain with the contented king in *The Arabian Nights* who, when Alexander offers to share his empire with him, refuses. He says because of his possessions all men are Alexander's enemies, while since he himself is very poor, all men are his friends.

He is equally forbearing to the tutors of his youth, particularly to Aristotle who continues to lecture him throughout his life. On one occasion, observing Alexander's devotion to his mistress, Phyllis, Aristotle warns him against submission to women. Phyllis asks to be given to Aristotle, and so charms him that at her request he allows himself to be saddled and bridled so as to carry her around on all fours. She arranges for Alexander to surprise them. Aristotle

74

quick-wittedly explains that he complied only to prevent her making Alexander even more ridiculous. In some Arabian variants, the woman is sent away, and the two men congratulate themselves on their lucky escape from fascination. This incident is also popular in the West, in facetiae and in a widespread fabliau, *Le Lai d'Aristotle*. Another example of Alexander's generosity man-to-man is found in the account of Apelles, the master painter. He employs Apelles to paint his favourite courtesan Campaspe with whom he is much in love. In the course of the sittings, Apelles too falls in love with her. When Alexander hears of this, he gives the girl to him. The sacrifice of a mistress or wife to a friend is a widespread Levantine folk theme, presumably based on practice, which we meet again in the *Disciplina Clericalis*, whence to the *Decamerone*, among others.

In other anecdotes of Arabic origin, Alexander is shown in a democratic-cum-princely style recognizable as Arab from, say, Saladin to Harun al-Rashid of *The Arabian Nights*. He sees one of his officers on a sorry-looking horse. 'What good canst thou do me in action on such a poor beast?' 'Please, your majesty, I mean to keep my post; but you seem to me from the choice of your charger already prepared to run away.' Alexander is so pleased with this repartee that he gives the officer his own horse with its rich trappings.[3]

Again, at an evening out with his men, he asks a riddle. 'What did not come last year, has not come this year, and will not come next year?' Someone calls out, 'It must be our arrears of salary!' He is rewarded amidst laughter. Alexander's companionship with his troops is evident everywhere. He risks himself rather than them. He eats what they eat, refuses drink when they are parched with thirst, gives his seat by the fire to a frozen soldier. He says, 'I will not live or die except with my men'.

The third source for western Alexander material is Christian legend. As usual, this is a world in itself. It may be startling to hear that Alexander figures in the Bible: allegorically in Daniel VIII and specifically by name in I Maccabees. In Daniel he is a leopard with four heads and a he-goat which attacks and conquers a ram with two horns, lines which led St Jerome to an interpretation which was upheld by later commentators. 'When Alexander appears as the leopard . . . the four heads are his four successors; as the goat, he attacks Darius, the ram whose two horns represent his two empires of Media and Persia, and destroys his might.' These two prophetic passages, in conjunction with a later reference to the king of Greece who shall come to destroy Persia, are of very great importance in the theological conception of Alexander, for they might only be interpreted as St Jerome interpreted them: 'Alexander's conquests were due not to his own power but to the will of God.'⁴ I Maccabees begins with a capsule account of Alexander's career and death, as a preamble to reflections on his successor, Antiochus, under whom the Jews were persecuted. Because of this passage, and through the intermediary of Jewish comment, medieval typology assigned the Maccabees as types of the faithful Christian and Antiochus as the Antichrist. At the same time, the legend of Alexander's reverence in Jerusalem and his mild treatment of the Jews led to Jewish tales that he worshipped the God of Israel. These in turn favourably affected the Bible commentators, first Jewish and then Christian.

We have already seen in the case of Solomon and Sheba the effect of Bible references and their interpretations. Here there are two conflicting ecclesiastical schools of thought: first, Alexander the instrument of God; and secondly, Alexander associated with Antichrist, which led eventually to his identification with the sin of demonic pride. But as we have noted, clerical adumbrations *per se* do not affect the Alexander Romance. It is in church iconography that the mixture of the religious and the legendary occurs, much as it did with Sheba and the True Cross.

We can trace one instance of this in the material about Alexander's ascent to the sky. The Armenian version of the Pseudo-Callisthenes, the accepted translation, as near as may be, of the Graeco-Egyptian original romance, does not contain or merely hints at adventures which were later interpolated into its recensions and are commonly included in European versions. As we have noted, the most prolific branch of Pseudo-Callisthenes was the one beginning with Leo of Naples which was known as *Historia de Proeliis* and was translated into almost all European languages. It is in this group of romances that the marvellous and marvellously popular episode of the ascent is found. It developed perhaps from a brief passage in the parent Pseudo-Callisthenes which tells of Alexander's coming upon two large birds with human faces who asked him, 'Why do you wish to ascend into the skies, which is not within your power?' He was seized with fear and trembling on hearing them.⁵ Whether arising from these lines or not, the fascinating report of an actual bird-assisted flight swept the West in the forty-odd Alexander books traced to Leo and in the even more numerous pictorial representations of this ascension in churches and illuminated manuscripts and elsewhere. In the West today, this has become one of the best-known episodes of Alexander's life:

Specialists apart, those who know anything of Alexander the Great as a hero of medieval romance know him usually as an airman. Representations of his flying-machine, varying between two and sixteen griffin-power, are found in every age from the 11th century to the 16th, and in nearly every medium – on a marble relief on the North Wall of St Mark's in Venice, on relief panels and capitals at Basel, Caen and Matrice, in a much restored mosaic in Otranto Cathedral, in a Tournai tapestry in the Palazzo Doria in Rome, on English misericords from Wells to Beverley and in manuscripts in Latin, French, Russian and German.[6]

Typically, the tale is as follows: Alexander writes to his mother about his travels. After giving the details of many monstrous beings and unnatural terrains, he describes coming to a place which he thinks might be the end of the earth where the heavens bend down. To find if this is true, he starves some large white birds, or else griffins, for three days, and then fastens them to a wooden cage which he has had made. He gets into the cage. He then takes two spears; at the end of each is meat. He holds these just out of the reach of the griffins. When the spears point up, they fly up, bearing the cage. A winged human shape warns Alexander to turn back. 'Look at the earth', it says. The earth appears as small as a boat on a big sea. Even higher up, Alexander is told to look again. Now the sea seems like a girdle; its limits can be seen. The third time the sea itself looks like a tiny pond. Alexander fears and trembles and points the spears down. The griffins fly downwards, and he lands ten days' journey away from his camp.

The white birds, the fearing and trembling, and the warning recall the Pseudo-Callisthenes. The three vistas of the dwindling world are a common motif in magic flights in Near Eastern legends, for example, the ascent of the originally Babylonian hero, Etana, on the back of an eagle. and the flight of Dhu al-Qarnain (Alexander himself) under the wing of the angel Raphael as recounted in a fifteenth-century *aljamiado* text,[7] as well as in Levantine folktales still current. But the basic idea here must reflect the Arabic Namrud (ultimately derived from the Nimrod of Genesis 10) who, in order to attack God, lifted himself to heaven in a chest flown by four young eagles, with spears and meat as in our tale (he fell down) as well as a mythical Persian king Kai-Kaus who, persuaded by demons, makes an identical trip except that the eagles are attached to his throne (he falls too).

It is interesting that in the Middle Ages this adventure and its image, so dependent on Arabian tradition, should become, after the Bible, the single most pervasive argument for Alexander as the instrument of the Christian God. Its development was made possible first by Alexander's Far Eastern travels to an unknown world, which allowed scope for any rumour or report. The historical Alexander wanted to prolong his campaign in India to see if the Ganges river did indeed flow into the eastern sea. But his soldiers refused to go any further, possibly because of the belief that the edge of the world on the shore of Ocean was a place of dread. Alexander acquiesced to this 'mutiny'. (It was then that they joyfully cried that their king had vanquished the world but permitted his men to conquer him.) Sending the rest of his army home by the regular northerly route, Alexander kept only light troops with him and went to explore a way across the desert. Thus it was quite justifiable that the expedition to India 'provided the opportunity for the insertion of legendary material in the later Graeco-Egyptian prose romance, which led to the artistic elaborations in medieval Europe'.[8] But of the many wonders and narrow escapes contained in these insertions, the aerial ascent is the only one commonly shown in monumental art. Perhaps this is because the lay-out of the scene as usually pictured is very heraldic, reminiscent of extremely ancient eastern ring-seals which show a man or a sacred tree flanked on each side by a griffin or sphinx. It was a favourite motif in Greece, Egypt, Persia and India. The lay out alone would have evoked age-old symbols of divine power. In many of them Alexander is not in a cage but on a throne and crowned, looking like a god and king and possibly suggesting to the medieval faithful the Ascension rather than the ascent.

In the Byzantine world, these connections with divinity are striking. For one thing, tradition in the Near East ascribed to great monarchs not merely control of one or many kingdoms but of the whole cosmos, and Alexander of course fulfilled this concept as no one else had. To the Byzantines, the aerial journey was the symbol of utmost triumph. Then, with the establishment of Christianity, previous illustrations of power were absorbed and reinterpreted. Settis-Frugoni[9] points out that Constantine was identified with Alexander and both of them with the theme of imperial saintliness. The image of the ascent was adopted by the Russian churches as an emblem of Christ enthroned, and purely secular royal objects were decorated with it as well, as can be seen in the crown at Kiev, the Innsbruck cup, the Venetian golden oars, all of eastern provenance.

'Alexander, therefore, precisely because he was the model of the Byzantine emperors, came to be transformed himself into a Byzantine emperor',[10] and as emperor he was the protected of God. Thus both secular and sacred tradition in the eastern Christian empire took up Alexander's celestial journey as endorsing his supreme position among men, a belief based ultimately on St Jerome's interpretation of Daniel VIII and reinforced later by the Islamic view of him and by Islamic iconography.

On the other hand, in western Christendom his reputation suffered from the twelfth century onwards, when especially in Germany and in the *Historienbibeln* he was accused of the sin of pride, the target at that time of most contemporary moralizers. His ascent was seen as the chief example of this, comparable to the similar wickedness of the Tower of Babel. The Church used the derogatory legend as if it too were biblical and therefore irrefutable, and it was so accepted. Conveniently, the same heraldic representations which could signify enthronement heavenwards could teach the fall of pride.

The Koran and Koranic commentary supported the view that Alexander was protected by God, was in fact divine, by identifying him with a pre-Islamic figure known as Dhu al-Qarnain, i.e. Two-horned. This pre-Islamic hero may indeed have been Alexander, who is often pictured wearing ram's horns. Historically, he did not wear them until his triumphant visit to the Temple of Zeus-Ammon in Egypt, where the oracle made it clear that Ammon was Alexander's father. A ram's head, sometimes represented by ram's horns on a man's head, was the distinctive feature of Ammon. A Syriac legend which arose in the sixth century is thought to be the source of the Koranic identification of Alexander with Dhu al-Qarnain. According to this, Alexander said to God, 'I know that thou hast caused horns to grow upon my head, so that I may crush the kingdoms of the world with them.'[11] But on the other hand, horns were an ancient sign of divinity, and the two-horned Arabian figure may simply mirror this, as may the two-horned Moses of Michelangelo. Michelangelo's is the most famous example of a general medieval concept of Moses which in turn was based on St Jerome's Vulgate translation of the Bible (fourth century). Jerome's effort was to be as literal as possible. Thus he translated a Hebrew word as 'horned' which could also mean 'glorified' (as it was rendered in the Septuagint) – 'his face was horned as a result of conversing with God'. As we have mentioned, in ancient Egypt and elsewhere there was already an association of

79

horns with deity. At some remove, then, this reflection of a piece of Near Eastern iconography affected Moses as well as Alexander.

Sura XVIII in the Koran speaks of Dhu al-Qarnain and al-Khadir, the Green One, in a way that shows familiarity with the Pseudo-Callisthenes. In one of his marvellous adventures, Alexander is said to have sought for the Water of Life with his servant al-Khadir in attendance. (Sometimes, instead, the servant is named Andreas.) In Alexander's absence, al-Khadir, preparing their meal, washes a salted fish in a spring. The fish comes to life and swims away. Al-Khadir jumps in after it and so becomes immortal. When Alexander returns and hears the story, they search for the spring but are unable to find it again. The same passage associates al-Khadir and the fish with Moses – who is not two-horned in the Koran. This *sura* also refers to Dhu al-Qarnain walling-in Gog and Magog in response to God's instructions. He appears to be invested with a divine mission to punish infidels and reward believers.

Thus Islam and Christianity might be said to join in regarding Alexander as divinely directed; the god-king attributes of Byzantine emperors are an instance of this. The Alexander Romance and folklore in general saw him as a superman, a godlike man, which the great supernatural deeds ascribed to him bore out. Even one of the Roman writers of the historic life, Arrian – the first, most scholarly, and most reliable – ends his summary of Alexander on the same note:

He was masterly in marshalling his army, without equal in commanding his troops . . . dispelling their fears by giving them the example of facing danger with unshakeable courage. In doubtful enterprises his daring decided the victory . . . he was most reliable in keeping promises, most guarded in not being trapped by the fraudulent, very sparing of money for his own use, most generous in gifts to others. *It is not without the special will of the gods that he appeared among men, not one of whom can be compared with him.*

King John and the Abbot

1 I'LL tell you a story, a story
   anon,
   Of a noble prince, and his
   name was King John;
   For he was a prince, and a
   prince of great might,
   He held up great wrongs, he
   put down great right.
   Derry down, down hey,
   derry down

2 I'll tell you a story, a story
   so merry,
   Concerning the Abbot of
   Canterbury,
   And of his house-keeping
   and high renown,
   Which made him resort to
   fair London town.

3 'How now, father abbot?
   'Tis told unto me
   That thou keepest a far
   better house than I;
   And for [thy] house-
   keeping and high
   renown,
   I fear thou has treason
   against my crown.'

4 'I hope, my liege, that you
   owe me no grudge
   For spending of my true-
   gotten goods:'
   'If thou dost not answer me
   questions three,
   Thy head shall be taken
   from thy body.

5 'When I am set so high on
   my steed,
   With my crown of gold
   upon my head,
   Amongst all my nobility,
   with joy and much
   mirth,
   Thou must tell me to one
   penny what I am
   worth.

6 'And the next question you
   must not flout,
   How long I shall be riding
   the world about;
   And the third question thou
   must not shrink,
   But tell to me truly what I
   do think.' . . .

9 And as the shepherd was
   going to his fold,
   He spy'd the old abbot
   come riding along:
   'How now, master abbot?
   You'r welcome
   home;
   What news have you
   brought from good
   King John?'

10 'Sad news, sad news I have
   thee to give,
   For I have but three days
   space for to live;
   If I do not answer him questions three,
   My head will be taken from
   my body.

11 'When he is set so high on
   his steed,
   With his crown of gold
   upon his head,
   Amongst all his nobility,
   with joy and much
   mirth,
   I must tell him to one penny
   what he is worth.

12 'And the next question I
   must not flout,
   How long he shall be riding
   the world about;
   And the third question I
   must not shrink,
   But tell him truly what he
   does think.'

13 'O master, did you never
   hear it yet,
   That a fool may learn a
   wiseman wit?
   Lend me but your horse and
   your apparel,
   I'll ride to fair London and
   answer the quarrel.'

14 'Now I am set so high on
   my steed,
   With my crown of gold
   upon my head,
   Amongst all my nobility,
   with joy and much
   mirth,
   Now tell me to one penny
   what I am worth.'

15 'For thirty pence our

   Saviour was sold,
   Amongst the false Jews, as
   you have been told,
   And nine and twenty's the
   worth of thee,
   For I think thou are one
   penny worser than
   he.'

16 'And the next question thou
   mayst not flout;
   How long I shall be riding
   the world about.'
   'You must rise with the sun,
   and ride with the
   same,
   Until the next morning he
   rises again,
   And then I am sure you will
   make no doubt
   But in twenty-four hours
   you'l ride it about.'

17 'And the third question you
   must not shrink,
   But tell me truly what I do
   think.'
   'All that I can do, and 't will
   make you merry;
   For you think I'm the
   Abbot of Canter-
   bury,
   But I'm his poor shepherd,
   as you may see,
   And am come to beg pardon for he and for
   me.'

18 The king he turned him
   about and did smile,
   Saying, 'Thou shalt be the
   abbot the other
   while:'
   'O no, my grace, there is no
   such need,
   For I can neither write nor
   read.'

19 'Then four pounds a week
   will I give unto thee
   For this merry jest thou hast
   told unto me;
   And tell the old abbot,
   when thou comest
   home,
   Thou hast brought him a
   pardon from good
   King John.'

The King and the Potter

One day the king summoned his wazirs and said: 'I will ask you certain questions. If you answer them, I will add to your pay and increase your power; but if you fail, I will cut off your heads. Tell me these three things: *First*, What is the number of the stars in the heavens? *Second*, What sum of money does the sun earn daily by his labour for each human being? *Third*, What does God almighty do, every day?' Not knowing what to answer they besought the king to give them a little time, and he granted them a month.

They used to go every day outside the city of Memphis, and stand in the shade of a potter's kiln where they would consult together. The potter, noticing this, asked them what they were doing. They told him. He replied: 'I can answer the questions; but I have a kiln and cannot afford to leave it idle. Let one of you sit down and work; and give me one of your beasts to ride, and furnish me with clothing.' They did as he asked.

Now there was in the city a certain prince, the son of a former king, whom ill fortune had overtaken. The potter proposed to him that he should try to regain his father's throne. But he replied, 'There is no way of getting this fellow outside the city.' 'I will get him out for you,' answered the potter. So the prince made ready.

Then the potter went and stood before King Baulah, and announced himself ready to answer the questions. 'Tell me, then,' said the king, 'the number of the stars in the sky.' The potter produced a bag of sand and poured it out saying, 'Here is just the number.' 'How do you know?' demanded the king. 'Order someone to count it, and you will see that I am right.' The king proceeded: 'How much does the sun earn each day by his work for each son of Adam?' He replied, 'One qirat; for the day-labourer who works from sunrise to sunset receives that amount.' 'What does God almighty do every day?' 'That I will show you tomorrow.'

So on the morrow he went forth with the king until they came to the wazir who sat in his place. Then he said: 'What God almighty does every day is this; he humbles men, and exalts men, and ends the life of men. To illustrate this: here is one of your own wazirs sitting down to work in a potter's kiln; while I, a poor potter, wear the garments of the court. And further, such a one has just barred the gates of Memphis against you!'

The king turned back in haste; but lo! the gates were already barred. Then the people, led by the prince, seized King Baulah, and deposed him.[1]

IV

'ANTAR AND 'ABLA

The *Sirat 'Antar* or the Romance of 'Antar (or 'Antara), who lived in
the sixth century, is connected with western tradition in two ways:
it looks back to the heroic age and it looks forward to the knightly
hero. As Clouston perceived a hundred years ago, it is 'the prototype of the European romances of chivalry'.[1]

Folklore of course includes many kinds of heroes. The best
known are the undifferentiated hero of fairytales, who does not
claim any actual historic existence, and the folk hero, who does,
although his life reflects and conforms to recognized folk motifs –
'Antar is one of these. The motifs may be characteristic of the heroic
age – a literary term which like the cultural terms Stone Age,
Bronze Age, etc., can vary geographically by millennia but is
nevertheless worldwide – and of more recent folklore as well. The
ultimate source of common eastern and western folk motifs is that
primitive capital, that reservoir of tradition in the Near and Middle
East which both drew from and supplied, among others, the Greeks
in the ancient world. This channel, which is largely what is meant
by 'western tradition', went through the Greeks to the Romans, and
through the Romans to Latin Europe and to us. The same reservoir
also drew from, mingled together, and supplied Egyptian, Indian,
Persian, Hellenistic, late Roman, Syrian, Jewish, Christian, Byzantine, early Arabian and above all that composite of composites,
Muslim, lore. Thus analogies between the folk heroes of western
cultures and 'Antar in the East are inevitable, although they have
not often been made.

The folk hero starts as an actual being. But in the process of
making him into a hero the facts of his historic life, which set the
scene, are gradually enlarged over the course of many years to

85

conform to already familiar heroic stereotypes. These are known to the folk from tradition – they were enshrined in myths, tales and songs, and often compiled into long oral narratives in verse known as epics or in prose known as sagas. Their age is the heroic age. In the case of the most ancient, a similar process built folk heroes into godlike culture heroes and into gods, in myths which depict divine magic and marvels. These enshrined figures – epic heroes, culture heroes, heroes of myth, and deities – are sometimes termed heroes of tradition. What may have been actual, in aeons past, was thus slowly transformed into super-historic or divine incidents along lines apparently fairly universal to mankind, lines which reflect the conditions and beliefs of primitive and early times. The definition of a hero was archetypically, and still is, one who is a great fighter or warrior beneficent to his people. It was of course the stereotyped events in the lives of these most ancient heroes and gods which formed in the minds of subsequent men the notions of what to expect from a hero. The question of how those things which became stereotypes were first formed is not settled. A range of origins has been suggested: magic and ritual from the beginnings of society; basic psychological drives and satisfactions which still operate, and so on. The international story of the hero has at any rate resulted.

Thus, in any era or place the process of making a hero must begin with the folk, who accept, or do not, and circulate, or do not, tales about outstanding men known to them. The accepted stories could be on a clan or national level about a king (Alexander, Arthur, Charlemagne) or about a more local warrior or protector (Finn, Robin Hood, Davy Crockett). As one of the last, 'Antar is especially interesting because his legend evolved for over five hundred years. We can compare the earliest part of the *Sirat 'Antar*, which we call *'Antar and 'Abla*, with later parts and see the progress of the narrative towards the general heroic pattern. Doubtless it is still growing and changing. On the other hand, the western folk hero-making process appears to be a thing of the past, since literacy and mass media have arrested its development. Davy Crockett and Abe Lincoln, for example, did not get past the first phase of their cycles; Robin Hood reached ballads but never arrived at the epic stage.

Unlike the international hero of folklore, the hero of chivalry is a special creation of one period, the Middle Ages. He evolves from folk heroes and king-heroes and is found in works about individual warriors as well as in all three of the great divisions of medieval literature: the Matter of Rome which included Greek subjects too, such as the Trojan War and Alexander; the Matter of France which was concerned with Charlemagne and his counts; and the Matter of Britain which dealt with King Arthur and his knights. In the light of fresh information about Arab contributions to the West in science and literature, a fourth class, the Matter of Araby, is well proposed.[2]

The folk hero comes from the folk and, as we have seen, the folk in the pre-Muslim East had their very rich reservoir to draw on when retelling the life-story of a hero. In short, they had the folklore of our civilized world, as the West of the time did not. In 'Antar's life there was an additional inspiring influence, that of Muslim equalitarian ideas, since 'Antar 'provided proof that a person of mixed race could . . . achieve the status of a full-blooded Arab'.[3] The folk also knew the historic 'Antara through his famous poetry, which formed 'the substream of the biographical legend'.[4] The three main themes of his verse were those of his valorous acts, of his love for 'Abla, and of his efforts to be worthy of her, themes which fit most appropriately into the *'Antar and 'Abla* section of the *Sirat* and which are found there. Especially in the later Romance, inferior verse appears which is falsely attributed to him. One of his poems, his *Qasida* or Ode, according to legend had the high honour of being one of the Seven Golden Poems suspended in the Temple at Mecca before the days of Muhammad. The *Sirat*, although not in our excerpt, praises this victory on equal terms with 'Antar's other exploits. His works were collected in the ninth century by scholars in Basra, notably by al-Asmaii who was a courtier of Harun al-Rashid.

However, the starting point for the folk would have been the facts of the actual 'Antara's life. He is known to have belonged to the Abs tribe of central Arabia, the son of an Arab father and a black slave. He would therefore have spent his youth in slavery as a shepherd, but the conflicts between the Abs and neighbouring tribes gave him the opportunity to show his ability as a fighter. He seems to have distinguished himself in the War of Dahis and al-Ghabra and was probably emancipated as a result. He is thought to have died as a very old man at around A.D. 600, on a raid against the Tayyi'.

From this bare outline the *Sirat 'Antar* is the end result. Given a warrior-poet who lived in the sixth century, the folk commenced on the creation of his saga from motifs common to folk heroes. He would not have been recognizable as a hero, would not have become a hero, without them. A whole class of professional storytellers grew up whose business it was to tell tales only of

THE PAST WE SHARE

'Antar; in fact, they were called ' 'Antari'. Even today the *Romance of 'Antar* is the most popular of all in Arab oral tradition and is still to be heard in the desert and in market-places.

That its composition was well under way as early as the eighth century we know from a religious dialogue which survives from that time. A monk and a Muslim converse, and the monk mentions the deeds of 'Antar. Within the story itself, the appearance of Bohemund the Frank and Jufran (Godfrey of Bouillon) brings us to the period after the First Crusade, that is, the first half of the twelfth century. B. Heller sums it up in his definitive article on the *Sirat* in the *Encyclopedia of Islam*:

> An original *'Antar* can be reconstructed with philological probability. In vol. xxxi the dying 'Antar reviews his heroic career in his swan-song. He proudly recalls his victories in Arabia, Irak, Persia and Syria. But he makes no mention of Byzantium or Spain, of Fez, Tunis, or Barka, of Egypt, or Hind-Sind, of the Sudan or Ethiopia. This original 'Antar may have arisen in Iraq (under Persian influence or perhaps in emulation of Persian epic poetry). The swan-song makes no mention of children, and knows of only one love of 'Antar's. This original 'Antar therefore should be called 'Antar and 'Abla. Following a genealogical stimulus, the later epic made royal ancestors be found in the Sudan and royal descendants in Arabia, Byzantium, Rome, and the land of the Franks. The Crusades next found an echo and a reaction in the 'Antar story. The Crusaders came from the land of the Franks via Byzantium and Syria. 'Antar goes in a kind of reversed crusade from Syria via Byzantium to the land of the Franks and brings about the victory, if not yet of Islam, at least of Arab ideals and culture over European Christianity.

'Antar's later deeds, not in *'Antar and 'Abla*, bring him into association with the kings of Iraq, Persia and Syria. He is made the guardian of the new Syrian king, a minor, and as such is the *de facto* ruler. Here he comes into contact with the Franks, sometimes as ally and sometimes as foe, and with the Byzantine court to which Syria is subject. He helps the Christians of Byzantium and is entertained and honoured by them; later he leads them against the Franks and the Spaniards. Rome is oppressed by Bohemund the Frank; 'Antar kills him and liberates Rome. On a reprisal against the Sudanese, he goes into Africa to the land of the Negus and finds that the Negus is the grandfather of his mother Zabibah. He also fights campaigns in the land of the demons. Although he has no children with 'Abla, he has several through secret marriages and love affairs, including two Christians. One is born of his marriage to the sister of the king of Rome; he is none other than Coeur-de-Lion, the Crusader. The other is his son with a Frankish princess; he is Godfrey of Bouillon, the leader of the First Crusade. On 'Antar's death, which is as described in *'Antar and 'Abla*, his sons avenge him and then return to Europe.

The *Sirat 'Antar* was in print in Arabic in the early nineteenth century in thirty-two small volumes, each ending in suspense to be continued in the next, like the tales in *The Arabian Nights*. Terrick Hamilton translated an abridgement of the first part of the *Sirat*, the part we have called *'Antar and 'Abla*, in 1819–20. Clouston in 1881 included an 'epitome' of Hamilton's translation in his *Arabian Poetry for English Readers* which is therefore an abridgement of an abridgement. This work of Clouston's is the basis for the selection which follows here; some passages have been condensed and others, including many poems, omitted.[5]

'Antar and 'Abla

Ten famous horsemen of the tribe of Abs went forth on a plundering expedition. They travelled by night and lay concealed during the day. When they reached a valley between two hills, they came upon the flourishing tribe of Jazrila. They avoided an open attack and went instead to the pasture ground where they saw a large number of camels which a beautiful black woman and her two sons were herding. The Absians seized them, and driving the camels before them, beat off the warriors of Jazrila.

Back at home they sat down to divide the spoils. One of them, Shedad by name, had fallen in love with the black woman, whose name was Zebeebah. Leaving the plunder to the others, he took her and her sons, Jarir and Shibub, for his share.

In the course of time Zebeebah gave birth to a boy who was dark of skin but otherwise resembled his father. Shedad was delighted with his son and called him Antar. Antar helped his mother watch the flocks, and as he grew, became noted for his great strength and courage. When he was only nine, he killed a wolf that harried the sheep, and soon after that, a lion. He became an expert horseman and taught himself to throw the javelin with unerring aim.

Zoheir, king of the Absians, had many sons, each of whom had two hundred slaves. His eldest son and heir was Shas, whose favourite slave was a bully named Daji.

One day the poor of the tribe, the widows and the orphans, were driving their flocks to the waterside to drink. Daji took possession of the water for his master's cattle. He abused one old woman who pleaded with him to let her sheep drink. When another old woman approached, he struck her down. Her rags of clothing were disarrayed and all the slaves taunted her.

Although only a boy, Antar ran up to Daji. 'You bastard!' he cried. 'How dare you do this to an Arab woman!'

Daji struck Antar in the face. Antar waited till he recovered his senses, then ran at the slave and threw him down. He raised him up high again and dashed him to the ground – a mass of flesh. Antar roared in fury like a lion. The other slaves turned on him, and he had to defend himself as best he could. Fortunately Prince Malik, one of the king's sons, happened to come along and promised Antar his protection. Thus when King Zoheir heard of Antar's deed, he approved and applauded it. 'He has defended the honour of women,' he said. 'He will be a noble warrior.'

When Antar returned home that day, all the women crowded round him and praised him, and among them was Abla, the daughter of Malik, his father Shedad's brother.

The Dawn of Love

Antar had frequent opportunities of seeing Abla, one of his duties being to serve the women of his father's and uncles' families with the camel's milk which, previously cooled in the wind, it was the custom of Arab women to drink every morning and evening. Coming into his uncle Malik's tent one day while Abla's long flowing hair was being dressed by her mother, Antar's soul was filled with the image of her beauty, and when he retired he thus expressed his feelings:

That fair maid lets down her ringlets, and she is completely hid in her hair, which appears like the dark shades of night.

It is as if she were the brilliant day, and as if the night had enveloped her in obscurity.

It is as if the full moon was shining in its splendour, and all the stars were concealed by its lustre.

Her charms bewitch all around her, and all are anxious to offer their services:

They live in her beauties and loveliness; and they are imbued with sweetness from her perfections, and receive new spirit from her graces.

Revile me not for my love of her, for I am distracted for her, and live but as the victim of my love.

I will conceal my affection in my soul, till I can see that I am sufficiently fortunate one day to serve her.

And on another occasion, seeing Abla playing and singing among other maidens at a feast, Antar addressed her in eloquent verses:

> The lovely virgin has struck my heart with the arrow of a glance, for which there is no cure.
>
> Sometimes she wishes for a feast in the sand-hills, like a fawn whose eyes are full of magic.
>
> My disease preys on me; it is in my entrails: I conceal it; but its very concealment discloses it.
>
> She moves: I should say it was the branch of the tamarisk, that waves its branches to the southern breeze.
>
> She approaches: I should say it was the frightened fawn, when a calamity alarms it in the waste.
>
> She walks away: I should say her face was truly the sun when its lustre dazzles the beholders.
>
> She gazes: I should say it was the full moon of the night when Orion girds it with its stars.
>
> She smiles: and pearls of her teeth sparkle, in which there is the cure for the sickness of lovers.
>
> She prostrates herself in reverence towards her God; and the greatest of men bow down to her beauties.
>
> O Abla! when I most despair, love for thee and all its weaknesses are my only hope!
>
> Should fortune or my father assist me, I will requite myself for its vicissitudes by my fearless spirit.

Love had now become the master-passion of the hero's soul; for all his subsequent exploits as a warrior were undertaken and performed mainly with the view of raising himself above the circumstances of his birth, and of becoming worthy of his cousin. But already Antar had many bitter enemies among his own people, who sought every means of depriving him of the favour and protection of King Zoheir, and of his son Prince Malik. Wandering one day far from the tents of his tribe, and brooding over his forlorn condition and his love for Abla, he composed the following verses:

> Abla's spirit appeared to me in my sleep, and thrice I kissed her within her veil.
>
> It bade me adieu, but it deposited in me a flame that I feel burning through my bones.
>
> Were I not left in solitude, and could I not quench the fire of my passion with tears, my heart would melt.
>
> But I do not complain; though all my fears are on thy account, O thou perfect full moon!
>
> O daughter of Malik! how can I be consoled, since my love for thee originated from the time I was weaned?

But how can I ever hope to approach thee, whilst the lions of the forest guard thy tent?

By the truth of my love for thee, my heart can never be cured but by patience.

O thou noble maid! till I exalt myself to the heights of glory with the thrusts of my spear, and the blows of my sword, I will expose myself to every peril wherever the spears clash in the battle-dust – then shall I be either tossed upon the spear-heads, or be numbered among the noble

Early Warlike Exploits

King Zoheir having summoned Shedad, the father of Antar, with his other warriors, to accompany him on an expedition against a neighbouring tribe, Antar was left behind in charge of the women; and here follows a graphic description of the amusements of Arab women in those days:

'The horsemen being now absent, the children, and women, and slaves, male and female, were left behind. Semeeah, the wife of Shedad, gave a magnificent entertainment at the lake of Zatool Irsad. Sheep were slaughtered, and wine flowed, and the girls carried their instruments. Antar stood amongst the attendants, and was in transports on seeing Abla appear with the other women. She was indeed like an amorous fawn; she was decorated with variegated necklaces; and when Antar was attending her, he was overwhelmed in the ocean of his love, and became the slave of her sable tresses. They sat down to eat, and the wine-cups went merrily round. It was the spring of the year, when the whole land shone in all its glory: the vines hung luxuriantly in the arbours; the flowers shed around ambrosial fragrance; every hillock sparkled in the beauty of its colours; the birds in responsive melody sang sweetly from each bush, and harmony issued from their throats; every ear was enchanted; the ground was covered with flowers and herbs; whilst the nightingales filled the air with their softest notes.

'They now formed a dance and took off their robes: the damsels danced while the servants sang, and carried round the goblets of wine. Roses were spread over their cheeks, and their bosoms heaved. And Abla joined her associates in the dance, and exhibited her charms, and laughed. Fire shot from their eyes, and the cups of wine were united to the honey of their mouths. The imagination of Antar was inflamed and overpowered in the sea of anxiety; he hesitated whether he should violate the modesty of love by the fingers of passion, when lo! on a sudden there appeared a cloud of dust; and a vast clamour arose, and in a moment there came forth a troop of horses and their riders, about seventy in number, armed with cuirasses, and coats of mail, and Aadite helmets, crying out, "O by Cahtan!" and rushed towards the women. At the instant joy was converted into grief, and smiles into tears: in a moment they seized the women and the virgins, made them prisoners, and placed them on their horses behind them.'

Antar, however, was not the man to stand by and allow the enemy thus to ravish his fair charges before his eyes. To rush after and overtake the horseman who had captured Abla, and to hurl him a lifeless and shapeless mass on the ground, and to take possession of his horse and armour, was to Antar mere child's play. Then he overtook the rest of the enemy, and with his single arm performed such wonders, that those who escaped the stroke of his death-dealing sword fled in dismay, leaving the women and the plunder they had taken.

This was Antar's first warlike exploit; and when King Zoheir returned, and heard of his prowess, he publicly praised him, and presented him with a robe of honour.

Shortly afterwards Antar put to flight a large party of a hostile tribe that had surrounded the King's sons and their attendants.

The King was naturally grateful for the good service which Antar had thus rendered, and at a grand feast held in celebration of the escape of the princes, he caused the hero to sit beside him, and commanded Shedad no longer to employ his son as a keeper of camels, but to allow him to take rank among the warriors of the tribe.

Antar and Abla's Mother

Antar was now become celebrated for his verses as well as for his remarkable strength and courage; and, as may be readily supposed, he was making considerable progress in winning the affection of his beloved Abla. But in the eyes of the maiden's father, Malik, he was far from being a desirable match; and even her mother ridiculed Antar's amorous poetry, and his love for her daughter. One day she sneeringly asked him to recite some of his verses about Abla, and he thus complied:

I love thee with the love of a noble-born hero; and I am content with thy imaginary phantom.

Thou art my sovereign in my very blood, and my mistress; and in thee is all my confidence.

O Abla, my description cannot portray thee, for thou comprehendest every perfection.

Were I to say thy face is like the full moon of heaven – where, in that full moon, is the eye of the antelope?

Were I to say thy shape is like the branch of the erak tree: O thou shamest it in the grace of thy form.

In thy forehead is my guide to truth; and in the night of thy tresses I wander astray.

Thy teeth resemble stringed jewels; but how can I liken them to lifeless pearls?

Thy bosom is created as an enchantment; – O may God protect it ever in that perfection!

To be connected with thee is to be connected with every joy; but separated from all my world is the bond of thy connection.

Under thy veil is the rosebud of my life, and thine eyes are guarded with a multitude of arrows: round thy tent is a lion-warrior, the sword's edge, and the spear's point.

O thy face is like the full moon of heaven, allied to light, but far from my hopes!

Antar Offends His Father

To a wedding among a friendly tribe Antar had the honour of escorting a party of Absian women of rank, among whom was the fair Abla, with their attendants. On the way thither some brigands attack them, but Antar, crying, 'O by Abs! I am ever the lover of Abla!' dealt his sword-blows among the enemy to such good purpose that many were slain, and the rest fled in dismay. The return of the party from the wedding feast furnished the hero with further opportunities for the display of his prowess; and after encountering several hostile parties, and killing many renowned horsemen, Antar brings home the women of Abs in safety and in triumph.

Shedad naturally exulted in the fame of his slave-son, and even declared his intention of ennobling Antar forthwith; but he was dissuaded from this by his brother Malik, who threatened to quit the tribe should Antar be raised above the condition of a slave. And one night, when Antar, emboldened with wine, presented himself before his father, and demanded the rank of an Arab chief, Shedad was enraged at his presumption and threatened to kill him. Antar seeks the counsel and protection of his friend Prince Malik, who expresses his regret that he should thus have offended his father. There is a deal of nature in Antar's reply: 'Do not, my lord, reprove my ambition, which often robs me of my wits and discretion; but had I not been intoxicated, this would not have happened, and I should have concealed my wishes, and submitted patiently to my misfortunes till death had overtaken me. But in all circumstances, thou art my master. Ah, my lord!' continued he, 'how often have I relieved them from their foes, and no one ever assisted me! Know, too, that I love Abla, the daughter of my uncle Malik, and she drives away sleep from my eyelids, and in my sleepless nights I am united to her; but my father Shedad has cut off all my hope, and misfortunes upon misfortunes overpower me. I only demanded to be recognized as his son, that I might be united to her; but truly all my hopes of her are completely destroyed. No joy now remains for me, and the light of the day is the darkness of night in my eyes. I have no home but among the wild beasts and the reptiles!' And tears gushed from the eyes of the hero as he expressed his anguish and passion.

The Prince endeavoured to soothe Antar's distress, by the promise of his influence and protection, and Antar remained all that night with Prince Malik.

How Antar Obtained His Horse Abjer

At daybreak Antar stole out of the Prince's tent, and mounting his horse, wandered into the desert, where he chanced to meet forty Absian horsemen. Antar joins them, and the Absians proceed to the land of Cahtan, where they saw 'a great quantity of cattle, with some high raised tents and lofty pavilions; many horses running about and camels grazing; and the people unsuspicious of a reverse of fortune'. Antar, while his companions were engaged in plundering the tents, drove away the cattle, and had proceeded some distance, when he discovered a knight, 'mounted on a dark-coloured colt, beautiful and compact; and it was of a race much prized by the Arabs: his hoofs were as flat as the beaten coin; when he neighed he seemed as if about to speak; and his ears like quills: his sire was Wasil, and his dam Hemama'. Perceiving the beauty and speed of the horse, Antar eagerly longed for it, and pursued the rider till sunset, when the strange knight stopped, and Antar, coming up to him, made overtures for the purchase of the beautiful steed. The knight, however, would only part with it in exchange for the cattle taken from his tribe, to which Antar very readily agreed; and thus he became possessed of Abjer, the famous horse on which he performed so many wonderful exploits.

A Bridal Party Attacked

Next day Antar and his companions meet with a numerous bridal party; the bride's howdah – richly ornamented with velvet, and on its top a crescent of gold – was preceded by damsels and slaves wearing bright-coloured robes, and behind came a troop of seventy horsemen. The Absians attack the escort, and take the bride prisoner. But while Ghegadh and the others are disputing with Antar about his share of the plunder, the father of the damsel, Yezid the son of Handhala, surnamed the Blood-drinker, arrives, with 300 warriors. 'In a moment swords clashed; every heart was roused: heads flew off like balls, and hands like leaves of trees. The Teyans rushed upon the race of Abs; the Blood-drinker assailed them in his courage, and released his daughter. The Absians quitted their plunder, for their souls could not stand fire, and they fled over the wilds.' Antar, to punish his sordid companions, had thus far remained an inactive spectator of the conflict, but seeing the Absians give way, he rushed down on the Teyans, and slew with his own hand eighty of their bravest warriors; and the rest, with the renowned Blood-drinker and his daughter, spread themselves over the plain and escaped. The Absians had hardly returned from pursuing the Teyans, when Nakid, the husband of the bride, came up, with a large body of horsemen, and a fierce battle immediately ensued. The tribe of Abs were overpowered, and were about to retreat, when Antar turned the fortune of the day, by encountering and slaying Nakid.

Meanwhile King Zoheir had sent a slave in search of Antar, who returned with the news that he was engaged with the tribe of Maan in deadly conflict. The King at once despatched his son Prince Malik with a party of warriors to Antar's assistance, but when they reached him, the enemy was already vanquished. Antar and Prince Malik then returned to their own land.

King Zoheir and the chiefs of the tribe came out to meet Antar, and congratulate him on his return. The hero, after the King had greeted him kindly, ran to his father Shedad, and asked his forgiveness; and the whole tribe were astonished at his prowess.

Plots Against the Hero

Old Malik, Antar's uncle, and his faction were, however, more than ever resolved to thwart the hero's union with Abla; and, envious of the honours bestowed on him by the King, and enraged at his presumption in professing love for his daughter, Malik proposes to his son Amru that Antar should be put to death. Other and more formidable enemies lay plans for his destruction. Antar's mother, Zebeebah, in the simplicity of her heart, advises him to resume his old occupation of tending the flocks and the camels, and no longer expose his life to perils. The hero smilingly replies that she should yet be proud of her son.

Prince Shas (who had never forgiven Antar for killing his insolent slave) complains to his father of his favour of Antar, and of the hero's presumption in desiring union with Abla. King Zoheir reproves his son for his evident ill feeling towards the hero, telling him that it may be decreed of God that Antar should be the recipient of divine favours. Antar, overhearing this conversation, entered the tent, and thus recited:

This flame is for Abla, O my friend – her lustre illumines the darkest night. She blazes – her form is in my heart, and the fire of love is in my soul.

Her gently-waving form has kindled it like the branches whose motion refreshes the breeze.

Her breath diffuses a lively odour, and in her perfumes I pass the night in paradise.

She is a maid whose breath is sweeter than honey, whenever she sips the juice of the grape.

When I taste a coolness from her lips, she leaves in my mouth a hot burning flame.

The moon has stolen her charms, and the antelope has borrowed the magic of her eyes.

O grant me thy embrace, O light of my eyes! and save me from thy absence, and mine own griefs.

Be just, if thou wishest, or persecute me: for in thee is my paradise, and in thee is my hell.

No happiness is there for me in my troubles, but my lord, who is called the generous Zoheir.

The King courteously thanked Antar for his verses, and confessed his inability to adequately reward him – 'even were I to give you all I possess; for my property will pass away, as if it had never been; but thy praises will endure for ever'. He presented Antar with two virgin slaves, beautiful as moons, two rows of rare jewels, and some perfumes; after which Antar withdrew, and going to the tents of the family of Carad, found the men absent, and the women sitting up to hear an account of his exploits, and the fair Abla most anxious of all.

Abla was deeply moved by Antar's evident distress, for she loved him both for his courage and his eloquence. 'Where,' said she, playfully, 'is my share of thy plunder, cousin? Am I now of no consequence to thee?' – 'Truly,' replied he, 'I gave all to thy father and thy uncles.' He then gave her the two female slaves and the jewels he had received from the King; but the perfumes he divided among his aunts, telling Abla that she had no need of them, her breath being sweeter than any perfumes.

Antar Rescues His Father and Uncles

Antar then learns that his father Shedad and his uncles are gone in pursuit of a knight, called Kais, who had taken some cattle from their tribe, and immediately mounts his horse Abjer and sets off to their assistance. He finds his father and uncles tied ignominiously across their horses, prisoners of Kais, at which he roared, 'Ye dastards! – come forth!' and Kais no sooner heard the challenge than he pricked on his horse till he came up to Antar, and thus addressed him:

> I am renowned in every nation for the thrust of the spear and the blow of the sword.
>
> I am the destroyer of horsemen with the lance, when the spears are interwoven under the dust.
>
> How many contests have I waged on the day of battle, whose terrors would turn grey the heads of infants!
>
> Long ago have I drunk the blood of horsemen, with which they fed me before I was weaned.
>
> This day will I prove my words when the blood streams from my sword.
>
> This foul wretch will I slay with the edge of my sword, that cleaves through the flesh before the bones.
>
> His dwellings shall this eve be found waste and desolate, and I will not swerve from my word: his body shall lie on the deserts, cut down, and his face thou mayst see grovelling in the dust.

To these insolent verses Antar replied, saying, 'Silence! – may thy mother bewail thee.' –

> Let him repent who has shown his vanity; and let him prefer flight to resistance.
>
> I am Antar; and my name is far spread for the thrust of my spear and the blow of my sword.

97

Having thus exclaimed, Antar 'drew forth his sword and struck Kais between the eyes, and split his helmet and wadding, and his sword worked down to his thighs, down even to the back of his horse: and he cried out – "Thou wretch! I will not be controlled! I am still the lover of Abla!" ' He then rushed among the tribe of Dibgan, who fled in dismay, leaving all their plunder behind.

A Gallant Knight of Mazin

The Absians return home in triumph, and King Zoheir comes to meet them at the lake Zatool Irsad, where he gives a grand feast to celebrate the exploits of Antar. In the midst of the entertainment a gallant knight of the tribe of Mazin, with a hundred followers, comes riding up to the royal pavilion, and implores the King's succour. He is Hassan, the foster-brother of Prince Malik. He had, he informs the King, long loved Naeema, the beautiful daughter of his uncle Nedjem. A wealthy chief named Awef had come as a suitor for his fair cousin, and her father feared to offend so powerful a knight by a refusal. Hassan, however, had settled the matter in his own favour by encountering Awef and dismounting him, and only spared his life on the intercession of his uncle Nedjem, who reminded him that Awef had eaten his bread and been under his protection; but he cuts off his hair and sends him away in ignominy. Thus far, all was well; but Hassan had nothing for his cousin's dowry; so he sets off to procure one in the usual way, by plundering some other tribe. He returns with immense wealth, and finds that Oosak, a still more powerful chief, had demanded his betrothed in marriage, and had been refused by her father; and now Oosak, with all the warriors of Cahtan, was on his way to attack the tribe – and therefore he had come to beg the help of King Zoheir in repelling the threatened invasion.

No sooner had Hassan finished his story than Antar started to his feet, and eagerly offered his services, and Zoheir gave Prince Malik leave to accompany the hero, with a thousand chosen warriors.

How Antar Found the Sword Dhami

'They travelled on for three days, and on the fourth (for the Lord of Heaven had decreed the glory of Antar, and that none should exceed him in prosperity), Antar, happening to stray a little out of the way, descended into a deep valley, and lo! there were two horsemen engaged in desperate combat. Antar urged on his steed, and coming up to them, "Stop, ye Arabs!" he cried, "and tell me the cause of your quarrel." At the instant one of them stepped aside, and came up to Antar. "Noble horseman of the desert and the town," said he, "I refer myself to you, for you are able to protect me." – "I will take your part," said Antar, "I will protect you – I pledge myself to you. But acquaint me with your story, and what has rendered necessary this combat between you."

' "Know, then, noblest knight of the age," said the youth, "that I and this horseman are brothers, of the same father, and the same mother; he is the eldest and I am the youngest; and our father was one of the Arab chieftains, and he was called Amru, the son of Harith, the son of Teba; and Teba was our ancestor. And one day as he was sitting down, his flocks strayed away, and one of his camels was lost, and as he was very partial to it, he questioned some of the herdsmen about it. One of them said: 'Know, my lord, yesterday this camel strayed away from the pasture; I followed behind it, and it still continued to run away, and I after it, till I became tired, and perceiving that it lagged behind, I stretched out my hand and took up a stone, black in appearance, like a hard rock, brilliant and sparkling. I struck the camel with it, and it hit the camel on the right side and issued out on the left, and the camel fell to the ground dead. On coming up to it I found the stone by its side, and the camel was weltering in its blood.'

' "On hearing this my ancestor mounted his horse, and, taking the herdsmen with him, went to find out the pasture. They passed on till they came to the camel, which they found dead, and the stone lying near it. My ancestor took it in his hand, and considered it very attentively, and he knew it was a thunderbolt; so he carried it away and returned home. He gave it to a blacksmith, and ordered him to make a sword of it. He obeyed, and took it and went his way; and in three days he returned to my ancestor with a sword two cubits long and two spans wide. My ancestor received it, and was greatly pleased when he saw it, and turned towards the blacksmith and said: 'What name have you given it?' So the blacksmith repeated this distich:

'The sword is sharp, O son of the tribe of Ghalib, Sharp indeed:
but where is the striker for the sword?

And my ancestor waved the sword with his hand, and said: 'As to the smiter – I am the smiter!' and struck off the head of the blacksmith, and separated it from his body. He then cased it with gold, and called it Dhami, on account of its sharpness. He laid it by amongst his treasures, and when he died it came in succession to my father with the rest of the arms; and when my father perceived his death was at hand, he called me to him privately. 'O my son,' said he, 'I know your brother is of a tyrannical, obstinate disposition, one that likes violence and hates justice, and I am aware that at my death he will usurp my property.' – 'What measures shall I take?' said I. – He answered: 'Take this sword and conceal it, and let no one know anything about it: and when you see that he takes forcible possession of all my property, cattle and wealth, do you be content, my son, with this sword, for it will be of great benefit to you: for if you present it to Nushirvan, king of Persia, he will exalt you with his liberality and favours; and if you present it to the Emperor of Europe, he will enrich you with gold and silver.'

' "When I heard these words I consented to what he demanded, and took it out in the darkness of the night, and having buried it in this place, I returned to my father and stayed with him till he died. We buried him, and returned home; but my brother took possession of all my father had, and gave me nothing – not a rope's end; and when he searched for the arms, and saw not the Dhami, he asked me for it. I denied knowing anything about it; he gave me the lie, and abused me most violently; at last I confessed, and told him I had buried it in such a spot; so he came with me hither, and searched for it but could not find it. Again he asked me where I had buried it; and when he saw me roaming about from place to place, he rushed upon me, and cried out, saying: 'Vile wretch! you know where the sword is, and act thus to deceive me.' He attacked me, and sought to slay me. I defended myself until you arrived, and now I demand your protection.'

'When Antar heard this his heart pitied him; he left the youth, and turning to his brother, said: "Why do you tyrannize over your brother, and do not divide with him the property your father left!" – "Base slave!" cried he, highly incensed, "look to yourself, and interfere not so arrogantly"; and he turned upon Antar, thinking him a common man; but Antar gave him no time to wheel, or direct his reins; ere he pierced him through the chest with his spear, and thrust it ten spans through his back, and threw him down dead. "And now, young man," said he to the other, "return to your family, and assume the rank of your father; and should any one molest you, send and inform me: I will come and tear his life out of his sides." The youth thanked him and expressed his gratitude: "Now my brother is no more," said he, "I have no other enemy"; and he departed home.

'But Antar fixed his spear in the ground, and dismounted from Abjer, and sat down to rest himself; and as he was moving the sand with his fingers, he touched a stone; on removing what was about it, behold! the sword the youth had been seeking! He still cleared away, and drew it forth, and seized hold of it, and it was a sword two cubits in length, and two spans wide, of the metal of Almalec, like a thunderbolt. And Antar was convinced of his good fortune, and that everything began and ended in the most high God.'

Rescue of the Tribe of Mazin

On the following day the Absians encountered five hundred horsemen, all clad in steel, and led by Gheidac, a haughty chief, whose father Antar had killed in one of his former expeditions. Gheidac and his troops were advancing to assist Oosak in his purposed attack on the tribe of Mazin, when they fell in with the warriors of Abs. 'They all rushed forward, and horsemen encountered horsemen. Cowards fled, and the weak-hearted were disgraced; but the bold were firm in the assault, and the equals in courage met each other in the field. The earth trembled under the trampling of the horses; the heavens were obscured with the clouds of dust; the warriors were covered with wounds, and the swords laboured in the cause of death: exertion was alive, and all jest was at an end.' Thus the battle raged till mid-day, when Antar and Gheidac met, and after a desperate combat, the Absian hero, having wearied his antagonist, at length struck him a blow with Dhami, and cleft him – and his horse as well.

On seeing their chief fall, Gheidac's warriors took to flight, and the Absians, after collecting the horses and plunder, resumed their journey and proceeded until they reached the tribe of Mazin. Here all was confusion and dismay; for Oosak and his horsemen were already busy plundering the women's quarter, and Antar, who was ever 'solicitous in the cause of women', rushed with his warriors upon the dastards, scattering them to the right and left – 'mighty was every act, and fate descended among them'.

'Antar eagerly sought after the plume that floated above the head of Oosak, and he stopped not in attack until he was beneath the standard where Oosak was waiting for his people to bring him Naeema; neither could he be roused till Antar came before him and encountered him. Then ensued a dreadful engagement. The combat lasted an hour; when nerveless sunk the arm of Oosak. Antar, seeing the state he was in, clung to him, and grappled him; and drawing his sword from the scabbard, he aimed a blow at his head, but Oosak received it on his shield. The sword of Antar came down upon it and shivered it in two, and split his vizor in twain, and it penetrated even to his thighs, down to the back of the horse; and the rider and the horse fell in four parts; and he cried out – "O by Abs! I am ever the lover of Abla! never will I be controlled! I will not be restrained!" '

Oosak's followers then wheeled about their horses and sought security among the rocks of the desert. The horsemen of Abs and of Mazin, having pursued them out of the land, returned to the tents, where Hassan entertained Antar and his comrades at feasts during seven days, and on the eighth night he was married to his beloved Naeema. Next day the warriors of Abs returned to their own country.

Another Suitor for Abla

While Antar was gone to assist the tribe of Mazin, something happened which marred his hopes of winning his beloved Abla, and commenced a series of troubles to himself, to his family, and even to the whole tribe of Abs. This was the betrothal of Abla to a noble Absian named Amarah; 'a conceited coxcomb, very particular in his dress, fond of perfumes, and always keeping company with women and young girls'. The fame of Abla's beauty having reached this Bedouin exquisite, he sent a female slave to the tents of the family of Carad, to discover whether Abla was as beautiful as was reported of her; and the girl returning with a glowing account of Abla's charms, Amarah conceived a violent passion for her – 'his ears fell in love before his eyes'. He visits old Malik, and demands his daughter in marriage, promising a handsome dowry. Malik the perfidious is overjoyed at the prospect of such a son-in-law, and very readily gives his consent – hoping, no doubt, that Antar is by this time become food for the ravens and the vultures.

Next day, as Amarah was hastening to Abla's father with the dowry and marriage presents, a messenger arrived to announce the return of Antar and Prince Malik, and the whole tribe went out to welcome them. Antar remained that night with his mother Zebeebah, from whom he learned that Abla was betrothed to Amarah; and 'the light was darkened in his eyes'. In the morning he acquaints Prince Malik of his uncle's perfidy, and the Prince offers to secure Abla for his friend, by 'putting his name on her', and thus keeping off any suitor till Antar was in possession of his wife. Prince Malik then goes to Shedad, and requests him to formally recognize Antar as his son, that he may take rank among the chiefs of the tribe. But Shedad would not consent to do what no Arab chief had ever done before – enoble his slave-son. The Prince replied that no other chief ever had such a son as Antar: 'Let other Arabs follow your example,' said he; 'good practices are to be admired, even though they are new.' But all that the Prince's arguments could effect in favour of Antar was a promise from Shedad that 'he would consider the matter'.

In the meantime, Antar meets his rival riding away from old Malik's tent, where he had been visiting. Amarah, in the excess of his vanity, addressed the hero in insolent language, to which Antar replied by seizing the coxcomb, and dashing him senseless to the ground. Amarah's followers rushed upon the hero, who would probably have been soon overpowered had not Prince Malik, returning from his interview with Shedad, come to his rescue, and, gallantly crying, 'Verily Antar is a rare onyx among a people who know not his worth! – Come on, Antar! – now for the family of Zeead!' lustily plied his sword among them, until the King came up and separated the combatants.

Although the coxcomb Amarah richly deserved the punishment he received from Antar, yet for a slave to raise his hand against a noble Absian was an unpardonable offence in the opinion of the hero's enemies; and his father Shedad was therefore compelled to send Antar back to his former occupation of tending the flocks and camels. At the same time Antar had to endure the mortification of seeing the warriors of Abs prepare to resist a threatened attack of the tribe of Tey. But his mother Zebeebah brings him a message of love and consolation from his faithful Abla: 'Soothe the heart of my cousin Antar; and tell him that, if my father even makes my grave my resting-place, none but him do I desire – none but him will I choose.'

Battle of the Tribes of Abs and Tey — Antar to the Rescue!

The Absians meet the Teyans, and are defeated; their bravest warriors retreat, and the women of Abs are taken captive. In their extremity the Absian chiefs recollect the prowess of Antar, whom their envy and malice have caused to be degraded from the rank of the foremost warrior of the age to the condition of a keeper of flocks and camels. A messenger is despatched to solicit his assistance. Antar puts on his armour, girds his sword Dhami to his side, and mounting Abjer, joins the chiefs of Abs. His father Shedad solemnly promises, if he will pursue the enemy and rescue the women and plunder, to recognize him as his son; and his uncle Malik swears that, if he will but rescue Abla, he shall have her for his wife. On these conditions Antar agreed to redeem the honour of the tribe.

The first object of his attack was the horseman who had captured Abla. Antar pierced him through the side with his spear, and he caught Abla in his arms, like a frightened bird, but unhurt. He then rushed upon the enemy with irresistible impetuosity – his sword Dhami played among them, causing the heads of warriors to fly through the air like balls, and scattering their limbs like the leaves of trees. The Absians are again collected together and attack the Teyans, who, seeing their leader Rebeeah fall, slain by Antar, fly in terror of the hero's sword; and the tribe of Abs, after driving them out of their country, return to their own tents, with Antar at their head, chanting his song of triumph:

> I have abused fortune, but how can she humiliate such as I? – I, too, that have a spirit would cut down mountains!
>
> I am the warrior of whom it is said, 'He tended the he and she camels of his tribe!'
>
> When I assaulted Kendeh and Tey, their hands brandishing the long spears, with armies, that when I thought of them, I imagined the whole earth filled with men;
>
> And as their hardy steeds trampled our lands, whilst you might see them talking and exulting – 'twas then their steeds fled away horrified at me, and the redoubled thrusts that gored them as they sought the fight.
>
> The noble hero feels no fatigue: him no challenger need call to the combat.
>
> It was the slave alone that drove back the horsemen whilst the flame of battle was blazing!

Antar Proclaimed Champion of Abs

At length the hero is duly admitted by the Absian warriors to the honour and rank of an Arab. King Zoheir causes a great feast to be prepared to celebrate the overthrow of the Teyans, at which he presents Antar with a robe worked with gold, girds on him a trusty sword, and placing in his hand a pike of Khata, and mounting him on a fine Arab horse, proclaims him the champion of Abs and Adnan. And thus, apparently, was removed the chief obstacle to Antar's union with Abla; moreover, the maiden's father had solemnly sworn that she should be married to the hero if he rescued her from the Teyans. But the treacherous Malik never meant to keep his word; although, the King favouring Antar's cause, he had no choice but to profess his willingness to bestow his daughter on the saviour of the tribe. Old Malik, however, was a perfect master of craft and cozenage; and he devised a plan of exposing Antar to almost certain death. He requires him to procure for Abla's dowry a thousand Asafeer camels – the property of Monzar the son of Massema, king of the Arabs, and lieutenant of Chosroe Anoushirvan, the King of Persia: if Antar once venture among the tribe of Shiban, Malik confidently assures his co-plotters, he will never return to trouble them again. For such a prize as Abla, however, Antar would willingly encounter even greater dangers, and therefore he undertakes the desperate enterprise with alacrity.

Antar's Expedition for the Asafeer Camels

Accompanied only by his faithful brother Shiboob, – his trusty henchman, who frequently rendered the hero important service by his dexterity as an archer, and whose fleetness of foot had gained him the *soubriquet* of Father of the Wind, – Antar departed at night from the tents of Abs, and proceeded towards the land of Iraq. Traversing the wilds and the deserts by secret paths, well known to Shiboob, one day they came upon a single tent pitched beside a spring, and near it was an aged sheikh, bent with years:

> An old man was walking along the ground,
> And his face almost touched his knees.
> So I said to him, 'Why art thou thus stooping?'
> He said, as he waved his hands towards me:
> 'My youth is lost somewhere on the ground,
> And I am stooping in search of it.'

Antar and Shiboob journeyed until they came to the land of Hirah, where they discovered 'populous towns, plains abounding in flowing streams, date-trees, warbling birds, and sweet-smelling flowers; and the country appeared like a blessing to enliven the sorrowing heart; and the camels were grazing and straying about the land'. Here was every sign of wealth and power; but, nothing dismayed, Antar despatched his brother to look after the Asafeer camels while he rested Abjer.

    Shiboob, disguised as a slave, proceeded to the tents of the slaves who had charge of the camels, and telling them a plausible story of his having run away from his master, and feigning sickness, he spent all the day with them; and when the slaves were all fast asleep, he stole away, and rejoined Antar, to whom he communicated the results of his observations regarding the numbers of the camels and of the slaves who guarded them. Antar stations Shiboob with his bow on the road to Hirah; he then cuts off a thousand of the Asafeer camels, and compels some of the slaves to drive them towards his own country. He is overtaken by King Monzar and his hunting party, and defends himself manfully against them all, until Abjer stumbles and brings him to the ground. Shiboob, seeing his brother fall, supposes him to be killed, and speeds homeward.

Antar, however, was not dead, though taken prisoner, and brought bound into the presence of King Monzar, who demanded to know whence he came. Antar replied that he was of the tribe of noble Abs.

'One of its warriors, or one of its slaves?' inquired the King.

'Nobility, my lord,' said Antar, 'amongst liberal men, is the thrust of the spear, the blow of the sword, and patience beneath the battle-dust. I am the physician of the tribe of Abs when they are in sickness; their protector in disgrace; the defender of their wives when they are in trouble; and their horseman when they are in glory, and their sword when they rush to arms.'

He then relates the occasion of his enterprise which had thus miscarried. The King expresses his astonishment that he should have exposed himself to such dangers for the sake of an Arab girl.

'Yes,' replied Antar, 'it is love that emboldens man to encounter dangers and horrors; and there is no peril to be apprehended but from a look from beneath the corner of a veil'; and thinking of Abla's charms, and his present condition, he continued,

'The eyelashes of the songstress from the corner of the veil are more cutting than the edge of the cleaving scimitars.'

The King was expressing his surprise at the eloquence and fortitude of the prisoner, when there arose a great commotion among his followers, caused by a savage lion that had rushed from the desert, and was busy mangling the boldest of the king's warriors. Antar offers to slay the lion, if only his hands are set free, leaving his legs still fettered, and he was given a sword and a shield. This feat he performs to the admiration of all; and Monzar sees in the hero one well qualified to aid his ambitious design of rendering himself independent of Anoushirvan, the King of Persia.

Monzar had been made the subject of a practical joke, which he little relished, at the court of Persia – by eating dates, stones and all, at dinner, in imitation of the King and his courtiers, who he supposed were also eating dates, but in reality simply almonds and sugar-plums prepared to resemble dates. On returning to his own country he resolved to revenge this insult, and secretly incited several Arab tribes to plunder Persian towns. Chosroe Anoushirvan commanded him to punish these marauders; but Monzar had the hardihood to send back the royal messenger with a letter, stating that, in consequence of the insult that had been offered him at the Persian court, he had now little or no influence with the Arab tribes, and that Chosroe must look after his own kingdom. And Monzar was awaiting the result of his answer to Chosroe when Antar fell into his power.

The Satrap Khosrewan Sent to Chastise Monzar

Immediately on receiving Monzar's audacious message, the King of Persia despatched his satrap Khosrewan (the original cause of all the trouble), with a large army, to chastise his Arabian vassal. On the approach of the Persians, Monzar collected all the clans of the tribe of Shiban, and all the Arab hordes, and, giving battle to Khosrewan, was signally defeated. In his extremity he thought of his prisoner, the lion-slayer. Antar was freed from his fetters, and brought before Monzar.

'I am now in your power,' said the hero; 'and I demand of you the marriage dower of Abla, my uncle's daughter: restore my sword, my cuirass, my arms, and my horse, and give me a thousand men to defend my rear; and you shall see what my courage and force will effect against your foes.'

Monzar swore, by the sacred Kaaba, that if Antar proved successful in destroying the Persian army, all his camels should be at his disposal, and ordered the hero's horse and arms to be restored to him.

Early on the morrow the Arabs went forth against the Persians, and at their head was Antar, who, exclaiming, 'By thine eyes, O Abla!' received the attack of the enemy 'as the parched ground the first of the rain'. The Persians were mowed down by the irresistible Dhami: terror seized upon their hearts at the sound of his voice, 'like the thunder's peal'; and his sword-strokes were more rapid than the flashes of lightning; the army of Monzar was victorious.

Combat Between Antar and Khosrewan

Next morning both parties prepared to renew the contest; and Antar, having engaged to challenge Khosrewan to decide matters by single combat, mounted on a mare ('for his horse Abjer, wounded the day before, was still unfit for the day of encounter'), rushed between the two armies, and thus spoke:

> Sally forth – ay, every lion warrior! Taste a draught at the edge of my sword, more bitter than the cups of absinthe.
>
> When Death appears in the crowded ranks, then challenge me to the meeting of armies; – ye Persians, I heed ye not – I heed ye not!
>
> Where is he who wishes to fight me, and wants to make me drink the liquor of death?
>
> Bring him forth! – let him see what he will meet from my spear under the shades of the war-dust; – I swear, O Abla! he shall eat of death!
>
> By thy teeth, luscious to the kiss, and by thine eyes, and all the pangs of their enchantment, and their beauty – were thy nightly visionary form not to appear to me, never shall I taste of sleep!
>
> O thou, my hope! – O may the western breeze tell thee of my ardent wish to return home!
>
> May it waft thee my salutation, when the sparkling dawn bursts the veil of night!
>
> May God moisten thy nights, and bedew thee with his rain-charged clouds!

May peace dwell with thee as long as the western and northern breeze shall blow!

No sooner had Antar concluded than Khosrewan appeared on the plain, 'mounted on a long-tailed steed, marked with the new moon on his forehead, and on his body was a strong coat of mail well knit together, the workmanship of David; and armed with an imperial casque and a glittering sword; and under his thighs were four small darts, each like a blazing flame.

'And when he came forth on the field of battle he roared aloud, and contemptuously of the Arabs. Antar assailed him: high arose the dust about them, so that they were hid from the sight. They exhibited most extraordinary prowess; they separated, they clung to each other; now they sported, now they were in earnest; they gave and took; they were close; they were apart; until it was mid-day, and both had severely toiled. But whenever Khosrewan attempted to assail Antar and strike him with his mace, he ever found him vigilant and on his guard, and aware of his intent. So he darted away from him in order to gallop over the field, and would exhibit all his manoeuvres and stratagems.

'But Antar kept him employed, and wearied him, and prevented his executing his designs, so that the chieftain's wrath became intense. He snatched up one of his darts, and shook it and hurled it at him – it flew from his hand like the blinding lightning, or descending fate. Antar stood firm; and when it came near him he met it, and dexterously turning it off with his shield, it bounded away, and fell upon the ground far off. Khosrewan snatched out a second dart and levelled it at him; but Antar sprang out of its way, and it passed harmless. He aimed a third; but Antar rendered it fruitless by his dexterity and his persevering activity. He hurled the fourth; but it shared the same fate as the others.

'When Khosrewan saw how Antar had parried the darts, his indignation was extreme. Again he took up his mace, and he roared even as a lion roars; – then stretching himself out with it he hurled it, backing it with a howl that made the plains and the air rebellow. Antar threw away his spear, and met the mace, and caught it with his right hand in the air; then, aiming it at Khosrewan, he cried out: "Take that, thou son of a two thousand-horned cuckold! – I am the lover of Abla, and am alone – the Phoenix of the world!" Khosrewan saw him grasp the mace in the air, and was horrified, for his strength and force were exhausted. He retreated, and attempted to fly from his antagonist, for he was now convinced of his destruction. He moved round his shield between his shoulders; but he felt that his fate was nigh at hand, for the mace fell upon his shield more forcibly than the stone of a sling; furiously it rattled on the Persian chief, and hurled him off his saddle to the distance of twelve cubits, and broke his ribs and snapped his spine.

'Every warrior was intensely agitated at this surprising deed; and when the Persians saw it they were bewildered: they rushed upon Antar, agonized as they were at this calamity, and exposed their lives to certain death. The Arabs received them with undaunted courage at the points of their spears, and their spirit was exhilarated by the acts of Antar. The two armies assailed, and the earth was pounded under the trampling of the horses. The horsemen and the clans encountered; clouds of dust thickened over their heads. And their fury increased till they were like the waves of the boisterous ocean. Spears penetrated through hearts and waists; heads were flying off; blood was boiling; cowards were scared; the courageous full of fire: the King of Death circled round the cup of mortality; and the commands of the Most High were executed upon them.'

Antar at the Court of Chosroe

Encouraged by his success, Monzar now resolved to formally declare war against Chosroe; but he was induced to defer his purpose by the counsel of his sagacious old vizier, Amru, who undertook to proceed to the Persian capital, and ascertain how the tidings of Khosrewan's death had been received. Amru finds the courtiers of Chosroe in a state of great excitement, in consequence of the arrival of a renowned knight, called Badhramoot, who had recently come thither, as the champion of the Emperor of Greece, to do battle for the Christian faith against the knights of Persia. The Emperor was preparing to send his yearly tribute of treasure to Chosroe, when Badhramoot arrived at his court, from Syria, where he had long been distinguished for his warlike prowess; and the indignation of the Christian champion was roused at the sight of so much wealth intended for a prince who was not of the true faith. Badhramoot proposed to convey the tribute, and deliver it only if he was vanquished in single combat by a Persian knight. The Emperor accepted his offer, and the champion accordingly departed for Persia with 500 horsemen in his suite. Monzar's vizier learns that Badhramoot had been engaged during fifteen days in single combat with the flower of Persian chivalry, and had overthrown all his antagonists. Chosroe was almost in despair: should none of his knights be able to vanquish the champion of the Emperor, his supremacy was gone. Amru contrives to acquaint him, through a friend at court, of the lion-hero Antar, who had lately slain his satrap Khosrewan, and routed his warriors, sent to chastise Monzar; and he sends to Hirah for Antar.

In the meantime Bahram, the famed knight of Deelem, encounters Badhramoot, and holds his own against the Greek for two successive days. On the morning of the third day, when the champions were about to renew the combat, King Monzar and Antar, accompanied by a hundred Arab horsemen, appeared on the plain.

The Arabian prince and the Absian hero having been ushered into the presence of Chosroe, after Monzar had duly saluted him, Antar stepped forward, and thus addressed the Persian monarch in verse:

May God avert from thee the evils of fortune, and may thou live secure from calamities!

May thy star be ever brilliant in progressive prosperity, and increase in glory!

May thy sword be ever sharp, and cleave the necks of thy foes, O thou King of the age!

May thy renown be ever celebrated in every land; for thou art just and beneficent!

So mayst thou ever live a sovereign in glory, as long as the dove pours forth its plaintive note!

Chosroe was filled with admiration at the hero's eloquence, and was astonished to perceive his prodigious form: here, at last, thought he, was come the destined conqueror of Badhramoot. The king then gave orders that Monzar and Antar should be treated with all kindness and hospitality. But when it was proposed to pitch the tents, in order that they might repose till the next day, Antar declared that he would not rest until he had slain the Greek chief, and at once prepared for the combat. Badhramoot, having been apprised of the new champion who was come to oppose him, eagerly entered the lists, and Antar, as he advanced towards him, exclaimed:

This day will I aid King Monzar, and I will exhibit my powers and my prowess before Chosroe:

I will break down the support of Greece from its foundations, and I will sever Badhramoot's head with my scimitar.

I will exterminate every lion-hero with my sword; – let him vaunt, let him boast, let him scoff!

Is it not known that my power is sublime on high? – is it not among the stars in the vicinity of Jupiter?

I am he whose might is uncontrollable in battle; – I am of the race of Abs – the valiant lion of the cavern!

If thou art Badhramoot, I am called Antar among men!

It was easy for me to vanquish the armies of Chosroe in the contest; and soon will I overthrow Caesar's self with my spear.

Hear the words of an intrepid lion – resolute, undaunted, all-conquering:

I am he of whom warriors can bear witness in the combat under the turbid battle-dust.

My sword is my companion in the night-shades, as are also my Abjer and my lance and my spear in the conflicts.

Night is my complexion, but Day is my emblem: the sun is unquestionably the mirror of my deeds.

This day thou shalt feel the truth of what I have said; and I will prove that I am the Phoenix of the age!

He then rushed down upon the Greek, and wonderful was the combat that ensued. Badhramoot soon found that in the Absian hero he had met with no common warrior; – all his skill and prowess were of no avail when opposed to the agility and strength of Antar, who evaded his most deadly spear-thrusts with the utmost ease. Bahram, the knight of Deelem, an envious spectator of the combat, foreseeing that Antar should achieve a victory which had been denied to himself, basely threw a dart at him while both combatants were obscured in a cloud of dust. But Antar's ever-watchful eyes saw the action, and catching the missile as it approached him, he hurled it against Badhramoot with such force that it pierced his chest and issued out at his back, and the Greek fell lifeless from his horse.

Antar would then have taken a terrible revenge on the treacherous Bahram, had not Chosroe prevented him by despatching his satraps to conduct the hero before him; when, having presented Antar with an imperial robe, he commanded that all the gold and jewels and beautiful slave-girls that came with Badhramoot should be delivered to him.

Next day, at a magnificent feast, the slave-girls employed all their blandishments to divert Antar, but in vain; for his heart was filled with the image of Abla; which his friend Monzar observing, he rallied the hero on his attachment to an absent Arab girl, reminding him that he was now raised to a station of glory which all the chiefs of Arabia would envy. Antar replied that even the grandeur which surrounded him had no charm in his eyes: nothing could cause him to forget his own land, and his beloved Abla.

The hero's return to his own land, for which he so eagerly longed, was delayed from day to day by the grateful hospitality of Chosroe. He accompanies the king on a hunting expedition, and narrowly escapes being foully slain by Bahram, still envious of his good fortune in having vanquished the Greek champion. Antar eludes his stroke, and dashes him senseless to the earthy. Bahram's myrmidons rush upon the hero, who defends himself against them all, until Chosroe comes up, and orders his satraps to seize the dastards and strike off their heads. They were accordingly taken and pinioned. 'But Antar, seeing Bahram's attendants thus disgraced, dismounted from Abjer, and advanced towards the great King, and kissing the earth before him, begged him to pardon them, saying: – "O my lord, pardon is becoming in you, and most suitable for such as you – here I kiss your noble hands, praying you to forgive them this crime, for tomorrow I intend to return home; my objects and wishes with respect to you are accomplished, and I do not wish to be mentioned after my departure, but for virtuous deeds; and let it not be said of me, I went unto a tribe, and left it in disgrace, and clothed with shame." ' The king, admiring Antar's magnanimity, granted his request, and set Bahram's followers at liberty

The same day Antar was present at a great feast given by Chosroe in a splendid pavilion erected in the royal gardens: 'It was a superb palace, like a fairy pavilion, ninety cubits in length, and seventy cubits wide, built of marble and red cornelian. In the centre was a fountain filled with rose-water and purest musk; in the middle of it was a column of emerald, and on its summit a hawk of burnished gold; its eyes were topazes and its beak jasper; around it were various birds, scattering from their bills, upon Chosroe and all that were present, musk and ambergris. The whole edifice was scented with perfumes, and the ceilings of the palace glittered with gold and silver. It was one of the wonders of the period, and the miracle of the age.'

Chosroe pressed the hero to drink freely of wine, and to take pleasure in the strains of the singing-girls; but amidst all this regal splendour Antar's heart was far away, in the land of Shurebah, and thus he recited:

Wine cannot calm my heart; sickness will not quit my body; my eyelids are ever sore – tears ever stream in torrents from them.

The songstress would soothe my heart with her voice; but my love-sick heart loathes it.

The remembrances of Abla draw off my mind from her song, and I would say to my friend: This is all a dream!

Pleasures have succeeded to difficulties; and I have met a monarch whom no words can describe:

A King to whom all the creation is a slave, and to whom Fortune is a vassal; whose hand distributes bounties, so that I know not whether it is the sea or a cloud.

The sun has invested him with a crown, so that the world need not fear darkness.

The stars are his jewels, in which there is a moon, brilliant and luminous, as at its full.

Mankind is corporeal, and he is spiritual; – let every joint and every member laud his name!

Live for ever! Prince of the horsemen! – long as the dove pours its plaintive note, live for ever!

Delighted with these beautiful verses, Chosroe took the tiara from his brow and presented it to Antar, as a gift to Abla on her bridal day; he also gave him a canopy of pure silver, richly adorned with the rarest gems. And Antar took the opportunity of interceding for his friend king Monzar, who was graciously pardoned, and reinstated in power.

Rostam, the king's famous wrestler, envious of these princely honours bestowed upon a stranger, challenges Antar to wrestle with him before Chosroe. But Antar is reluctant to accept his challenge, lest it should be said of him that, after being the recipient of Chosroe's bounties, he had slain one of his subjects in his own presence – for, if he did wrestle with Rostam, who sought his life, assuredly he would kill him. The king advises Rostam to withdraw his challenge, but the wrestler insists upon the contest, and Anoushirvan at length grants his permission. Rostam then stripped off his clothes, but Antar merely tucked his skirts into his waist-band, and advanced to his antagonist.

'Rostam bent himself like an arch, and appeared like a burning flame. He rushed upon Antar with all his force, for he looked on him as a common man, and he did not know that Antar, even in his youth, used to wrestle with he and she camels in the plains and the rocks. They grasped each other with their hands, they butted with their heads, they assaulted with their whole might, like two lions, or two elephants. Then Rostam stretched out his hand at Antar's waistband, and clung to it, and attempted to lift him up in his arms, but he found him like a stone fixed in a tower, and he tottered before him. Then he repented of what he had done, and of having provoked Antar. He slackened his hold, and he ran round him for an hour, in the presence of Chosroe and his attendants. He then sprang behind him, and thrust his head between his legs, and attempted to raise him on the back of his neck and to dash him on the ground; but Antar knew what were his intentions and his secret designs; so he closed his knees on Rostam's neck, and almost made his eyeballs start from their sockets, and nearly deprived him of life. Rostam was terrified, and wished to escape from between his legs, but he could not; every attempt failed: Antar was like a block of stone growing on a desert or a mountain. Antar seized him and clung to him, and raised him up in his hands like a sparrow in the claws of a bird of prey, and walked away with him among the multitude, wishing to wrestle quietly before the king. But Rostam, when he saw his life was in Antar's hands, like a young child, was abashed and mortified before the warriors and satraps and the great King. He clenched his fist, and struck Antar on the ear. Antar soon recovered from the blow, – he returned to the threshold of the palace, and dashed him on the ground, and smashed him to atoms.'

The king then announced that Rostam had been justly slain for having transgressed the laws of fair battle, and assigned to Antar all the wrestler's property and wealth.

Shortly afterwards, the eventful day being spent, Monzar and Antar retired to their lodgings, where they were presently joined by Mubidan, the chief-priest of the Fire-worshippers, who, in compliance with the hero's urgent request, introduced him to the Temple of Fire.

'There he beheld a magnificent building, of yellow brass, raised on pillars of steel, with precious stones in the interstices, – the wonder of the age, to astonish the wisest of men. It had three storeys, and to each storey were three portals, and to each portal were slaves and servants, stationed over the edifice. Antar gazed at these men with glittering forms; and round the waists of each were leather coverings in the form of short breeches; and they were standing at the doors of the Temple, some near, and some at a distance. In their hands were pokers of steel, with which they raised the flame, heedless of the God of the two worlds, and uttering Magian words that ravished the soul; whilst their sheikh, seated on a bench of skin, chanted in his own tongue. The fire blazed before him; the fuel was of aloe-wood; towards which they all addressed their prostrations, saying: "I and you, we laud the adored God!" '

At length Antar obtains permission of Anoushirvan to return to his own country; and the king bestowed on his hero, as his parting gifts, a vast quantity of treasures, in gold and silver, and precious jewels; a thousand embroidered velvet robes, and a thousand rich silk vests; four hundred white male slaves and four hundred strong black slaves, fit for battle, with all their horses and accoutrements; four hundred Georgian female slaves, four hundred Copht and four hundred Persian slaves, and four hundred slaves of Tibah, each slave mounted on a mule, and under each were two chests of rich silk.

'Thus Antar departed with boundless wealth. The great king also mounted, with Mubidan and all the satraps, to take leave of Antar. And when they were at some distance from Modayin, and had plunged into the barren desert, Antar dismounted from Abjer, and, moving towards the king, kissed his feet in the stirrup, and begged him to return with his attendants, thus addressing him:

O thou, whose station is sublime – in thy beneficence above the heights of Sirius and Aries! –
Thou art the King like whom there is no king, and whose munificence is renowned over hill and dale!
O thou, my hope! – thou hast overwhelmed me with favours!
O thou, whose largesses resemble the bounteous rain-cloud! – thou hast bestowed gifts on me whose extent I cannot count:
So liberal is thy hand, O thou, my life and my hope!
Thou art he to whom all kings must submit; and in thy justice thou hast surpassed all thy predecessors!

' "Do not imagine," exclaimed the King, with augmented delight, "that we have been able duly to recompense you. What we have given you is perishable, as every thing human is; but your praises will endure for ages."

'He then kissed Antar between the eyes, and bade him adieu, giving him as a last token a rich robe; and begging him to visit him frequently, he departed.'

King Monzar and Antar journeyed on till they reached Hirah, where the hero was sumptuously entertained for some time; and when he was about to depart for his own land, Monzar gave him a thousand Asafeer camels, besides many other valuable gifts. Antar then began his journey homeward, attended by the troops of slaves presented to him by Anoushirvan and Monzar. As he traversed the deserts, he reflected on all the adventures and perils he had encountered for the sake of Abla, and on approaching the land of Hejaz, he gave way to his feelings in verse:

Is it the breeze from the heights of the land of Shurebah that revives me and resuscitates my heart, or is it the gale from the tamarisks?

Is it the flame that consumes me for Abla, or is it the lightning flash from her dwelling that deprives me of my senses?

O thou spot where she resides! May thy hillocks be ever inhabited by thy families, and may thy plains be ever crowded with friends!

Have thine eyelids been seen to watch at night, as my eyelids have watched ever since I quitted thee?

And has the turtle-dove's moan filled thee with sorrow in thy sleeplessness, as the turtle-dove's moan has distressed me?

I departed from thee not uneasy, or much in anguish; but my uncle has outraged me, and coveted my death.

He has exposed me to a sea of dangers, but I plunged into it with my glittering two-edged blade.

I have cut through the neck of Fortune, and the nocturnal vicissitudes and the nightly calamities have trembled.

My good fortune has seated me in a mansion of glory, man and genii could never attain.

I have encountered in Irak horsemen that may be accounted as whole tribes when the battle rages.

I am returning with the wealth of Chosroe and Caesar – with he and she camels, horses, and slaves;

And when I reach home, my enemies shall weep, as one day they laughed, when Shiboob announced my death.

They indeed sought my destruction in a distant land; but they knew not that Death was – my sword and my spear!

Abla's Trials During Antar's Absence

After it was spread abroad that old Malik had maliciously despatched Antar on the desperate enterprise to procure the Asafeer camels for Abla's dowry, he soon found himself the object of scorn and contempt among his tribe, and resolved to depart secretly, with fifteen horsemen, on a marauding expedition, and not to return until the scandal had been forgotten. But instead of plundering others, Malik and his party were taken prisoners by Vachid, a famous horseman of the tribe of Kenanah. This chief being informed by his mother that Malik had a beautiful daughter called Abla, he demands her in marriage, to which Malik readily consents, and offers to go and bring her to him as his bride. On this condition Vachid releases Malik and his son Amru, who at once depart for the land of Shurebah; and on approaching the habitations of their tribe, they find all the people in grief on account of the reported death of Antar. They skulk along until they reach their own tents, where they discover Abla, clothed in black, and seated in the deepest affliction, beside a newly-made grave.

Malik then enters the tent of his wife, who informs him that Shiboob had brought tidings of Antar's death, adding that all the tribe execrated himself as the cause; and after attempting to soothe the anguish of Abla, who refuses to be comforted, and calls him the murderer of her cousin, he next visits his brother Shedad, and hears him bitterly lamenting the loss of his heroic son.

Altogether the wretched Malik found matters very unpleasant, to say the least, and there was nothing for it but to emigrate with his family; – meanwhile concealing himself, lest Amarah, to whom he had also betrothed Abla, should suspect his design, and prevent his departure. But presently Amarah, now that his formidable rival was dead, resolves to lose no time in claiming his bride; and, accompanied by Oorwah the son of Wird, and ten other horsemen, he departs for the land of Yemen, to procure the dowry (by plunder, of course); and Malik resolves to take advantage of his absence and remove with his family. But when he acquainted Abla of how he had promised her in marriage to Vachid, she protested that she would never become the bride of either Amarah or Vachid, since her heart was buried in the grave of Antar.

In spite of Abla's tears and agonies, however, Malik caused the tents to be struck, and at midnight he quitted the tribe, and proceeded with his family to the Springs of Zeba, where Vachid lay concealed with Malik's companions, whom he held as hostages. On Malik's arrival, Vachid released his prisoners, who returned home; and the party of Vachid, including Malik's family, commenced their journey back to their own land.

On the fourth day of their march they were attacked by a party of brigands, led by a chief who rejoiced in the name of the 'Nocturnal Evil'. Eager to display his prowess in presence of Abla, Vachid encounters this formidable robber, and is slain. Malik and his son Amru are taken prisoners and securely bound; but while the brigands are engaged with Vachid's followers, Abla and her mother release them, and they all escape into the desert, where they meet with Amarah and his party, returning, exulting and victorious, with plunder, from the land of Yemen. Malik was giving Amarah an account of their misfortunes when they were surprised by the appearance of the Nocturnal Evil and his gang, who, having defeated the Kenanians, and turned back in quest of the howdah containing Abla, and finding it empty, had hastened to overtake the fugitives. Amarah and Oorwah prepare to resist the brigands, but are speedily overpowered and pinioned; and once more the fair Abla and her family are in the power of the dreaded 'Evil'. Having rested in that spot for the night, at daybreak the Nocturnal Evil sent before him five slaves in charge of Abla, with orders to proceed to a place called Zatool Menahil, and there pitch the tents – 'for there,' said the foul wretch, 'I intend to remain three days with this lovely damsel'.

Abla and Her Family Rescued by Antar

Now it happened that Antar, pursuing his journey homeward, reached the Zatool Menahil shortly after the five slaves in charge of Abla's litter had pitched the tents there; and he was not a little surprised to hear the voice of a woman within the litter, calling upon his own name in her distress, saying, 'Woe to these dastard slaves! O Antar! where are thine eyes, that they might behold me?'

Antar was now assured that the distressed damsel could be none but his own beloved Abla; and furiously assailing the slaves with his spear, he slew three of them, while the two others fled, to carry the news to their chief.

Abla was naturally overcome by the sudden apparition of her brave lover, whom she had long regarded as dead, but at length her spirits revived

She then told Antar how Shiboob had brought the doleful news of his death, and of all that had occurred to her during his long absence; and Antar, in his turn, briefly recounted his own adventures, and the perils he had been exposed to since he quitted the land of Shurebah to procure the Asafeer camels for her dowry.

Thus the lovers were conversing when the Nocturnal Evil was seen rapidly approaching, having heard, from the two slaves that escaped Antar's spear-thrusts, of the irresistible champion who had come to the rescue of their fair charge. Antar, mounted on Abjer, impetuously assailed the brigand with his spear, and, crying 'O by Abs! O by Adnan! – I am the lover of Abla!' forced it through his breast, so that he fell lifeless to the earth. The hero then hastened to disperse the followers of the Nocturnal Evil and release the prisoners; and while expressing his gratification at meeting his uncle Malik, he reminded him that all his late sufferings were but a just punishment for his past conduct.

Then were the tents pitched, and a grand feast prepared by Antar's slaves; and the hero entertained his friends with his adventures in Iraq and the honours and princely gifts bestowed on him by King Anoushirvan. After the feast was over, Antar rejoined Abla, who threw herself into his arms, and kissed him repeatedly; and when he told her of all the riches he had brought home with him, 'Truly,' she replied, 'thy safety is more acceptable to me than all thou hast described: I have felt no pleasure but in thy presence.' Antar smiled, and his bosom expanded with joy at the purity of her love.

The Hero's Reception by His Tribe

At daybreak the hero ordered the camels to be loaded and preparations made for continuing their journey home. Decorating Abla with magnificent robes studded with jewels, and placing on her head the diadem of Chosroe, he raised her into the silver litter, with her mother, and commanded the slaves to proceed with them in advance and guard them on the journey.

'When Abla was seated in the litter, her countenance became radiant and illumined; she smiled in the loveliest manner; every charm was heightened, and from her eyelashes she shot arrows that penetrated the slayer of men and heroes.' It was therefore no wonder that the coxcomb Amarah should be tortured with envy and rage at thus beholding the bride of Antar!

When the party were within one day's journey of the tribe of Abs, Malik, with his son Amru and Abla's mother, went in advance to apprise King Zoheir of Antar's return. All the warriors of Abs, with the King at their head, came forth to meet the hero, – and never was there such another meeting – such a glorious day! 'The noble Absians all surrounded him, whilst, in reply to King Zoheir, he related his adventures. His mother and his brothers wept, and clamoured at the ecstasy of meeting, and in the excess of their happiness after all past alarms and afflictions.' Antar then distributed rich presents to Zoheir and his sons, and to all the noble horsemen of Abs; to his father Shedad he gave abundance of gold and silver, and many stout slaves; and the remainder, with the Asafeer camels, he delivered to his uncle Malik. After this every one sought his own tent. 'But Amru, Abla's brother, made the camels that conveyed his sister kneel down; he lifted up the curtain of the litter – but *Abla was not there!*'

Antar's Grief for the Loss of Abla

'Fortune builds up, and throws down!' – Antar's cup of happiness, filled to overflowing, was in an instant dashed from his lips, by the mysterious disappearance of his beloved Abla, for whose sake he had braved the perils of the deserts and the wastes, and fought with savage lions, and with warriors all but invincible. This was a calamity for which the heroic son of Shedad was totally unprepared; it fell upon him with a force that threatened to deprive him of his reason. In vain the kind-hearted King Zoheir tried to soothe him with the assurance that he would soon clear up the mystery. The grief-stricken lover bitterly accused himself of having, in his anxiety to meet the King, carelessly left his heart's idol in charge of slaves who knew not her worth. The King sent forth parties to scour the country in every direction, but they all returned without having obtained tidings of the beautiful daughter of Malik. As to Antar himself, the calamity had quite unmanned him: his 'native hue of resolution was sicklied o'er with the pale cast of thought'; and the slayer of heroes was for the time being unfit for 'enterprises of great pith and moment'. He despatched his brother Shiboob, however, in quest of his lost bride, and awaited his return with anxious expectation, that banished sleep from his eyelids.

Shiboob Brings Tidings of Abla

Antar endured many days and weeks of torturing suspense, his only source of consolation being the society of King Zoheir, until at length Shiboob returned – with news of Abla.

'After I had passed through various cities of Yemen,' said Shiboob, 'I came to Sana and Aden, and encountered numerous difficulties until I reached the tribe of Tey. It was there I found Abla, in the power of Moofrij: there she attends on the camels and the sheep. He has clothed her in garments of raw leather, and makes her serve in the meanest offices day and night. His mother too threatens her, and treats her harshly in her speech; so that she weeps both when she rises and lies down. She calls on your name, and seeks her wonted succour from you both night and day.'

'Well, Shiboob,' said Antar, while the tears gushed from his eyes; 'but what was the cause of her falling into the power of Moofrij? – How came he, of all people, to obtain possession of her?'

'Son of my mother,' replied Shiboob, 'the cause of all this is Amarah, in whose mind are ever harboured evil and deceit. His envy at last over-powered him, at the sight of the vast wealth you had with you. He turned aside into the desert; but his love for Abla was so violent, that he followed your traces, and watched her after you had quitted her in the morning. Fate and destiny overcame her. He seized her; and, though he was desirous to vanquish her, Moofrij overtook him in the desert. He tore her away from him, and reduced him to a most pitiable state.'

'Brother,' said Antar, whose heart was almost bursting as he listened to this narrative, 'how did you obtain this information?'

'Know,' continued Shiboob, 'that, when I quitted you, I made the circuit of every tribe and horde, and made inquiries of every one I met, whether on horseback or on foot, until I came to Aja and Selma, and the waters of the tribe of Tey. With every family I passed one night, saying to myself, peradventure I may learn something. On the last night of my stay I slept in the dwelling of Moofrij, and my place of rest was close to that of one of his slaves, called Moobshir. He invited me to converse with him, and was very kind to me; and to his questions about my connections, "Son of my aunt," I replied, "I am of the tribe of Jalhema, of the family of Saad, son of Khoozrej – and this is the family of Hatim Tey." So he com-plimented me.

'But when all was still and quiet, and every one asleep, the voice of Abla struck upon my ears. She was loudly wailing, and exclaiming through the calmness of the night – "O for the joys of Mount Saadi and the land of Shurebah!" and she was expressing her regret at being separated from her native soil, and her loss of friends; adding – "O protector of the tribe of Abs, how often have I called on thee! Where is the path by which I can give thee news of myself and meet thee? O son of my uncle! for torments distract me. My eyes are ulcered with weeping, O son of my uncle! Thy foes triumph, and watchful are the eyes of thy enemies. It was the very moment of meeting, when separation closely followed its traces; and thou hadst but just arrived from Irak, when we were again scattered over the globe! Woe to me! my lot is nothing but tears and sighs. What a misery it is to put on raw leather for a garment! Cruel is this grievous state! Hasten, then, thy arrival, son of my uncle; – rescue me by thy exertions, that laid low the lions of the caverns. Let me hear thy shouts in the tumults of spearsmen and swordsmen."

'After this doleful effusion, my brother, she sobbed and sighed so bitterly, it might almost be said that she was dead, and that her soul had departed.

'I immediately turned,' continued Shiboob, 'towards the slave near whom I was lying: "Son of my aunt," said I, "why is this damsel grieving? Does she not sleep? Does she pass her nights generally thus?" – "Young man," replied the slave, "she is a foreigner, and she is a captive; it is thus she passes her mornings and evenings. Her name is Abla, daughter of Malik, the Absian."

'I soon contrived to draw from him the whole story; how Moofrij happened to meet Amarah and her; how he took Amarah prisoner, and carried her home; and when he demanded of her what man demands of woman, how she used the most opprobrious expressions towards him – threatening him with her cousin, a fierce lion, who had raised himself from the state of a slave to that of a chief; how Moofrij upon this treated her most vilely – stripping her of her clothes, and overwhelming her with cruelties; how also he behaved in the same manner to Amarah – handcuffing and fettering him, until he should ransom himself with money and camels; and that he had sent to Rebia to rescue him from misery.

'At hearing this, O son of my mother, sweet sleep abandoned my eyes, and I anxiously waited for the dawn of day, that I might hasten to you, and return with my intelligence. But on my way I met the family of Zeead, travelling towards that tribe. I turned out of the road, so that they did not see me: and this is what I have seen and heard during my absence.'

Antar Rescues His Beloved

When Shiboob had concluded his story, Antar appeared to be stupefied with rage and grief; but recovering himself, he cried, 'I must be revenged on that family of Zeead! – I will deprive them of their sweet slumbers!' He hastened to his friend Prince Malik, who conducted him to the King, to whom he related Amarah's ungrateful return for his services in liberating him from the Nocturnal Evil. Zoheir was greatly exasperated at the infamous conduct of Amarah, and vowed vengeance upon the whole family of Zeead. But Antar tells Prince Malik that he will not put the king to any trouble on his account, for he will alone undertake the rescue of Abla. His friend, however, insists upon going with him; and, taking advantage of the king's absence at the chase, he musters his father's horsemen, while Antar summons Shedad and his brother Malik, with his son Amru; and the sun was not yet high when the warriors, to the number of two hundred, set out to revenge the insult that had been offered to the family of Carad, and to the whole tribe of Abs. On the way, Antar, turning to Prince Malik, thus addressed him:

'Truly, my lord, it is very absurd in me to set out to the assistance of my foes. This is the most grievous circumstance of all; for I am aware that, though they become victorious by my means, they will not let me be quiet. But it is on Abla's account that I act thus.'

Meanwhile Rebia, with two hundred horsemen of his family, is advancing to the rescue of his brother Amarah. But Moofrij has timely warning, and, assailing them, routs the party and takes thirty prisoners; and Rebia, with the remnant of his followers, retreats into the sand-hills. There they are in distress from want of water, and Rebia sends a messenger to Moofrij, asking his protection in order that they might surrender themselves and procure their ransom; or, if he will not consent to forgo the further shedding of blood, at least supply them with water. To this message Moofrij returns the grim answer, that he would furnish them with water only on the condition that they throw away their arms, and come dismounted before him; when he would shave off their beards, and cut off their noses and their ears; after which – by Lat and Uzza! – he would hang them all. In desperation Rebia and his followers descend and commence another attack; but, being weakened by thirst, the Teyans easily make prisoners of them all.

'The night was not far spent when Moofrij became intoxicated. The people had departed to their respective tents, and every one was asleep, when Moofrij happened to think of Abla; and as he was considering how he should complete his gratification, he repaired to his mother, and said: "I wish you would bring me that Absian damsel. If she will not consent, I will use her most cruelly; I will multiply her distresses, and slay her countrymen." Away hastened his mother to Abla. – "Go to your master instantly," said she, "that he may show some kindness to you and your countrymen; but if you still obstinately refuse to yield to him, dread his violence." – "Vile hag!" exclaimed Abla, "were your son even to hack my limbs with the sword, or to massacre the whole tribe of Abs, and all that the sun rises upon, never would he see me his property – never see me yield or submit to him. Wishes he my death? I will kill myself with my own hand." – "Accursed wretch!" cried the old woman. She struck her with her fist, and ordered the slave-girls to drag her forth, as she screamed out, "O by Abs! O by Adnan! who can now save me? who can assist me? who can redeem me from this captivity? Alas! is there any one to deliver me from this distress?" '

The same night Teyans were surprised in their tents by the renowned Antar and his warriors, crying, 'O by Abs! O by Adnan!' and sparing neither old nor young. While the horsemen were engaged in slaying or capturing the Teyans, Shiboob released Rebia and his companions; then roamed among the tents in search of Abla, whom he at length found covered with the bodies of the slain, and groaning like a woman bereft of her children.

Shiboob took Abla in his arms, and brought her to Antar, who pressed her to his breast, and kissed her between the eyes, saying, 'Grievous indeed it is to me that you should suffer such calamities, and I be alive in the world! But it is the misfortune of the times, against which no human being can find refuge.' He then desired his brother to convey her to the tent of Moofrij (who had escaped to the sand-hills); and here Shiboob has the satisfaction of discovering all Abla's property – her rich robes and strings ' of jewels – which he restores to her. 'Thus all her distresses and afflictions vanished, and her hopes and wishes were released.'

As the Absians are about to set out for their own country, Rebia and Amarah come up to Antar, and in the most abject manner implore his forgiveness for their infamous deeds. 'Antar pitied them; and, feeling favourably inclined towards them on account of his relationship, he embraced them, saying: "Although I am abused for being black, my acts are the acts of the noble born." '

Returning from the land of Cahtan, they encounter the tribes of, Jadeelah and Nibhan, and, after a dreadful battle, are victorious. When they had collected all the spoil, they returned to their tents, preceded by Antar.

'Abla rejoiced at his prowess and intrepidity, and smiled; and as Antar saw her smile,–"Daughter of my uncle," said he, "are you smiling at what you saw me perform this day in the carnage and combat?" –"By the faith of an Arab," she replied, "my sight was bewildered at your slaughter among these wretches!" – Her words descended into his heart sweeter than the purest water to the thirsty spirit.'

At midnight, the Absians, having first divided the spoil, mounted their horses and resumed their march home. When the sun's rays began to dispel the darkness they discovered the Teyans, headed by King Maljem, son of Handhala, and his brother, the Blood-drinker, in pursuit of them. On seeing the number of the enemy, they were disposed for flight, but Antar inspired them with courage, by rushing impetuously among the Teyans, dealing death and destruction with his irresistible sword Dhami. At this juncture the Absians are reinforced by troops which King Zoheir had despatched to Antar's assistance, and the Teyans are defeated with great slaughter.

The next day, Abla's father, acting upon Rebia's suggestion, begs Prince Shas to take Abla under his protection, to prevent Antar from marrying her, to which he consents; and sending for Antar, he intimates to him that henceforth Abla shall be under the protection of his wife; at the same time reproaching him for lusting after a woman to whom he has no claim. Tears filled the eyes of the hero as he replied, saying that it was his uncle Malik who had excited his passion; – for whenever Abla is a prisoner, he entreats him to liberate her; but when she is in safety, he calls him a slave, and the son of a slave-woman.

Antar then goes to his friend Prince Malik, and acquaints him of his uncle's new device to thwart his union with Abla. The Prince promises to carry her off for him – only let him wait until they return to King Zoheir, and he should obtain justice. But the hero, unwilling to burden his friend with his distresses, or to be the cause of dissensions in his tribe, resolves to set out secretly for Mecca, and there make his complaints to the Lord of mankind.

Antar Goes to Mecca

At night, when all was still, Antar, mounted on Abjer, and accompanied by his brother Shiboob, departs for the Holy Shrine.

Their journey was marked with no particular incident until they drew near Mecca, when Shiboob observed to his brother that it was strange they had met with no adventure on the way. Antar replied that he was harassed with encountering dangers, and his heart was disgusted at fighting.

But presently they hear, in the calmness of the night, a female voice crying out, evidently in sore distress; upon which Antar slackens his bridle, and gallops in the direction whence proceeded the cries. He discovers a lady, who informs him that she is of the noble tribe of Kendeh; her husband, As-hath, the son of Obad; that a famine having visited their land, they were proceeding, with their family, to the country of Harith, where they intended to settle, having a daughter married there, when they were attacked by a horseman of the desert, called Sudam, the son of Salheb, with forty plundering Arabs, who had slain her three sons, wounded her husband, and taken herself and her three daughters captive; and that the brigands were about to convey them to the mountains of Toweila, there to sell them as slaves. Consigning the ladies to the care of his brother, Antar grasped his spear, and turned to meet Sudam and his followers, whom he now saw hastily advancing towards him. The hero is assailed by several of the brigands at once, but he cuts them down on either side, and at length encounters Sudam, and, striking him on the breast with his cleaving Dhami, the chief falls to the ground dead, weltering in his blood.

The three damsels and their mother crowd round their deliverer, kissing his hands and thanking him for having saved them from dishonour; and Antar, desiring the damsels to veil themselves, and having bound up the old sheikh's wounds, sat down to rest himself after the fatigues of his conflict. The old sheikh, grateful for the good service rendered his family by Antar, offers him his choice of his three daughters, but Antar courteously declines the compliment, saying to the damsels:

Were my heart my own, I should desire nothing beyond you – it would covet nothing but you.
But it loves what tortures it; where no word, no deed encourages it.

Having escorted the old sheikh and his family to the land of Harith, Antar took leave of them, and, in company with Shiboob, proceeded to Mecca. 'He alighted in the Sacred Valley, and there he resided; passing his days in hunting, to relieve his sorrows and afflictions, and his nights with Shiboob, in talking over old stories and past events.'

Prince Shas in Captivity

The friends of Antar were much troubled at his departure, and searched for him in all directions; but his uncle was especially gratified, since it left him free, as he thought, to dispose of Abla; and accordingly she is again betrothed to Amarah – the contract being formed by Abla's father and Amarah shaking hands. But Prince Malik, grieved at this great injustice to his absent friend, vows that he will never permit Amarah to marry Abla, while he lives to thwart his wicked plans, and those of the maiden's sordid and crafty father; and he predicts that evil will befall his brother Shas for his share in the infamous transaction.

When the Absians reached the lake of Zat-ul-irsad, Prince Shas with ten horsemen went into the desert in pursuit of the antelope. There they are met by a troop of warriors led by Maisoor, son of Zeead, of the clan of Hazrej, a branch of Harith, and the little band of Absians are all slain, with the exception of Shas, who is taken prisoner, and barbarously treated by Maisoor, whose brother the Prince had killed in the conflict.

Prince Malik and the others arrive in safety at the dwellings of their tribe, and the King is indignant when he learns how the noble Antar has been again deceived by Abla's father. He severely rebukes him for his scandalous conduct, and causes Amarah to be scourged as a punishment for espousing Abla, when he knew that she was already betrothed to Antar, and that her father was in possession of the rich dowry which the hero had brought from Irak. The absence of Prince Shas causes the King great uneasiness. Having sent horsemen into the desert in quest of him without success, his affliction increases, and he declares that if Shas is slain, he will strike off the head of Amarah, and hang Malik, the son of Carad, because they had incited his son to act basely towards Antar.

In the meantime Shas is a prisoner in the land of Harith, and daily tortured by Maisoor, who 'enclosed him between four bars of iron, and stationed a guard of slaves over him; and whenever he went out he kicked him, and whenever he entered he thumped him with his fists'. The chief of the clan, however, hearing of this shameful treatment of a noble Arab, sends for Maisoor, and advises him to relax his severities towards his prisoner, which he does, in this manner: he hastens back to Shas and unties his hands, but binds his feet; then he kicks him in the rear, and places a slave over him.

Antar Summoned from Mecca to Rescue Shas

The unhappy Prince, however, finds a friend in need in the old lady of Kendeh, who, with her family, had been rescued from the brigand Sudam, by Antar, on his way to Mecca. Misfortune had taught Shas a salutary lesson, and he now bitterly repented of his conduct towards the noble hero: he assured the old lady that if ever he gained his freedom he would henceforth befriend Antar, and further his union with Abla. Perceiving the advantages which Antar would derive from the friendship of Shas, the good old lady despatches her husband, As-hath, to Mecca, to acquaint the hero of Shas' condition.

'With all haste he traversed the plains till he reached Mecca, where he inquired for Antar; and being directed to his residence, he introduced himself, and told what had happened to Shas, and how he had left him in despair. – "May God never deliver him from peril or death!" cried Shiboob; "for my brother has no such enemy among the Absians as he." – "Brother," said Antar, "bear malice against no man"; and he repeated these verses:

> Do not bear malice, O Shiboob! – renounce it, for no good ever came of malice.
>
> Violence is infamous: its result is ever uncertain, and no one can act justly when actuated by hatred.
>
> Let my heart support every evil, and let my patience endure till I have subdued all my foes.

'When Antar had finished, the old man was amazed at such clemency towards his enemies, strong and powerful as he was. That night they reposed; but early next morning Antar said to As-hath, "Let us depart, O Sheikh, before my lord Shas be reduced to the last extremity and be killed." The sheikh and Antar were soon mounted, and Shiboob started in front of them, making the wild beasts and antelopes fly before him.'

But before Antar can come to his deliverance, Maisoor has determined to hang Prince Shas without further delay, and the old lady of Kendeh therefore enables him to escape in the disguise of a slave, directing him to take the road to Mecca. Having rested during the night in a mountain-cave, the Prince resumes his flight at daybreak, and meets with a party of the tribe of Riyan, one of whom mistakes him for a slave who lately stole his horse. He tells them that he is Shas, the son of Zoheir; but unfortunately his captors are enemies of his tribe; and they are about to put him to death, when they discover a man running towards them with the speed of the wind, and close behind him two horsemen. These are Shiboob and the noble Antar and As-hath. The hero, with his sword Dhami, and Shiboob, with his arrows, soon make all the warriors to bite the dust, save one, who escapes on a swift camel.

Prince Shas expresses his contrition to Antar, and promises to make him ample amends for the past. Antar having presented to As-hath all the horses and plunder, the old sheikh takes his leave, and departs for his own country; while the hero and Prince Shas begin their journey to the land of Hejaz, with the trusty Shiboob for their guide. On the fifth day they reached the waters of the tribe of Akhram, where they rested for the night.

The Hero Encounters Roudha, a Gallant Horseman, Going A-wooing to Abla

Shiboob continued to guide his brother and Prince Shas in safety past many hostile tribes, and on the eleventh day they reached the country called Zat-ul-ialam. 'In the middle of the plain they met six howdahs, upon six camels; and over each howdah was a crescent of polished gold, with hangings of magnificent velvet; and round the howdahs rode a troop of sturdy slaves, armed with shields and sharp swords. The whole cavalcade was preceded by a knight in whom fortitude and intrepidity shone conspicuous. He was close-vizored and broad-shouldered; over his body was a corslet that enveloped his limbs; upon his head was an Aadite helmet, like a raised canopy; he was girt with a well-watered scimitar, and a well-proportioned spear was slung round him; and beneath him was a white horse, of the noblest breed; and, like a ferocious lion, he marched in front of the howdahs and the camels.'

This horseman was Roudha the son of Meneea, who, like Amarah, had fallen in love with the daughter of Malik, from descriptions he had heard of her beauty; and he was now on the way to the tribe of Abs, with rich presents for Abla, and accompanied by his mother and his five sisters – eager to encounter Antar, or any other famed knight who would oppose him, for Abla's sake.

A combat, of course, ensues between Antar and Roudha, in which the Absian hero unhorses his antagonist, but spares his life and grants his liberty on the intercession of his mother and sisters; and Roudha, full of admiration and gratitude for his clemency, begs Antar's acceptance of the presents he had intended for Abla, and returns home.

Prince Shas and Antar at length reach the land of their tribe, and are heartily welcomed by the King and all the noble warriors of Abs. The hero's time-serving uncle congratulates him on his return, and declares that Antar shall be married to Abla that very night. 'Shedad thought the world too narrow for the extent of his joy on the arrival of his son: his mother, Zebeebah, kissed him, as she said, "If you would but stay and tend the camels with me, my heart would be relieved from the pain of all these terrible events." Antar smiled, and composed her.' The King celebrates the return of Shas and Antar with a grand feast, at which all the sons of Zoheir warmly profess their friendship for the hero.

Antar Undertakes Another Enterprise for Abla's Sake

Thus, once more, every obstacle to Antar's marriage appears to be removed; but in reality his treacherous uncle is as much averse as ever to his union with Abla, and he soon devises another stratagem to bring about the hero's death. Artfully instructed by her father, Abla demands of Antar that at her marriage she should be exalted as was Jaida, the daughter of Zahir: when she was married to her cousin Khalid, the son of Moharib, the bridle of her camel was held by the daughter of Moawiyah, son of Nizal. The hero boldly promises that at Abla's marriage Jaida herself shall hold her bridle, with Khalid's head slung round her neck. To this wild proposal the father of Abla pretends opposition; but, as he had anticipated, Antar is resolute; and that same night the hero, eager to gratify the wishes of his darling Abla, set out on his perilous enterprise, exclaiming:

I traverse the wastes, and the night is gloomy: I stray over the wilds, and the sands are parching; I desire no other companion but the sword, whether, on the day of horrors, the foe be few or numerous.

Ye beasts of the desert! beware of the warrior; for when he brandishes his scimitar, caution avails not.

Accompany me: ye will behold prostrate carcasses, and the birds darting at them as they hover and look on.

Now that I am going in quest of him, no eternity is there for Khalid.

No, no; let Jaida no longer boast; – short will be the happiness of their country – soon will the tiger come!

O Abla! may the riches that come for thee rejoice thee, when Fortune casts me among thy enemies!

O thou, who, with one glance of the eye, hast exposed my life to deadly arrows, whose wounds are frightful – it is well; for thy embrace is an unadulterated paradise, and the flames of separation from thee cannot be endured.

O Mount Saadi! may showers from the rain-cloud ever moisten thee, and may the dew ever refresh thy lands!

How many nights have I travelled in thy society, and lived in happiness, unalloyed by pain, with the damsel who circles the goblets, and whose form shines among them like the flame of wine!

The maiden who passes them round is of the daughters of Arabia, elegantly formed, and Paradise is in her eye.

If I live, it is she whom I will ever remember: if I die, a night in death with her will be existence.

Story of Jaida and Khalid

Moharib and Zahir, the fathers respectively of Khalid and Jaida, were brothers. Moharib was chief of the tribe of Zebeed, and Zahir was his counsellor. The brothers quarrelled, and Zahir struck his tents, and cast his lot with the kindred tribe of Saad. Zahir's wife becoming pregnant, he said to her that if a son was born, he would be most welcome; but if a girl, then she was to conceal the fact, and let it appear to the world that they had a male child, in order that his brother should not exult over him. In due course a daughter was born, and was called, in private, Jaida, but Jooder in public, that it might appear she was a boy. About the same time Moharib had a son born to him, whom he called Khalid. The daughter of Zahir was brought up as a boy, and taught to ride on horseback; and soon she became famous in all the exercises befitting a noble warrior – accompanying her father to battle, in which she ever took a prominent part. Khalid was also one of the most illustrious horsemen of the age, universally acknowledged as an intrepid warrior and a valiant hero.

The fame of his cousin Jooder (Jaida) having reached him, Khalid, after his father's death, visited his uncle, and spent ten days in jousting with the horsemen of the family. Jaida became deeply enamoured of him, and her mother, on learning this, revealed the secret of her sex to Khalid's mother, and suggested that their children should be united in marriage. But when Khalid was told by his mother that his cousin was a woman, he was greatly chagrined, slighted her love for him, and hastened back to his own tribe.

Jaida, enraged at finding herself thus scorned, resolved to be revenged on her cousin, and disguising herself, she set out for the land of Zebeed. Arrived there, she entered a tent of public entertainment, close-vizored, like a horseman of Hejaz. After proving her superiority over the best horsemen in the course, she encountered Khalid for three days in succession, without either of them obtaining any advantage; when she discovered herself to her cousin, his hatred was now suddenly converted into love. But Jaida rejected him, and returned home.

Khalid hastened to his uncle and demanded Jaida in marriage. His cousin at length consents, on condition that he provide for slaughter at her wedding-feast a thousand camels belonging to Gheshm, son of Malik, surnamed the Brandisher of Spears. These Khalid procured by plundering the tribe of Aamir; but on his return, Jaida imposed a further condition – that her camel should be led by the captive daughter of a prince. Khalid again set out with his horsemen, and, assailing the family tribe of Moawiyah, son of Nizal, took captive his daughter Amimah; and his marriage with Jaida took place immediately after his return; when the daughter of Moawiyah held the bridle of her camel, 'and the glory of Jaida was exalted among women and among men'.

Antar in the Land of Zebeed

On reaching the country of the Zebeedians, Antar finds Khalid absent on a plundering expedition, but he is met by Jaida on horseback, armed as a knight. The warlike lady boldly encounters Antar; she is vanquished, and taken prisoner. Zoheir having summoned his warriors and set out to join Antar, the father of Abla avails himself of this opportunity of again quitting the tribe, and accordingly Malik emigrates with his family, and accompanied by Rebia, to the tribe of Aamir. But here his usual ill-fortune follows him; for the Aamirites are presently attacked by Khalid and his warriors, and Malik and Rebia are taken captive. Returning home, Khalid meets the Absians, and a desperate battle ensues, with great slaughter on both sides. During the following night Antar and Khalid keep watch over their respective tribes: the two chiefs meet; Khalid is slain by the all-conquering hero, and Shiboob cuts off his head as a trophy to grace Abla's wedding. Meantime a general battle takes place, in which the Absians are completely victorious. After the horsemen of Abs had returned from pursuing the enemy and collected the spoil, Antar inquired for Jaida, but she had escaped; Malik and his daughter too were nowhere to be found;

and the hero passed a sleepless night, lamenting the loss, once more, of his darling Abla.

At daybreak the noble Absian warriors set out for home, and as they drew near the tents of their tribe, 'high and low came out to meet them, and it was a grand day for them all'. When friends had greeted friends, all retired to their tents; but Antar remained gazing sorrowfully upon the abandoned and ruined dwelling of Abla; and leaning on his spear, in a voice expressive of his poignant grief, he recited these verses, which form the opening of his famous *Moällacah*:

> Have the poets left aught to be repaired in song? Canst thou recollect the abode of thy love, after long meditation?
>
> O dwelling of my Abla! Speak to me from Jiwa! Hail to thee, dwelling of my Abla! secure and safe be thou!

The Matrimonial Schemes of Abla's Father Again Come to Naught

Shiboob having been despatched by the sorrowing hero to obtain tidings of Abla, after many days he returns with a message of love from her to Antar; but also with the unpleasant intelligence that her father, now dwelling in the tribe of Shiban, had promised Abla in marriage to Bostam, the son of Prince Kais, on condition that he brought him Antar's head as her dowry.

Bostam accordingly sets out for the land of Abs, meets Antar, and is vanquished in combat with the hero. Shiboob comes to report the capture of all the women of Shiban by the tribe of Temeen. Bostam offers his assistance in rescuing Abla; Antar releases him; and together they proceed to take vengeance on the despoilers. Again the hero rescues Abla from captivity.

His uncle Malik also wept (crocodile's tears), and once more renewed to him his promise of Abla's hand. The crafty old fellow, however, persuades Antar to return home, on a vain errand, and as soon as he is gone, again flees with his daughter; but Antar gets word of this, and pursues him. Malik places himself and his family under the protection of King Amru, of Kendeh, and espouses Abla to Mas-hil, the king's nephew.

Shiboob in Masquerade at the Tents of Kendeh

Shortly before the appointed day of Abla's bridal, Antar arrived in the neighbourhood of the tribe. Shiboob disguised himself as a woman, and, with a water-bag slung over his shoulders, sought the tents of Kendeh.

'He perceived the tents destitute of horsemen, for they were gone out to the plain, and the families were occupied in festivities. The unmarried girls were playing about, and beating the cymbals and musical instruments, and the slaves were brandishing their swords and shields, and their countenances appeared glistening with joy. When Shiboob saw this, he advanced towards them, and mixing with them, looked towards a tent, on the outside of which was a brilliant illumination of lamps and candles. Being convinced that this must be the nuptial pavilion, he made a great noise, and began to play, and mingled with the women and slave-girls, and danced till he attracted the attention of all present, and they all crowded round him, staring at him while he sang, for he knew his voice would reach Abla:

Fawn of the huntsman, thy captor is come: say not he is not come; lo! here he is – certain are all thy hopes! – rejoice in the aid of the sword of thy hero!

Understand the tale I tell thee: how long wilt thou delay? Joy is now descending on thy home, and will ever endure, summer and winter.

'Now Abla was at that moment listening to the music from the tent. She signified her wish to sing and play with the other damsels, and thus addressed Shiboob:

O wanderer of the desert, dancer of the tent! – the lion is the noble animal that affords refuge after excess of pain – this is indeed a period of my joy in thee!

All my sorrows and griefs have vanished. My joy depends on thee, O Chief! Approach, for I am here as one dead!

'When Shiboob heard these words, he pretended being tired, and sat down near the tent. Just at that time Abla also appeared and looked at him, and, as he was dressed in woman's clothes – "This damsel cannot be a Kendeyan maid," she said: "she must be a damsel of Shedad's." Then went pit-a-pat Shiboob's heart; but he turned towards her, and calmed her mind, and uncovered his face. She recognized him. "O Shiboob!" said she, "where is my cousin Antar?" – "Here he is," replied Shiboob, "hard by; and with him his friend Oorwah, and a hundred horsemen. We arrived here last night, and I am come to procure intelligence of you: I shall return and inform him." – "Shiboob," said she, "there are still three days for the marriage with Mas-hil, son of Tarak; but let that rather be the means of separation. Return immediately and tell him my situation; but let him not think of assaulting the tribe; he must lie in wait for me till I set out: then let him rush forth, and slay all that are with me. Do you seize the bridle of my camel, and we will return to our native land. All – all must taste of death; bid Antar not to spare even my father."

'Shiboob, having heard this, returned to Antar, and related to him all that Abla had told him.'

Antar forms his plans accordingly; and, waylaying the bridal party, slays Mas-hil, and seizes his uncle Malik. The Kendeyans are attacked by Bostam, and the Absians, led by Zoheir's sons, arrive to the aid of Antar.

The Princes reproach Antar for leaving them, and abuse his uncle for his infamous conduct. Antar magnanimously offers to make no demand upon his uncle, if he will go back to the land of Abs with his daughter; but he must marry her to no one else. Malik is thus compelled to return with Abla to his own tribe; while Antar determines to reside for some time with his friend Bostam in Shiban. But his passion for the daughter of Malik soon sends him forth again in quest of her.

Antar finds his uncle lying in the desert, desperately wounded, his party having been attacked by Anis, son of Madraka, the Kitaamite, and Abla and her brother taken prisoners. He pursues this chief, rescues Abla and Amru, and returns to the land of Abs with his uncle's family.

Attempted Murder of Abla

A fresh plot is formed by Rebia, the brother of Amarah, to thwart Antar's marriage. Rebia employs a female slave to decoy Abla to the lake, one evening, on pretence of her meeting with Antar, when she is carried off, and concealed in the land of Shiban. The slave-girl soon afterwards discovers the iniquitous affair, and Rebia is compelled to leave the tribe. He proceeds to Shiban, where he finds Mooferrij, the friend who had charge of Abla, in terror lest Antar should come to know of his share in the transaction. They determine to have Abla murdered and buried in the sand-hills, so as to leave no trace of her. A slave, named Basharah, accordingly carries Abla into the desert, and is about to deal her a fatal blow with his poniard, when a man suddenly pounces upon him, strikes him with a dagger between the shoulders, and the assassin falls to the earth, bathed in blood.

The deliverer of Abla was Shiboob, who chanced to pass that way in quest of her. Basharah, however, was not killed, though badly hurt. He disclosed the chief actors in the murderous plot, and, with Shiboob's consent, he placed Abla under the care of his own mother, living at a distant place; and there she remained until Antar found an opportunity of exposing Rebia's guilt to the King.

The Hero Quits His Tribe

But at length Antar's love for Abla is the cause of so many dissensions in the tribe that King Zoheir requests hiim to depart. The noble hero, with his father and uncles, accordingly quits the land of Abs. After plundering the tribe of Fazarah, the warriors of Carad, led by Antar, invade the land of Shiban, before assailing Mooferrij, who had concealed Abla from him, and whom he took prisoner.

Numan, King of Hirah, Makes War Against King Zoheir – the Hero Saves His Country

King Zoheir had soon cause to wish for the presence of the champion of Abs and Adnan. Having refused to give his daughter in marriage to

Numan, King of Hirah, the latter sends his brother, Prince Aswad, with a large army to lay waste the land of Abs; and Antar partriotically resolves to assist his sovereign and old friend in repelling the invaders. The army of Prince Aswad was destroyed by a strategem of Shiboob, who contrived to obtain access to their water-bags, and, cutting them open, allowed all the water to escape. Weakened by thirst, they were easily vanquished by a very small force of Absians, and, among others, Prince Aswad was taken prisoner.

Meanwhile the renowned female warrior, Jaida, who had been captured by Antar and afterwards escaped, set out from her own country to take vengeance on the hero for the death of Khalid. She did not meet Antar, however, but, attacking a party of Absians, she took Malik and Abla prisoners; then she went to Irak, and delivered them to Numan, who declared that he would hang Abla beside Antar, and would not leave a single Absian alive. But when he heard of Antar's great victory over his brother's army, he despatched a satrap to the hero, offering to exchange Abla and the other Absian women for Prince Aswad and his companions. The royal messenger returned with the answer, that Abla and all her jewels must be restored before he would release Prince Aswad; and Numan, hearing from his satrap a fearful account of Antar's exploits and prodigious courage, at once complied with the hero's demand. As soon as Abla and her father were restored to their tribe, Antar proceeded to release his prisoners, among whom was Maadi Kereb, a cousin of Jaida.

'Having now entered the mountains, Antar ordered Shiboob to set at liberty Prince Aswad and his people. And Shiboob released them. But Antar cut off Maadi Kereb's hair with his own hands, saying: "O Maadi Kereb, I have cut off your hair in revenge for Jaida's insults towards my cousin Abla"; and he ordered the slaves and attendants to turn out the prisoners bare-footed, and naked, and bare-headed. And as they were executing Antar's commands, – "Art thou not ashamed, O son of Shedad," cried Aswad, "to drive us away in this condition? We have not a horse to ride on! We have nothing to eat or drink!" – "By the faith of an Arab," said Antar, "reproach me not for my conduct towards any one of you; for you are all going to assemble in a body against me, and you will return a second time to fight me, and the horses I should give you, verily I shall have to fight you for them. As to eatables, you will find on your way green weeds that you may graze on, and drink out of the puddles; but we at all events are a tribe entrenched within the mountains, and in the day of battle a small supply will feed us. Ay, and most of you say of me that Antar is a black slave and a bastard; – these are the expressions you and others make use of towards me, and would do so were I to release you a thousand times: my best plan would be to kill you all at once – thank God you are alive." – "Do not act thus, O Aboolfawaris," said Aswad; "for indeed I cannot walk on foot, no, not a quarter of a mile; so do give me something to carry me, or put me instantly to death, and deliver me from this ignominy." – "Hola, Ebe Reah!" said Antar to Shiboob, "bring here a she-camel; let him mount it and quit my presence, or I shall never be able to keep my sword off his neck." So Shiboob ran off, and, with his usual ingenuity and sagacity, he chose out a she-camel, foundered and quite worn out – born lame and blind – weary and broken-winded – grunting, loose-lipped, and toothless – crop-eared and spavined. When it was presented to the Prince his soul was most indignant. – "Come, Prince," cried Shiboob, "mount, whilst I hold the bridle, for I am terribly afraid she will fly away; for indeed she is one of the celebrated breed of Asafeer camels!" – "May God curse the bowels that bore thee!" cried the Prince; "away with it, for I want it not"; and he rushed out from the mountains, blaspheming the fire.'

Anoushirvan, King of Persia, hearing of Antar's exploits against his vassal, Numan, of Hirah, sends his satrap, Wirdishan, with a large army, to humble the champion of Abs. A fearful battle takes place between the Persians and the Absians, in the Valley of Torrents, in which Wirdishan (like his renowned predecessor, Khosrewan) is slain by the irresistible Antar, and the Persians are completely routed.

The hero's fair enemy, Jaida, still burning to avenge the death of her husband, Khalid, again takes the field at the head of the warriors of Zebeed.

'The tribe of Zebeed sent forth one general shout that made the mountains tremble – they remembered the death of their chief Khalid – they poured down upon Antar, uncovering their heads, and lightening their garments, to the number of five thousand, and about two thousand of the tribes of Lakhm and Juzam followed them; they all attacked, led by Maadi Kereb, bellowing like a lion.' But Antar, with only three hundred horsemen, resolutely received their attack, and defeated the whole seven thousand – Jaida and Maadi Kereb flying for their lives.

King Numan, having sent another army against Abs, which was driven back by the noble Antar and his lion-warriors, now became anxious for peace, and renewed his proposal for the hand of Zoheir's daughter. Antar, grateful to Numan for having released his father Shedad, who had fallen into his power, strongly advised Zoheir to consent, and peace was proclaimed, and Numan duly married to Zoheir's daughter.

But Prince Aswad misrepresents his brother Numan's conduct in the late war to Anoushirvan, who deposes him, confers his kingdom on Aswad, and sends his son Khodawend with fifty thousand Persians to destroy the Absians. At the same time the chief Hijar and the warriors of Kendeh advance to lay waste their lands. Antar obtains information of their movements from the ubiquitous Shiboob, and, putting himself at the head of three thousand horsemen of Abs (leaving Prince Cais with a party to protect the women and property of the tribe in the mountains), goes forth to give the enemy a warm reception. The noble hero's reflections on the march found expression in these verses:

> O Abla! my heart is rent with anguish on thy account: my patience is
> fled to the wastes!

O Hijar! – hey! I will teach thee my station: thou shalt not dare to fight me, disgraced as thou art!

Hast thou forgotten in the Vale of Torrents the deeds of my valour, and how I overthrew the armies, undaunted as they were?

I precipitated them with the thrust, and I abandoned them and their carcasses to be trampled on by the wild beasts!

Shall I not behold thee in anguish tomorrow? – ay! – thou shalt not escape from me to the arms of thy beloved!

I will leave the brutes of the desert to stamp over thee, and the eagles and the ghouls shall mangle thee!

I am Antar, the most valiant of knights – ay, of them all; and every warrior can prove my words.

If you have a milch-camel, milk her; for thou knowest not to whom her young may belong.

Antar takes Hijar prisoner, and his little army is victorious. But now Khodawend has come with his legions, and in the battles between the Persians and Absians, Antar performs many marvellous exploits. Khodawend, thinking the Absians would willingly surrender on almost any terms, causes his vizier to write a letter to King Zoheir, offering peace if he would give up to him that vile slave Antar. This letter he sends by a satrap, escorted by twenty Persian horsemen, and accompanied by an interpreter called Ocab, the son of Terjem. On reaching the Absian encampment, it chanced that only Antar and another chief were mounted.

'They were in conversation when the satrap came up to them; he did not salute them, but asked for King Zoheir. "He inquires for King Zoheir," said the interpreter, "for he has a letter from Khodawend for him." – "We, O Arab," said Antar, "have read your letter before its arrival: in it your Prince orders us to surrender ourselves without fighting. – Pull that satrap off the back of his horse," said he to Shiboob; "ay, and the rest, too: seize all their property; and if any one dares to struggle with you, treat him thus," – and at the word he extended his arm, and pierced the satrap through the chest, forcing the spear out quivering through his back, and he hurled him down dead. When his comrades saw what Antar had done, they cried out for quarter, and surrendered themselves to Shiboob, who bound them fast by the shoulders. As to the interpreter, he shuddered. "May God requite you well," said he; "for you have answered us before even reading the letter! If this indeed is the honorary robe for a satrap, let it not be so for an interpreter; for I have children and a family, and I am but a poor fellow. I only followed these Persians but with the prospect of gaining some miserable trifle. I never calculated on being hung; and my children when I am gone will remain orphans." So he wept and groaned, thus expressing himself:

O knight of the horses of warriors that overthrow; their lion, resembling the roaring ocean!

By your awful appearance you have disgraced heroes, and reduced them to despair.

As soon as the Persian sees you he is dishonoured: if they approach you, and extend their spears against your glory, they must retreat, or there is no security.

Have compassion, then, on your victim, a person of little worth, whose family will be in misery when he is gone!

Not the thrust of the spear or battle is among my qualifications; – I profess no fighting – I have no cleaving scimitar.

My name is Ocab; but indeed I am no fighting man; and the sword in the palm of my hand only chases pelicans.

'Antar laughed at Ocab's verses, and let him go. "Return to your family," said he, "and go no more to the Persian, or you will be in danger; for when they see you safe they will accuse you, and perhaps put you to death." – "You are very right, my lord," said he; "By the faith of an Arab, had I known these Persians would have been thus worsted I would not have quitted you; and probably I might have managed to secure some of their goods, and return with it to my family." – "Sheikh," said Antar's companion, "this business has failed; but come, take the spoils of this satrap, and return to your family, and pass not your evening a dead man." – "Ay, my lord," said Ocab, "he is a wise fellow who returns safe to his friends." – So he ran up to the satrap and despoiled him. Round his waist was a girdle and a sword, and when Ocab saw all that wealth he was bewildered; and having completely rifled him, – "O my lord," said he to Antar, "I will never separate from you again. I wish you would present me to your king, that I may kiss his hand and offer him my services; then indeed I will for ever cleave to your party, and whenever you slay a satrap I will plunder him." Antar laughed heartily.'

A battle of seven days' duration ensued, which, despite of the heroic exertions of Antar, ended in the discomfiture of the Absians, who, however, still continued to contend with the enemy among the sand-hills and the defiles. Antar himself was wounded in three places, but his spirit remained undaunted, albeit afflictions were multiplied around him. At this crisis King Numan obtains an interview with Khodawend, and clears himself of the false charges brought against him by his brother: Aswad is degraded; Numan restored to power; and peace being proclaimed between the belligerents, the Absians return in joy to their homes. Antar and a select number of his comrades accompany King Numan to Hirah, where they are splendidly entertained for some time; and before they return to their own country, Chosroe Anoushirvan, having heard, from his son Khodawend, how the Absians had been saved by Antar's indomitable prowess, sends the hero a robe of honour and many other rich presents, in token of his renewed friendship.

1. Joseph and Potiphar's Wife (Chapter I) – three versions (two western, one eastern) of the seduction scene. This one, an etching by Rembrandt of 1634, is in striking contrast to the other, more romantic, depictions.

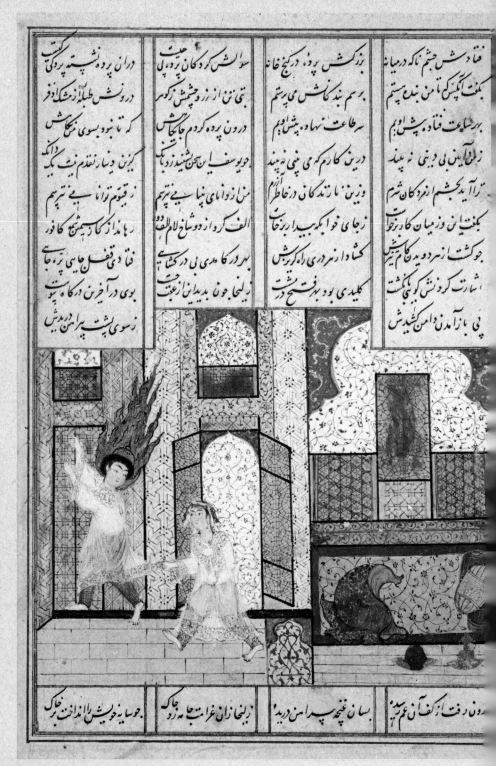

2. Yusuf wa Zulaikha as shown in a Persian manuscript from Trinity College, Cambridge. This is its first reproduction.

3. A sixteenth-century painting by 'The Master of the Joseph Legend'.

4.   Another scene from the Joseph/Yusuf story: the women of Egypt, overcome by Yusuf's beauty, accidentally cutting their fingers (see pages 10, 13-14). From a manuscript of a poem by Jami.

5. Solomon and the Queen of Sheba (Chapter II). This version, firmly in
the Christian tradition, is a stained-glass window from the north aisle of
Canterbury Cathedral, late twelfth century.

6. The Queen of Sheba with the hoopoe (page 23) from a Persian
manuscript, Qazvin style, *c.* 1590.

7. The 'Solomon' panel from Lorenzo Ghiberti's bronze Gates of Paradise
in the Baptistery, Florence, 1452. This panel is the last of ten Old Testament
scenes which begin with the fall of Adam, and was described by Ghiberti
as 'how the Queen of Sheba comes to visit Solomon, with a great
company. She is adorned, with many people about'.

8. Detail from Albrecht Altdorfer's *Die Alexanderschlacht*, reproduced
in full on the front of the jacket. It is contemporaneous (1520s) with the
miniature on the back. Altdorfer shows a western preoccupation with
military glory: massed armies, minute spectacular detail, unreal glowering
landscapes; Sheikh Zadeh an eastern interest in the poetic and personal: the
single combat of the champions with rank and numbers represented only
by symbols (canopy, a handful of warriors) and the landscape, too,
suggested and delicate. Altdorfer's painting is said to have been Napoleon's
favourite, an influence of the legend of Alexander on the modern world
(Chapter III).

9. Alexander wearing the horns
of Zeus Ammon. On a coin of
his successor Lysimachus, *c.* 290 B.C.

10. This is one of the earliest
surviving likenesses of Alexander,
a tetradrachm from the mint at
Amphipolis, *c.* 333 B.C. He is here
portrayed as Heracles with a lion's
mane head-dress.

COINS WERE STRUCK TO EMPHASIZE VARYING ASPECTS OF THE HERO. JUST AS
THE LION'S MANE OF HERACLES CONNOTATED ALEXANDER'S GREEK ANCESTRY
THROUGH HIS FATHER PHILIP, WHOSE FAMILY WAS OF THE HERACLEIDAE, SO THE
HORNS WOULD SUGGEST HIS EGYPTIAN DESCENT FROM AMMON. (OTHER COINS
SHOW HIM WITH AN ELEPHANT TO COMMEMORATE HIS VICTORY IN INDIA.)

11. Head of Alexander, second century B.C., found in Pergamon.

فخر الرجال سداسل دقيود
و كذا النساء خلاخيل وعقود
ابا الفوارس غتر

الأمير

12.   The story of 'Antar (Chapter IV) is still the most popular of all in
Arab oral tradition. Despite his sixth-century origins as a hero of oral, vs. literary
tradition, 'Antar has not been depicted before this century. This picture
(printed on cloth) was originally drawn by a Syrian artist and has recently
been popularized by his son, so that it now appears in different forms
throughout the Middle East.

13. The Half-Friend
(Exemplum I, page 168)

14. The Weeping Bitch
(Ex. XIII, page 181)

15. The Linen Sheet (Ex. X, page 175)

16. The Grape-Harvester and his Wife (Ex. IX, page 176)

WOODCUTS OF TALES FROM THE *Disciplina Clericalis* (CHAPTER V) WHICH
FIRST APPEARED IN A 1489 EDITION OF *Fabulos de Esopo*.

17. The Wolf and the Fox at the Well (Ex. XXIII, page 190)

18. The Sword (Ex. XI, page 230)

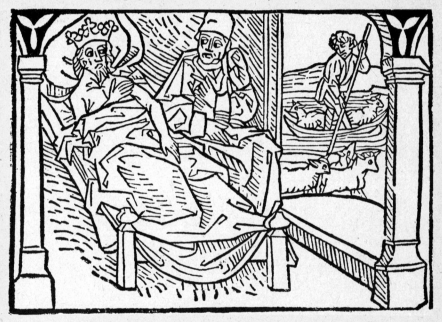

19. The King and his Storyteller (Ex. XII, page 189)

20. The Lovers in the Pear Tree or The Blind Man and the Adulterous Youth (Ex. XXXV, page 187)

21. The Barber's Story of his
Fifth Brother (page 200) by
Thompson

23. Dough for the King's Horse
(page 208) by Landells

22. Digging for Treasure from
A Dream (page 204) by Bastin

ENGRAVINGS ON WOOD ILLUSTRATING STORIES FROM *The Arabian Nights*
(CHAPTER VI) WHICH APPEARED IN E. W. LANE'S TRANSLATION, *The Thousand
and One Nights*, 1889

24, 25 (*overleaf*). Two view of the Alhambra (Chapter VII), published in 1833 and thus actually sketched at just about the time (1829) of Washington Irving's stay there. The simple life of the peasant tenants contrasts with the grandeur of Arabic architecture and decoration.

'ANTAR AND 'ABLA

Prince Harith in Love

Prince Harith, one of Zoheir's sons, while hunting, one day chanced to strray into a valley, at some distance from the land of Shurebah. There he saw a party of women of the tribe of Zohran, and conspicuous among them was the chief's beautiful daughter, Labna. They fell in love with each other at first sight. Shiboob contrived to carry off the damsel to her lover; but her father, breathing vengeance, pursued them, with his warriors. Harith was taken prisoner, but was soon afterwards released by Shiboob, who, however, in his turn, was captured. At this juncture, Antar, returning from Hirah, reached the place, and rescued his brother; and Labna and Harith were restored to each other.

King Zoheir and His Brother, Asyed

While Prince Harith was absent and in trouble on account of his love-affair, King Zoheir went to meet his brother Asyed, 'a learned man in that age of ignorance, who generally passed his time at the Sacred Shrine and the Zemzem. He was full of virtue and liberality, loving justice and equity, and detesting violence and oppression.' Asyed visited the tribe of Abs once every year, and on this occasion Zoheir, accompanied by three hundred horsemen, met him, by appointment, at a place called the Valley of Tamarisks.

The King was not a little surprised to hear his grave and learned brother refer to some secret love-episode of his youth, and earnestly desiring to know the particulars, Asyed thereupon related the following tale:

'Know, then, my brother, that the year our father, King Jazeema, made his pilgrimage, I accompanied him; and when our pilgrimage was expired, as we were on our way home, we happened to pass by this place, in which I saw a vast quantity of wild beasts and deer. My father rode on and went home, but I remained for the sake of the chase. Thus occupied, I stayed till the meridian heat overpowered me, and the sultry air became so excessive, I returned also, seeking the track of my father. I chanced to pass by this tree, and when I reached it, I saw a very old sheikh beneath it, and with him an immense quantity of camels, and also his daughter, who was tending them at the pasture – she was the most beautiful and most elegant of forms; and as soon as I came up to him I saluted him. "What do you want, young man?" said he. – I only said, "Will you accept of a guest when he comes?" – "Welcome, to me," said he, "in winter and in summer. But, young man, every one, according to his means."

'On hearing this, I resolved on alighting at the lake, in order to drink, and water my horse. But the sheikh prevented me, and called out to his daughter, who brought me some fresh camel's milk and gave me to drink, and also watered my horse. I remarked the beauty of the maiden, and I perceived her moving in the plains of loveliness. Her father, too, observing the symmetry of my horse, and my rich garments, brought me some victuals. "Excuse my scanty offering," said he, "for I am a poor man, and the liberal pardon, when they see the apology is sincere." – "O Sheikh!" said I, "this is the greatest charity; but if you will accede to my wishes, I would request you to accept my proposal, and gratify my desire with regard to your daughter, and you shall then go with me to my tribe. I am anxious you would receive me as her husband, and I will take you to my land and family; speak to me and bestow her. By Him who has created her and fashioned her," I added, "take all I have about me as part of her marriage dower"; and I took off my sword-belt and my horse-trappings, which were all of gold.

'The sheikh at the sight of this was much surprised and delighted, and came towards me without hesitation, and, giving me his hand for the marriage, drove away the camels and cattle, and went to his own dwelling, and I accompanied him; and on our arrival he slaughtered all the sheep he possessed, and some she-camels, and rejoiced in me as no one ever rejoiced before, and married his daughter to me that night. I tarried with them three days, and afterwards I informed them who I was. I stayed some time longer, and quitted them, bearing in my heart the greatest attachment for them, and intending to return to them with abundant wealth.

'Having reached home and joined my family, I despatched a slave to conduct my wife to me, and sent with him a great quantity of camels and sheep to this valley and desert. I remained anxiously expecting them, till my slave returned in despair, and brought back all my property. I asked him what was the matter. "I have seen no one there, my lord," said he. I stayed some time quiet, and despatched emissaries to all the Arab tribes, and expended amongst them much gold and silver, but I never could obtain any intelligence of her. And even now, my brother, I bear her in my memory. It was on her account I attached myself to Mecca and the Sacred Shrine, till I this day beheld these remembrances of her, and now all my sorrows come upon me anew; and whilst I meditated on the past, I was anxious that you should come with me to this spot, that I might renew the vows made so many years ago.'

Asyed having thus ended the recital of his pathetic story, the King caused the slaves to spread carpets beneath the tamarisk trees, and, the hunters presently returning with abundance of hares and deer, a sumptuous feast was quickly prepared. They passed the night in the same spot, but at break of day the party were surprised and taken prisoner by a troop of horsemen of Cahtan, led by a young chief called Nazih, who was returning in triumph to his own tribe, with his distinguished captives, when he was met by Antar. The noble champion of Abs impetuously assailed Nazih, and unhorsed him. Shiboob bound him securely, and then hastened to release the King and his brother. Antar proposed to put Nazih and his companions to death: and proceeding to strip off the young chief's clothes, he discovered on his wrist a bracelet of cornelian, on which were engraved images of Lat and Uzza. Asyed recognizes the trinket as being identical with one which he had given to his bride in the Valley of Tamarisks: he questions the young chief regarding his parentage, and discovers in Nazih his own son. Ultimately Asyed has the felicity of being re-united to his long-lost bride.

Death of Prince Shas and King Zoheir

About this time Prince Shas, while journeying through the land of Aamir, was foully murdered by a huntsman, called Thalaba. The Prince's attendant escaped to carry the tidings to King Zoheir, who immediately placed himself at the head of his warriors, and set out to avenge his son's death. Khalid, the chief of the tribe, being absent in Irak, the Aamirites feared to oppose the Absians, and offered to pay King Zoheir ten times the usual price of blood. The King refused to compound with them for the murder of his son, but after assailing the tribe, he was duped into granting a truce, of which the Aamirites availed themselves to occupy a strong position in the mountains, where they continued in safety during the few days that remained before the sacred month of Rejeb, when war ceased among the Arabs. Hostilities are renewed as soon as the sacred month is past; and Khalid, having in the interim returned from Irak, encounters King Zoheir, who is slain by a foul stroke from Jandah, one of Khalid's followers; and the Absians, being discomfited, return to their own land.

King Cais Avenges His Father's Death

Cais, the eldest surviving son of King Zoheir, having acceded to the supreme power, goes forth with his warriors to avenge the death of his father. But, acting on the advice of Antar's enemies, he leaves the hero behind. The Absians attack the tribe of Aamir, and are defeated. King Cais then sends a letter to Antar, begging him to come to their assistance. Meantime a fierce combat takes place between the young chief Nazih, on the part of the Absians, and Harith the son of Zalim, a renegade knight, on the part of the Aamirites. Just as Nazih is about to succumb to his antagonist, a strange knight makes his appearance, mounted on a meagre, foundered horse, and poorly armed. This Bedouin wanderer assails Harith and takes him prisoner; then he overcomes Jandah – who gave Zoheir his death-blow; the King Cais is the first to recognize in the person of the uncouth champion Antar himself. The King strikes off the head of Jandah with the assassin's own sword. After a period of repose, the Absians again made war upon the Aamirites, who were ultimately vanquished.

Abla's Father and Brother Again Rescued by Antar

Notwithstanding the great respect entertained for Antar by King Cais and the noble warriors of Abs, his uncle Malik was yet far from being reconciled to his proposed union with Abla. On one occasion the ungrateful wretch planned a murderous attack upon Antar by a party of the tribe of Fazarah, while the hero was carousing with himself in his own tent. But Antar, having been warned of the plot by Abla's maid, defeated his uncle's inhospitable designs. Enraged at his failure, and perhaps also a little ashamed, Malik resolves again to emigrate; but this time Abla firmly refuses to accompany her father and brother, and these two worthies have no help but to leave Abla behind, in the care of Shedad, the father of Antar.

A few days after Malik and his son had quitted the tribe, Antar determined to go in quest of them, and induce them to return. Accompanied by Shiboob and two trusty comrades, he sets out accordingly; and learning that Malik and Amru are prisoners of Ramih, chief of the tribe of Jibhan, they proceed thither with all haste. When they reached the tents of Ramih, Shiboob and Antar disguised themselves, and, each carrying a bundle of wood on his head, they approached the dwelling of the chief.

'It was almost dark when they entered the tents, through which they continued to pass, attentively observing everything, till they came to the tents of Ramih, where they saw Malik and his son, in extreme misery, tied up with the dogs. "Behold your uncle," said Shiboob; "let your grief be now assuaged." Antar threw his bundle of wood off his head, and Shiboob did the same; but they did not stop till Ramih, who was the chief of the Jibhanians, came out, attended by a troop of slaves, who laid out a sofa for him to sit on. He then began to talk to his shepherds, who were parading before him his horses and his cattle; and he inquired of them about the pastures and the grain.

' "O my lord," said one of the slaves, "I beheld a most extraordinary sight this day; for whilst I was in the Valley of Meadows, tending the flocks, I came upon the high road, where, behold! was a knight hunting the fawns. He was mounted on a black steed, and in front of the knight was a man on foot, girded with an Arabian bow, and round his waist was a quiver full of arrows, and both were in pursuit of a fawn, endeavouring to catch it. I stopped to look at them, when, lo! the man on foot outstripped the knight. He seized the fawn by the left horn, and the knight, catching it by its right horn and gazing in its face, thus in poetry exclaimed:

Depart, and, ever in the protection of God, may no evil e'er overtake thee! for thou resemblest my love in her eyes, and her beauty; so depart in security.

Although thy form resembles the damsel, no imagination can comprehend the virtues of her mind.

' "As soon as the knight had finished his verses, my lord, he let the fawn go out of his hand, and it went off skipping over the barren waste, when soon two more knights joined them." – "And what is there so wonderful in all this?" said Ramih. "I suppose they are of the tribe of Cahtan, and that the evening has surprised them, and consequently they must repose in my land, and will quit it in the morning." '

Malik, however, who had overheard this conversation, was convinced that the man on foot, spoken of by the slave, must be Shiboob, while the humane knight could only be Antar, on the way to rescue them; and he was right. Immediately there was great confusion in the tents; – the lion-hero struck off the chief's head with his sword Dhami, and having released Malik and his son, they all returned to the land of Abs.

A Horse Race, and its Consequences

King Cais having despatched some of his slaves to obtain tidings of Antar, one of them returned with a glowing account of a wonderful colt, called Dahis, which he had seen in the course of his journey. In beauty and in speed this colt had no equal in all Arabia. The King bargained for Dahis with the owner, and was delighted when he came to terms for his purchase. Soon after this Carwash, a cousin of King Cais, was present at a grand feast given by Hadifah; and the conversation turning upon horses, Carwash boasted of the racing qualities of Dahis. Hadifah offers to back his mare Ghabra for twenty camels, to run against Dahis, and a match is made accordingly. But the King takes the matter in his own hands, and visits Hadifah, to arrange the conditions of the race.

' "As to the first bet, Hadifah," said Cais, "I dissolve it, and I will lay you another, and let the wager be thirty." "Forty," said Hadifah. "Fifty," said Cais. "Sixty," said Hadifah; and they continued rising till they made the bet a hundred she-camels, and consigned the contract into the hands of a man called Sabik, son of Wahab, whilst a crowd of old and young collected about them. – "What distance shall we run?" said Hadifah to Cais. – "Forty arrow-shots," said Cais; "and we have an archer called Ayas, son of Mansoor" – for there was no Arab at that day could shoot like him0, and the Arabs had made him quite a proverb. King Cais was anxious indeed for a longer race on account of the strength of his horse's muscles; for the greater distance he went, the more his spirit and animation increased in his movements. "Determine, then," said Cais to Hadifah, "when the match shall take place." – "Forty days, I think," said Hadifah, "will be required to train the horses." – "Very well," said Cais; and the affair was mutually settled, that the horses should be trained forty days, and the race-ground should be near the lake of Zat-ul-irsad; and the horse that should arrive first should be the winner. Cais having given his consent, he returned to the tents.'

The race between Dahis and Ghabra came off at the place appointed, and Dahis would have won, but for foul play on the part of Hadifah, who caused the colt to be injured before reaching the goal; the consequence of which was the famous Forty Years' War between the tribes of Abs and Dhobyan, known as the War of Dahis.

Prince Malik's Marriage and Death

Prince Malik, while hunting, like his brother Harith, fell in love with a beauteous damsel of the tribe of Ghorab, and straightway asked her in marriage of her father, an old sheikh, who consented, after some little demur on the ground of his own poverty, and they shook hands for the nuptials.

'On the next day Prince Malik sent to the sheikh he and she camels, and variegated robes, and cattle, and precious jewels, and howdahs, brilliant with magnificent velvet, and servants and slaves, and with them horses and sheep, ordering them to be expeditious, on account of the passion that was in his heart; and he appointed a certain hour on the seventh day. When all these presents reached the tribe of Ghorab, the old and the young rejoiced; they passed those days in the greatest delight, and slaughtered the sheep and the camels, and filled the goblets with wine; and they were perfectly happy, to the exclusion of every sorrow.

'Soon after, Prince Malik clad himself in the robes of nobleborn kings, and his beauty was more dazzling than the new moon. On this expedition Antar accompanied him, fearful lest some enemy should waylay him; and he took ten horsemen and five of his brothers. They wandered through the Arab dwellings till they reached the tribe of Ghorab, and Prince Malik dismounted at the marriage canopy, his brothers also alighting round the tent. The feast immediately commenced; the damsels waved the cymbals, and the horsemen flourished their swords; exclamations of joy arose, and the cups went round; and thus they continued till the laughing day was spent, when the nymph was married to Malik.'

But who could guess that 'upon night so sweet an awful morn would rise'? – that the nuptial night of the good Prince Malik should be his last! – 'By morning their joys were converted into sorrows, and shots were precipitated at them from arrows for which there is no surgeon; – for Fortune never gives, but it pillages; is never stationary, but it revolves; is never merry, but it sorrows; never bestows, but it takes back; never joys, but it grieves; never sweetens, but it embitters.'

Early next morning, Hadifah, with a party of his kinsmen, attacked the marriage-guests. Antar was the first to start up on the alarm being given by the slaves; springing upon his horse Abjer, he hastened to meet the enemy, and soon the whole tribe of Ghorab were in motion. Hadifah advanced towards the nuptial tent. Prince Malik, half asleep, and his garments scented with musk and saffron, rushed out, and mounting his horse, cried, 'I am Malik, the son of Zoheir!' But his horse stumbled and threw him. As he was attempting to rise, Hadifah dealt him a deadly blow on the head with his sword; then, fearing the vengence of Antar, he rejoined his companions, and they all hastened away. When Antar returned from the conflict he found his friend in the agonies of death, lying bathed in blood beside his horse. The dying Prince opened his eyes and attempted to speak to Antar, but could not; and with a sigh his gentle spirit departed. 'Antar wrapped him up in his clothes, and tying him on the back of his horse, took him away, and sought the land of Abs.'

The shade of Prince Malik appeared to Antar one night in a dream; – beckoning with his fingers, he said: 'O Aboolfawaris! dost thou sleep, and I unrevenged? Hast thou forgotten our former friendship? Before thee many have been faithful to their friends; be thou faithful also to him who was slain but yesterday'; and then the apparition vanished. In the darkness of the night, then and there, the hero mounted Abjer, and taking his brother Shiboob in front of him, he sought the land of Fazarah. There he slew Awef, the brother of Hadifah, as a first sacrifice to the manes of his murdered friend.

Amarah Lampooned by the Girls

Antar returned to his tribe, and lived secluded in his tent, sorrowing for the loss of his first and ever steadfast friend. One day Khemisa, Abla's hand-maiden, came to him with a message from his darling, who desired him to watch over the safety of herself and her female companions while they passed some time at the lake during the evening. The hero was delighted with the duty, and readily promised Abla his protection against the wanderers of the night.

The girls set out for the lake at the hour appointed, and Amarah, disguised in women's clothes, followed them. When they reached the lake he pounced upon Abla like a voracious vulture. But help was at hand. Antar, concealed behind the sand-hills, heard Abla's screams. He rushed forth like a furious lion, grasped Amarah, and almost beat the life out of him; then he let him go, followed by the taunts and jeers of the girls.

'This circumstance with Abla soon spread abroad, and all the women, and men, and girls, and boys, and slaves, and slave-girls joined in the laugh against Amarah, singing these verses, whilst Amarah heard them: – the women and shepherdesses sang them at their spindles; for there was a girl among the Absians who could compose verses; she was very eloquent, so she repeated these verses on Amarah the cuckold, and they were recollected by all the women and girls':

Amarah, leave alone the beautiful, full-hipped damsels; – let alone all disputes about the lovely girls!

For thou canst not plunge into the sea of deaths, and thou art no horseman in the day of battle.

Aspire no more to Abla: if thou dost but look at her, thou wilt see horrors from the lion of the forests!

As to the thin quivering spear, touch not its strength, nor the cleaving scimitar.

Abla is a fawn chased by a lion, with eyes that afflict with disorder the stoutest in health.

Let alone all contest about her, or the unflinching Antar will make thee drink of death.

Thou didst not cease thy obstinacy, till thy foul condition gave evidence against thee!

All the girls laughed at thee; thou wast the carrion of the plains and deserts; thou wast the common talk of the merry, and the laughing-stock for every passenger!

Marriage of Antar and Abla

Many more wonderful exploits were performed by Antar in opposing the enemies of Abs – many illustrious warriors fell beneath the stroke of his irresistible sword Dhami, before he attained the chief desire of his heart. At length King Cais, grateful for his services, resolved that Antar should be married to his darling Abla without further delay, and his uncle Malik freely gave his consent. And never was there such another glorious wedding! From the most distant lands came famous knights to honour the nuptials of the renowned son of Shedad and the beauteous daughter of Malik, and rich and rare were the presents they brought with them. Each of these illustrious chiefs addressed verses to Antar, in praise of his prowess, and congratulating him on his marriage. 'It was now the season of spring, and the land was enamelled with the lustre of new-born flowers.' For several days the horsemen jousted with each other, with blunted spears. And then came the wedding night.

'Now there was a curious custom current among the Arabs at that period. The night on which a bridegroom should wed his wife, they brought a quantity of camel pack-saddles, and heaped them one upon the other, decorating them with magnificent garments. Here they conducted the bride, and having seated her on high, they said to the bridegroom: "Come on – now for thy bride!" And the bridegroom rushed forward to carry her off, whilst the youths of the tribe, drawn up in line, right and left, with staves and stones in their hands, as soon as the bridegroom dashed forward, began beating and pelting him, and doing their utmost to prevent his reaching his bride. If a rib or so were broken in the affair, it was well for him; were he killed, it was his destiny. But should he reach his bride in safety, the people quitted him, and no one attempted to approach him.'

This singular custom was, however, waived in the case of Antar, by order of the King, who feared lest some enemy of the hero might do him a mortal injury in the *mêlée*.

'And now, when the Arabs assembled for Antar's marriage had eaten their dinner, the cups of wine were brought round to them. The men and the women were promiscuously moving together; the girls came forth, and the slave-women were amusing themselves, enjoying the happy moments. "Hola!" cried the matrons and the virgins, "we will not remain covered on Antar's marriage." They threw aside their veils, and the full moons appeared in all their lustre; and they flaunted the branches of their forms in the excess of their delight; and it was a famous day for them. "By the faith of an Arab," said the matrons and virgins, "we will not remain thus concealed behind these curtains – the doors shall not be shut upon us; we will see Abla in her magnificence, and we will walk in her train, and make our offerings to her and Antar, and we will not keep a dirhem or a dinar to ourselves; for a happier night than this can never be, and no one but a madman would miss it."

'When the women of Carad heard this, they were alarmed for the scandal and censure that would thus be occasioned: so they resolved to finish Abla's ceremony. They clothed her in most magnificent robes and superb necklaces; they placed the coronet of Chosroe on her head, and tiaras round her forehead: Abla was remarkable for her beauty and loveliness: the tire-women surrounded her, and they requested Antar to let her come forth in state. He gave them permission, whilst his brothers and slaves stood round the pavilion with their swords, and javelins, and weapons. He ordered them to place a lofty throne for Abla in front of the pavilion. They executed his commands: they lighted brilliant and scented candles before her, and spread afar the odour of aloes and camphor, and scattered the perfumes of ambergris and musk; the lights were fixed in candlesticks of gold and silver – the torches blazed – and whilst the women shouted and raised their voices to whistles and screams, Abla came forth in state. In her hand she bore a drawn sword, whose lustre dazzled the eyesight. All present gave a shout; whilst the malicious and ill-natured cried: "What a pity that one so beautiful and fair should be wedded to one so black!" '

Thus, after all his trials and perils, the renowned son of Shedad was duly married to his darling Abla, and thus he expressed his satisfaction at the consummation of his wishes:

My heart is at rest: it is recovered from its intoxication. Sleep has calmed my eyelids, and relieved them.

Fortune has aided me, and my prosperity cleaves the veil of night, and the seven orders of heaven.

THE DEATH OF ANTAR

In the course of his exploits as chief of his tribe, Antar had conquered a horseman, called Jezar, who was a famous archer; and, to punish his aggressions upon his people, he had blinded him by causing a red-hot sabre to be passed before his eyes; then he granted him life, liberty, and even the supreme rank in his own tribe.

I

From that time Jezar, son of Jaber, meditated in silence on vengeance. Although his eyes were deprived of sight, he had in no way lost his skill in archery. His ear, practised in following the movements of wild animals by the sound of their steps, was sufficient to guide his hand: never did the arrow miss the mark. His hatred, always alert, listened eagerly for the news which fame spread about his enemy. He learned that Antar, after a distant and fortunate expedition against the frontiers of Persia, was returned to Yemen, laden with as much glory and booty as he had formerly brought from the court of Chosroe, and that he is about to pass into the desert adjoining his encampment. At this story Jezar weeps for envy and rage. He calls Nejim, his faithful slave:

'Ten years are passed,' says he to him, 'since a burning iron destroyed, by Antar's order, the light of my eyes, and I am not yet revenged! But at last the moment has come when to quench in his blood the fire which burns in my heart. Antar is encamped, they say, on the banks of the Euphrates. Thither I wish to go to seek him. I shall live hidden in the reeds of the river till Heaven delivers his life into my hands.'

Jezar orders his slave to bring him his she camel which rivals the ostrich in the race: he arms himself with his quiver of poisoned arrows. Nejim makes the camel kneel, helps his master to mount upon her back, and takes the end of the halter of the animal, to direct her steps toward the distant bed of the Euphrates. The blind warrior fills the desert with his wailings and his threats.

After a long day's march through a waterless space, Jezar and his slave reach the banks of the Euphrates, whose course is marked by the verdure of trees and the herbs along its bed.

'What seest thou on the other bank?' asks Jezar of his slave.

Nejim casts a glance to the other bank. He sees tents richly adorned; numerous flocks; camels wandering in groups on the plain; spears planted in the ground at the doors of the tents; harnessed horses, fastened by the feet, before the dwellings of their masters. A tent more splendid than the rest is erected at a little distance from the river. Before the door arises, like a mast, a long spear of steel, beside which is a horse blacker than ebony. Nejim recognizes the noble courser of Antar, the famous Abjer, and his terrible spear. He halts his master's camel behind the shrubs and reeds, which conceal them from all eyes; and they await the hour of darkness.

II

When night had covered with its shadows the two banks of the Euphrates –

'Let us quit this place,' says the blind Jezar to his slave; 'the voices which I hear from the other side seem to me too far off for the range of my arrows. Bring me nearer the edge: my heart tells me that a glorious stroke is about to immortalize my name and my revenge!'

Nejim takes the blind man by the hand; brings him close to the water; makes him sit upon the bank opposite the tent of Antar, and gives him his bow and quiver. Jezar chooses the keenest of his arrows, places it upon the string, and with listening ear awaits the hour of vengeance.

Meanwhile Antar, in the arms of Abla, his beloved wife, for whom ten years of possession have in no wise diminished his love, was forgetting within his tent his fatigue and exploits, when the dismal howling of the dogs – faithful guardians of the camp – cast a prophetic unquiet into his soul.

He rises and goes out of his tent. The sky is dark and cloudy. He wanders, feeling his way in the darkness. The louder voices of the dogs attract him to the river. Impelled by his fate, he goes forward, right up to the bed of the water; and, suspecting the presence of some enemy on the opposite bank, he calls to his brother in a loud voice to search the other side.

Scarcely does his resounding voice echo in the hollow bed of the valley of the Euphrates, reverberating in the rocks and mountains, when an arrow pierces his right side, and penetrates to his entrails. No cry – no groan unworthy of a hero – escapes him through his pain. He withdraws the iron with a firm hand.

'Traitor, who has not dared to attack me in the light of day!' cries he in a loud voice to his invisible enemy – 'thou shalt not escape my vengeance! – thou shalt not enjoy the fruit of thy perfidy!'

At that voice, which makes him think that his arrow has missed its mark, the blind Jezar, struck by terror at the thought of the vengeance of Antar, swoons upon the bank, and his slave, thinking him dead, flies upon his camel, leaving his inanimate master where he lay. Antar's brother swims across the river, stumbles against a body which he takes for a corpse, and bears it upon his shoulders, with the bow and arrows, to the camp.

III

Antar, stretched in his tent amidst his despairing friends, is suffering horrible torments: the tender Abla is stanching his blood, bathing the wound with her tears.

They bring the body of the assassin, the bow and the arrows, into the tent. Antar recognizes the mutilated countenance of his enemy: he no longer doubts that the arrow discharged by such a hand was poisoned. Hope leaves his heart: death inevitable presents itself before his eyes.

'Son of my uncle!' says Abla tenderly to him, 'why abandon hope? Ought a slight arrow-wound to alarm him who has confronted without fear so many swords and spears, the wounds from which cover his body?'

'Abla,' replies Antar, 'my hours are numbered. Look at the features of that face; – it is Jezar: the traitor's arrow was poisoned!'

At these words Abla fills the night with her sobs; she rends her garments; she tears her long hair, and picks up dust, which she scatters on her head. All the women of the encampment re-echo her lamentations.

'Dear wife!' says Antar to Abla, 'who will defend thy honour and thy life after the death of Antar, in that long journey which remains for thee to make through our enemies before reaching thy father's land? A second husband, another I, can alone save thee from the horrors of slavery. Of all the warriors of the desert, Zeid and Amnem are those whose courage will best protect thy life and liberty: choose one of those, and go and promise him thy hand.'

Abla replies not but by her tears to a thought which is to her horrible.

'To return to the land where dwell the children of Abs – to assure thy passage through the desert which separates thee from it – clothe thyself with my arms and mount my courser Abjer. In this disguise, which will

145

make our enemies think that I still live, fear not of being attacked. Reply nothing to those who salute thee upon the road: the sight of the arms and the horse of Antar will suffice to intimidate the boldest.'

IV

Antar after these words orders the departure. They strike the tents, fold them, and place them upon the camels. Abla, bathed in her tears, constrains herself, through obedience, to don the heavy armour of Antar. Girt with his sword, holding his straight spear in her hand, she mounts his courser Abjer, whilst the slaves lay the dying Antar in the litter in which Abla used to travel in happier days, when she crossed, like a queen, the desert.

Scarce have they lost sight of the verdant banks of the Euphrates to plunge into the immensity of the desert, when they perceive in the distance tents, like dark dots on the horizon, or a black fringe on the blue mantle of heaven. It is a numerous and powerful tribe. Three hundred horsemen advance to fall upon the caravan; but, on approaching, they recognize the litter and the horse.

"Tis Antar and Abla!' they say to one another in a low voice – 'see, there, his arms, his horse Abjer, and Abla's splendid litter. Let us return to our tents, and not expose ourselves to the anger of these invincible warriors.'

Already they are turning the rein, when an old sheikh, more reflective and more sagacious than the young men, says:

'My cousins, that is indeed the spear of Antar, that is indeed his helmet, his armour, and his courser, whose colour resembles a dark night; – but that is neither his lofty figure nor his manly bearing. It is the figure and the deportment of a timid woman, borne down by the weight of the iron which galls her frail limbs. Believe my surmises – Antar is dead, or else a mortal illness hinders him from mounting his horse; and this false warrior whom Abjer bears is Abla, who, to frighten us, has clad herself with her husband's arms, whilst the real Antar is perchance laid dying in the women's litter.'

The horsemen, recognizing something probable in the old man's words, retrace their steps and follow at a distance the caravan, without daring to attack it.

V

Now the feeble arm of Abla is bending beneath the weight of the iron spear; she is obliged to hand it to her husband's brother, who walks beside her. Soon, when the sun, arrived half-way in his course, had made the sand of the desert glow like fire, Abla, worn out with suffering and fatigue, raises the vizor of her helmet, to wipe off the sweat which bathed her forehead. The eyes of the hostile Arabs who are watching her catch a glimpse of the whiteness of her face:

'It is not the Black!' they cry; and they dash with all the speed of their horses upon the tracks of Antar's little troop.

At the gallop of their horses behind him – at the neighing of their steeds – at the voice of Abla, which calls him – Antar, who is lying half dead in the litter, rises, shows his head from between the curtains, and utters, for the last time, his terrible war-cry, known of all the desert. The manes of the horses stand erect: the horses bear their riders rigid with terror.

'Woe to us!' say the Arabs, enemies of Abs, – 'Antar still lives! It is a snare which he has laid: he has wished to know which is the tribe so bold as after him to aspire to capture his wife and his possessions.'

Only a small number, still trusting the voice of the old sheikh, continue to follow afar the caravan.

VI

Antar, in spite of his weakness, places Abla in the litter, and mounted upon Ābjer, clad in his arms, he marches slowly beside her.

At the close of the day, they reach a valley not far from the tribe of Abs. This place was called the 'Valley of Gazelles'. Surrounded by inaccessible mountains, one could only enter it from the desert side by a narrow and tortuous pass, where three horsemen could scarcely march abreast. Antar, stopping at the opening of this defile, causes first to enter his flocks, his slaves, and the camel which bears the litter of his dear Abla. When the whole caravan is in safety in the valley, he comes back, to stand alone as sentinel at the end of the gorge, opposite the plain and the Arabs who are following him afar. At this moment his agonies increase; his entrails are torn; each step of his courser makes him suffer torments like to the fire of hell. Death invades his limbs, and yet reveres his dauntless soul. He faces the Arabs; he stops Abjer; he plants the point of his spear in the ground, and leaning against the stem, like a resting warrior allowing his horse to breathe, he stands motionless at the entrance of the pass.

VII

At that sight, the thirty warriors who have hitherto followed the tracks of his caravan halt, hesitating, a few hundred steps from the hero.

'Antar,' say they to one another, 'has noticed that we were following his march; he awaits us there to slay us all; – let us profit by the shades of night which fall, to escape his sword and rejoin our brothers.'

But the old sheikh, steadfast in his opinion, keeps them still.

'My cousins,' says he to them in a low voice, 'heed not the counsels of fear. The immobility of Antar is the sleep of death! – What! do you not know his fiery courage? Has Antar ever waited for his enemy? Were he living, would not he fall upon us, as the vulture falls upon his prey? – Come on, then, bravely; or, if you refuse to risk your lives against his sword, at least wait till dawn arises, and clears away your doubts.'

Half persuaded by the old man, the thirty horsemen resolve to remain where they are; but, always troubled and alarmed at the least cloud of dust which the wind raises about the feet of Abjer, they pass the whole night on horseback, allowing not their eyes to close in sleep.

VIII

At length the day begins to lighten the sky, and to clear away the shades which cover the desert. Antar is still in the same attitude at the entrance of the pass; his courser, obedient to his thought, is motionless as his master.

At this strange spectacle the astounded warriors consult long before coming to a decision. All appearances say to their hearts that Antar has ceased to live; and yet not one of them dares advance to make sure: so strong is the habitude of fear which the hero inspires! . . . The old sheikh wishes to convince himself and them by a proof before flying or advancing. He descends from his mare, lets go the bridle, and pricking her haunch with the point of his spear, he drives her towards the entrance of the pass. Scarcely has she reached in her course the border of the desert next the gorge, when the fiery stallion Abjer darts neighing after the riderless mare. At the first bound of the courser, Antar, supported only by the stem of his spear, which slips away from under him, falls like a tower, and the clang of his armour resounds in the pass.

At that fall – the sound of a lifeless body falling upon the earth – the thirty horsemen flock round the corpse stretched at their horses' feet. They marvel to see lying motionless in the desert him who made Arabia tremble. They cannot resist measuring with their eyes his gigantic limbs and stature. Forgoing the attack upon the caravan of Abla – to which the stratagem of Antar had given an entire night to reach the tents of the tribe of Abs – the warriors content themselves with robbing the hero of his arms, to carry them to their tribe as a trophy conquered by death. In vain they endeavour to capture his courser. The faithful Abjer, having scented his master dead, feels that there is no longer a rider worthy of him: fleeter than the lightning, he escapes them, disappears from their eyes, and plunges into the freedom of the desert.

They say that the old sheikh, softened by the fate of the hero who had made himself illustrious by so many exploits, wept over his corpse, covered it with sand, and addressed to it these words:

Glory to thee, brave warrior! Who, during thy life, hast been the defender of thy tribe, and who, even after thy death, hast saved thy brethren by the terror of thy corpse and of thy name! May thy soul live for ever! May the refreshing dews moisten the ground of this thy last exploit!

The first common folk-motif in 'Antar and 'Abla is that of unpromising early circumstances. Slave-concubines were regarded with special disapproval in Islam, under which 'Antar's story took shape; the children of such unions had the lowest status. In addition, 'Antar was black-skinned at a time when raids and threats of Ethiopian rule were a recent memory. Of other unpromising childhoods, probably the best-known in folklore are those in male and female Cinderella fairy tales which have no true hero, and those of the heroes of tradition. In these latter, the child is exposed at birth, is saved and brought up by humble foster-parents, and in the end is revealed as the son of a king. Only the later redactions of the *Romance of 'Antar* contain this dénouement – his discovery that his mother is an Ethiopian or Sudanese princess – but this is an indication that his cycle as it grew was conforming to the pattern. Other heroes who suffer scorn of various kinds include Joseph sold as a slave, Arthur subject to his foster-brother Kay, the kitchen-boy Gareth humiliated by Lynette, Abe Lincoln hampered by homeliness and poverty.

The next heroic trait in 'Antar is his precocious strength and size. He demonstrates this when he kills the wolf, the lion, and the bullying slave. Additional incidents in the *Romance* though not in our résumé tell how as an infant he tore the strongest swaddling clothes and at age four killed a large dog – as did Cuchulainn who thus got his name, the Hound of Culann. Parallels are also found in Heracles who, not yet a year old, strangled two snakes; the infant Paul Bunyan whose huge cradle rocked the tides in the Bay of Fundy; and Davy Crockett who 'killed him a b'ar when he was only three'.

The hero's arms and accoutrements are traditional too. Thus 'Antar wins his horse Abjer, Alexander tames the horse Bucephalus, Cuchulainn is renowned for his chariot horse, the Grey of Macha. 'Antar has his sword Dhami, Arthur and Roland their swords Excalibur and Durandel. Fergus, Sigurd, Charlemagne, Siegfried and Ogier also carry celebrated swords. Dhami comes to 'Antar's hand under the desert sand in an almost magical way, not unlike Excalibur yielding only to Arthur or Gram to Sigmund. Roland and Robin Hood blow famous horns; Achilles, Cuchulainn, Crockett and 'Antar loose dreadful war-cries.

Boasting to the enemy is another custom shared by heroes. Examples are Antar's challenge on the plain before he fights the satrap Khosrewan, which begins:

Sally forth – ay, every lion warrior! Take a draught at the edge of my sword, more bitter than cups of absinthe.

Where is he who wishes to fight me, and wants to make me drink the liquor of death?

Bring him forth! Let him see what he will meet from my spear under the shades of the war-dust; I swear, O Abla! he shall eat of death!

And later his song before his combat with the Greek champion, Badhramoot:

I will exterminate every lion-hero with my sword – let him vaunt, let him boast, let him scoff!

I am he whose might is uncontrollable in battle; I am of the race of 'Abs – the valiant lion of the cavern!

Hear the words of an intrepid lion – resolute, undaunted, all-conquering.

My sword is my companion . . . as are also my Abjer and my lance and my spear in the conflicts.

This day thou shalt feel the truth of what I have said, and I will prove that I am the Phoenix of the age!

Compare, though it is from the sublime to the ridiculous, these lines from the lost American play, *The Lion of the West* (1831). The character, Col. Nimrod, who was modelled on Davy Crockett, is the lion. He is about to beat a typical backwoods boaster, a Mississippi raftsman who has claimed among other things that he can whip his weight in wildcats. Cries Nimrod, 'An't I the yaller flower of the forest! . . . My name is Nimrod Wildfire – half-horse, half-alligator and a touch of the airthquake – that's got the prettiest sister, fastest horse and ugliest dog in the District, and can outrun, outjump, throw down, drag out and whip any man in all Kaintuck.'[6] Similar in both are the lion comparison, the possessive reference to lady and horse, to each hero's particular talents in combat, and the war-cry and the exaggeration.

A speech from Crockett purporting to have been made in Congress carries on the message, beginning with a war-cry:

Who-Who-Whoop-Bow-Wow-Wow – Yough. I say, Mr Speaker, I've had a speech in soak this six months . . . I'm a screamer, and have got the roughest racking horse, the prettiest sister, the surest rifle and the ugliest dog in the district . . . My father can whip any man in Kentucky and I can lick my father. I can outspeak any man on this floor, and give him two hours start.

I can run faster, dive deeper, stay under longer, and come up drier, than any chap this side of the big swamp . . . I can walk like an ox, run like a fox, swim like an eel, yell like an Indian, fight like a devil, spout like an earthquake, make love like a mad bull, and swallow a citizen whole without choking if you butter his head and pin his ears back.[7]

But the *sine qua non* of the popular hero is his prowess in single combat. Even when battling within an army, he fights his foes one at a time. It is characteristic, too, that the hero always wins; he is invincible, supreme, at least until the end. But when the end comes he again has a folk pattern to follow: he dies as a result of treachery or poison, and dies heroically, often defending his people even beyond death. Achilles is unfairly shot in his vulnerable heel; Roland dies by Ganelon's treason and Arthur by Mordred's; Robin Hood is treacherously bled to death; Alexander, dying of poison, gives his last hours to his soldiers; at the Alamo Davy Crockett, shot from behind, continues in death to defend the fort. Closest to 'Antar is the dying Cuchulainn, who has himself bound to an upright stone and so keeps the foe at bay, until ravens settling on him reveal that he is dead. And like Abjer who will allow no one near him after 'Antar's death, Cuchulainn's horse, the Grey of Macha, charges his dead master's enemies and then escapes.

There seem to be special affinities between 'Antar and Cuchulainn. This is the more remarkable because the early literature of Ireland was not in the Greek-Roman-Latin-Europe channel, mentioned before, of general western culture, but along with the literature of the other British islands and Iceland is regarded as independent of the mainstream.[8] Perhaps some of the affinities come simply from what appears to be a similar social structure between Arabia and Ireland, although the Arabs are more organized, more gentle, more advanced and of course reflect a more recent period than the late antiquity in the Irish legend.

If we look at the way of life in *'Antar and 'Abla*, we see an environment of knighthood, class distinction, and respect for women, three components of later European chivalry. Although less legally feudal than European society, Arab society was none the less based on regional wealthy families to whose courts allegiance was owed. In *'Antar*, Monzar represents this class. He is the son of the high king of the Arabs who rules the local kings or chiefs and who in turn is ruled himself as a lieutenant of the Persian king. Arab loyalty, however, goes by tribe to each tribal chief or local king, whose position is sometimes but not always inherited; the leadership of an able man from the knight class is the crucial factor. Thus Monzar and his family are the uppermost class, but they are supported by the tribal chiefs; the chiefs' strength and wealth come through their armed horsemen, the knights; the knights have privileges over other, non-combatant members of the community; the poor come next; and the slaves are lowest of all.

In economic terms, livelihood as we see it in *'Antar and 'Abla* is based on the livestock which are necessary for sustenance, horses, camels, sheep, goats – and slaves – and other occasional plunder such as arms, jewels, gold and valuable garments. These are acquired by raids and defended from raids, but the nomadic life does not lead to the amassing of property. When wealth is needed, a knight or a group of knights goes out and gets it. It is quite normal for 'Antar and 'Amarah, for example, to find the dowries required of them in this way, and we hear in the story of other dowries captured, bride and all. The knights also make military excursions to rescue tribesmen, to assist allies, or to attack enemies. The Abs clan or tribe like other Bedouin nomads have a homeland, in their case about a hundred miles north of Medina. Here they hold property rights in common, such as for pasture and water as well as for dwelling. King Zoheir, their chief, and his sons have more property (two hundred slaves each) and thus more of the common 'rights' than the rest. The poor, the widows and the orphans (often referred to as one group), although full-blooded Arabs, have these rights only by grace of a code of behaviour in which the powerful protect the weak. The powerful are the knights, the mounted men, who are the productive, i.e., the raiding, members of the tribe.

This *modus vivendi* interestingly resembles that of Ireland as described in the *Tain Bo Cuailnge*, *The Cattle Raid of Couly*, in which Cuchulainn is the champion. The story is thought to have developed during the first centuries of our era but was written down in the first half of the eighth century. It is recognized as a source of the Arthurian cycle. But many identical narrative parts are found in the *Tain* and *'Antar and 'Abla*.

An illustration of this is livestock as livelihood. The *Tain Bo Cuailnge* is only one of many Irish sagas about cattle raids. As in *'Antar and 'Abla*, they are pictured as the single way of life, everyone's occupation. Under the leadership of chief or king (here a queen), schemes are laid and battles are fought for the possession of herds. Whether to call these battles war, sport, or business has long been debated; they were the permanent state of affairs, and the cattle of Ireland must have been lean as greyhounds from all the running.

Again as in 'Antar, in Irish heroic tales the weak are protected by the strong; social classes exist based on the fighting force which is also per se the working force; clan leaders succeed by election from within ruling families; women are respected. Women are even rulers like Medb, or athletes like Scathac. They are companions, equals; they have identities, fulfilled potentials, and various other liberations, but they are not passionately adored like 'Abla.

This is a main difference between the East and the West before the late eleventh century, when romance came to the south of France from Muslim Spain. The Arabs had a sensual interest in women and an acknowledgement of sexual love which the West had not. We see this in Yusuf as opposed to Joseph, in Olympias and Nectanebos, in the humorous exempla of the Disciplina Clericalis, in the tales of The Arabian Nights and in novelle and anecdotes in medieval European literature which were originally from the Levant. Passion was one of the refinements of living which the West was happy to adopt from the superior Arab civilization, along with bathtubs, carpets, brocades, velvet, silk, oranges, sugar, spices, chess, stained glass, mirrors of glass, new colours (lilac, crimson, carmine), heraldry, courtyards, pointed shoes, Moorish (or Morris) dances and musicians, guitars, lutes, rebecs and troubadors. In Europe, passion became Courtly Love.

Proto-chivalric Ireland and proto-chivalric Arabia are more alike in their heroes, as we have seen in folk-hero analogies between Cuchulainn and 'Antar. Details specifically related to medieval romances could be added to these. Not mentioned in Clouston's summary, 'Antar's eyes are described as growing monstrously red and protuberant in rage; Cuchulainn, warming up for battle, can withdraw one eye into his head and thrust the other out like a cauldron. Their youthful exploits, already noted, include the fact that each as a boy was trained by a woman (Zebeebah, Scathac) but because of extraordinary ability was conferred arms by a male relative ('Antar's father, Cuchulainn's uncle). 'Abla is promised to 'Antar if he will fight her father's enemies; Fand is offered to Cuchulainn if he will fight those of her brother-in-law. 'Antar and 'Abla describes a reunion without a confrontation with a son who is recognized by a bracelet (Asyed and Nazih); Cuchulainn meets his son Connla and slays him in combat prior to the recognition by a ring.

All of these Arab and Irish motifs are found also in the Matter of Britain. A feature of terrible ogres and giants is their bulging red eyes; Perceval, and knights cognate with him, as youths are brought up by women; the hand of a female relative is offered as pay for fighting (Gareth and Lyones); the father-son battle and/or recognition, long known of course to Arabs as a fatal combat from the Rustam-Sohrab story, provides the climax of two main Arthurian matières – Arthur-Modred and Lancelot-Galahad – and enters into others, Gawain-Lionel, Lot-Gawain and Nuc-Ider, where the ring recognition reappears. When we note that Irish traditions are accepted as the ultimate source of the Matter of Britain, and that the Cuchulainn saga plays a large part in this debt, we have also made a parallel between 'Antar's story and western chivalry in its pre-chivalric stage.

This stage is perhaps best termed knighthood, which in the West was the actual precursor and basis of the ideals, the institution, and the romances we call chivalry. 'Antar and 'Abla thus shares with European tradition elements commonly found in the tales of folk-heroes who are not yet chivalric heroes, and in aspects of chivalry as well.

In Europe, knighthood developed from the massed cavalry of Justinian's time who, armed with spears and bows, became the backbone of the Roman army. But they were slow and unwieldy and inadequate against the barbarian invasions, since those free-wheeling nomads, armed only with bows and arrows, struck swiftly and got away. But in the ninth century the West began to use heavy-armoured cavalry adapted from the Sassanid Persians (third to seventh centuries) who had learned the technique the hard way from the Parthians. Horsemen and horses with mail body-armour could withstand barbarian harassments and local raids, and in this way the advance of the barbarians was halted. From the Persians the new style had gone to Byzantium and from Byzantium to western Europe, where an aristocratic armoured cavalry became the primary force of local self-defence. The European knight was one who fought on horseback in war, and by virtue of this military service to his lord, held land in peace. He was required to supply his own horse and equipment. By the eighth century, horse-gear included the stirrup, which had been in Persia as early as the seventh, having come from further east. The stirrup, of course, made possible mounted fighting with lances, which was to be the typical combat of chivalry and later its typical game, the joust. Knighthood was awarded at first by dubbing, at court or sometimes on the field of battle, but by the thirteenth century it had become a matter of inheritance. The nobles were the knights, now by birth; they held the land, and thus the land was in the hands of one class only. Personal military service was a thing of the past; instead there was a legal contract between the knight and his feudal lord, and the knight became an administrator as well as a soldier and landowner – a road which led him to the king's court in France and to Parliament in England.

By the mid-thirteenth century, knighthood became the foundation for chivalry, that is, for the ethics of chivalrous behaviour. This included obligations to the social system that supported it, namely the aristocracy-monarchy and the Church; knightly descent as a test of nobility; the notion that baseness of birth meant baseness of motive; and from the two last a consequent prejudice against those who married beneath their station; the Crusade; knight-errantry; and courtly love. The chivalric code called for loyalty, courtesy which included respect for women and affability, largesse which included generosity of money and spirit, i.e. magnanimity, toughness and prowess.

In 'Antar and 'Abla we do indeed see the prototvpe for much of this. The baseness of 'Antar's birth makes him many enemies (Malik, Shas, 'Amarah, Rebia and others) who feel that because of it he is intrinsically unworthy. At the same time, the 'Abs warriors pride themselves on their pure-blooded descent which gives them the right to knighthood. Loyalty to their tribe is absolutely essential and is demonstrated in almost daily skirmishes and missions. At one point, 'Antar is even exiled as a possible cause of dissent within the 'Abs, and understands, accepts and forgives this. He is magnanimous again and again to 'Abla's father and to his own father, and even to bitter foes like Amarah and Rebia when they ask for forgiveness. He underlines this by calling their attention to his acts as those of the noble-born. He admonishes Shiboob when this loyal half-brother does not share his magnanimity to Shas. In battle he spares worthy opponents like Roudha, and when he punishes a leader, he spares the followers.

As for the protection of women, his career begins and ends with this. It is evident, and indeed he states it in his poems, that his love for 'Abla is the ennobling force in his life, inspiring him to the great deeds that later literally ennoble him. His achievement in winning her as his wife is the more remarkable because he is originally beneath her station. He is courtesy itself when he rejects the daughters offered him by the old knight whom he rescues, and a courtier above reproach when at Anushirvan's magnificent court he avoids the dancing-girls and sings of 'Abla. Single-handed, he guards and saves the women of 'Abs when they are attacked on the

way home from a wedding; he rushes to the defence when Usak
plunders the women's quarters of the tribe of Mazin. He saves the
'Abs women when they are captured by the Tayyi'. He repeatedly
rescues 'Abla. And the women recognize him as their protector – a
girl sings a song of praise to him, and all the women applaud when
he spanks 'Amara.

'Antar is also a model of chivalric prowess and practice. When
he slays Usak, he cuts him and his horse down the middle so that
they fall in four parts, a feat which foreshadows *Guy of Warwick* in
which Guy in killing Colbrand cuts his horse in two. King Arthur,
too, strikes a mounted giant, dividing him so that the sides hang
over his horse. Monzar's freeing 'Antar in return for his help against
Khosrewan is a motif repeated in tales of knighthood. Again in *Guy
of Warwick*, a king has Sir Heraud prisoner. When he learns that he
holds a famous knight, he frees him in return for his service. In both
cases, the hero turns the tide. A frequent device in Arthurian tales is
that of the hero who appears as a poor unknown knight only to
overcome all before him, as 'Antar does when he rescues Nazir
from the Aamir tribe. Also typical of chivalric romance are visits to
holy places and shrines. In the *Sira*, 'Antar goes to the Holy Shrine
in Mecca to pray to the Lord of mankind. Even apart from the Grail
stories where these visits are the substance of the narrative,
medieval romances record innumerable sojourns with hermits and
other holy folk. The theme of female warriors which enters with
Jaida into *'Antar and 'Abla* is not quite the same as Medb's role in the
Tain, in that Medb is a central character, a ruler and military
general, while Jaida is a female knight, one of many knights. But
Jaida is a precursor of the women warriors who are the companions
and lovers of knights in Renaissance epics, especially of course
Bradamante in *Orlando Furioso*, Clorinda and Gildippe in
Gerusaleme Liberata, and Britomart in *The Faerie Queene*.

Another similarity is found in the brief passage about the Arab
interpreter whom 'Antar captures with the Persians. 'Antar laughs
at the fellow's humorous promise, 'Whenever you slay a satrap, I
will plunder him', in a way that both looks back to Alexander's
enjoyment of wit and forwards to the medieval king and his jester.

Many of 'Antar's adventures are those of a knight-errant, as
when he follows the knight who rides Abjer and wins the horse for
his own, when he fights for Monzar, and when he finds his sword,
Dhami. Related to this are the granting of boons; 'Antar gives
boons as well as the Arab and Persian kings. Knight-errantry is an
historical fact East as well as West. Clouston cites the name of a

Persian knight, Razm Khah, which means one who goes in quest of adventures, and mentions two famous Arabian knights-errant of the eighth century, Abu Muhammad al-Battal and Jaifar al-Sadiq.[9]

Other elements as well have correspondences in western medieval narratives. For instance, Monzar is insulted at the Persian court. Khosrewan and the other courtiers arrange for false, edible stones to be put in their dates and so eat them completely; Monzar politely imitates them and so swallows the real stones left in his. Then the trick is revealed. This leads to Monzar's defection and to the death of Khosrewan at 'Antar's hands. We find an analogous anecdote in the *Disciplina Clericalis*, No. XXI. At a king's banquet a jester puts all the bones at the feet of another jester and says that he has eaten everything. The accused one replies, 'I have followed my nature, that is, human nature, in that I have eaten the flesh and left the bones. But my friend has followed *his* nature, which is obviously canine, since he has eaten both flesh and bones.' This attempted insult is as old as Josephus who tells it of Hyrcanus[10] and was later ascribed to many others, but inevitably it gravitated into association with Dante at the court of Can Grande della Scala, where *dog* and *Can* give the poet a pointed answer.

The ghost who demands revenge for his murder harks forward to *Hamlet*; the women ridiculing the dandy 'Amarah may hark back to a theme as old as the bickering of Helen and Paris in the *Iliad*. The incident of Badhramoot brings the Christian-Muslim conflict into the story in terms of champions and single combats on the international scale, a Syrian being the champion of the King of Greece.

Although these are events of chivalric romance rather than of courtly love, courtly love is also approximated in *'Antar and 'Abla*, in two aspects. One is that of 'Antar as the famous poet and singer, who praises his lady and the power of love. His poems anticipate twelfth-century troubador lyrics and subsequent western poetry. For example, glances from her eyes dart shafts by which champions are slain, her face is like the sun, or the moon, her smile is like wine and honey, she is graceful as the tamarisk tree, or the gazelle. The turtle-dove is invoked as the pattern of consummated love and of the grief of parted lovers. Folk lyrics even today echo this:

> And on my breast a turtle-dove
> To signify I died for love

It is one of the age-old images that float *ad lib* from song to song in western folk songs. The nightingale heralds spring and the lover. Both a poem by 'Antar and one by 'Abla call on the west wind as the messenger of love. They are ancestors perhaps of the anonymous and strangely allusive quatrain which is among the most enduring of English love poems:

> Western wind, when wilt thou blow,
> The small rain down can rain?
> Christ, if my love were in my arms
> And I in my bed again!

As a tradition shared by East and West, courtly love is the subject of many volumes. In 'Antar we simply touch on it, but nevertheless on two aspects in a controversial field which have won scholarly acceptance.[11] Poetry is one of them. Through Spain, Arabic verse introduced rhyme to Europe. Arabic forms underlay the Mozarabic kharjas and thus were the forerunners of troubadour songs. The Reader's Advisor, a standard reference work, in its section on Spanish literature lifts this long-debated matter into the realms of familiar fact. In 1948

S. M. Stern discovered in a Cairo synagogue twenty poems in Hebrew, the final verses of which were in Spanish, dated around 1040. Since that time fifty such poems have come to light, and they constitute the oldest known lyric poetry in a Romance language. These anonymous verses, born out of the mixture of Arabic, Hebrew and Spanish cultures, are an appropriate beginning for Spanish literature, which is characterized by its popular roots and deeply affected by eight centuries of occupation by the Arabs. Further, in their subject matter, the laments of a young girl for an absent love, and in their nostalgic tone, they introduce love as an important theme in Spanish poetry.[12]

The resemblances we have seen in 'Antar's poems point to this. When Dante used the lyrics of the troubadours as the model for the dolce stil nuova, the Arabs had successfully penetrated to the heart of western European literature.

The second suggestion of courtly love comes in 'Abla's request that she be honoured at her wedding as Jaida was at hers. This is an example of the dangerous task undertaken at the lady's whim, a service the lover is happy to accomplish or to die in attempting. The task is part of the 'feudal' aspect of the socially dominant woman, a significant element in courtly love. In 'Antar's case many hardships and battles ensue. The troubadour's love service is allied to vassalage too; there are many instances in troubadour poetry of the lady's being addressed as 'my lord'. But the same term also occurred earlier in Arabic poetry. We have seen how in 'Antar's case, penalties are imposed both by and for 'Abla within the class system of the 'Abs. His stature minimizes the burden, but it is illustrative of the feudal position as later envisaged by the troubadours, just as 'Antar's love poems with their metaphors from nature and springtime are harbingers of later lyrics.

Thus 'Antar may be regarded as an archetype for the West not only as hero, but also as poet.

The Taming of the Shrew

There was an ill-tempered young lady in pioneer days. All the boys were scared off, but a man back in a clearing needed him a wife. So he went on his horse and they got married; set her up behind him, and started home. He intended to teach her a lesson.

Well, they were riding along and the old horse stumbled. He looked at the horse's head right ill and says, 'That's once!' They gone on a piece further, and a rabbit run across the road and he shied. Looked at him ill again and he said, 'That's twice!' They came to a ford in the creek. The old horse balked. So he looked at him and said, 'Now that's three times!' Told his wife to get down. He gets down, takes the saddle off and sets it on the ground. And, stepped off a few steps, shot the old horse between the eyes with his rifle. Killed him!

And so his wife began bawling him out for killing the poor old horse. She just kept storming and storming at him, but he didn't say a word, just kept loading his old muzzle-loading rifle. So she finally wearied herself out and hushed, and he looked at her and said, 'Now that's once!' Now he said, 'We better get going, I guess.' Man says, 'Pick up that saddle and let's go.' She hesitated. He looked at her again, and said, 'That's twice.' Well, she picked up the saddle on her shoulder and away they tuck. Went home, and she made him a good wife.[1]

An Undesirable Match

There lived a Moor who was much respected, and who had a son, the most promising youth in the world. There also lived another Moor, who was very much richer and who had an only daughter of so violent a temper that no one would marry her. But the young man sought to enrich himself by such a marriage.

So they were married, and the bride taken home; the friends and relations waiting anxiously for the following day.

The young couple sat down to supper, when the bridegroom saw his mastiff and said to him, 'Bring me water wherewith to wash my hands.' The dog, naturally taking no notice of this command, the young man arose in a great rage, and, drawing his sword, commenced a savage attack upon the dog and cut off his head. Thus furious and blood-stained he returned to the table, and saw a cat. 'Bring me water for my hands,' said he. The animal not noticing the command, the master cried out, 'How, false traitor, did you not see how I treated the mastiff for disobeying me? If you do not do as I tell you this instant you shall share his fate.' The poor little cat continuing motionless, the master seized him by the paws and dashed him against the wall. His fury increasing, he espied his horse, and called to him fiercely to bring him water. The animal not obeying, he cried out, 'How is this? Think you that because you are the only horse I have that you dare thus to disobey my orders?' Saying this, he cut off his head.

He sat down to table, swearing he would kill a thousand horses, or men or women, if they disobeyed him. He looked around and ordered his wife to bring him water. She immediately rose and brought it to him.

Thus passed the night; she not daring to speak, but strictly obeying all his orders. After letting her sleep for a short time, he said, 'Get up, take care that nothing disturbs me.'

The following morning, the relatives came stealthily to the door. She went cautiously towards them, and exclaimed: 'Traitors, what are you doing? Speak not – be silent, or all of us are dead.' They were much astonished and, on learning what had taken place, they esteemed the young man very much who had made so good a commencement in the management of his household; from that day his wife became tractable and compliant, so that they led a very happy life.

A few days later, his father-in-law likewise killed a horse in order to intimidate his wife, but she said to him, 'My friend, it is too late to begin now; it would not avail you to kill a hundred horses: we know each other too well.'[2]

V

THE DISCIPLINA CLERICALIS

Of the Arabian books which have most affected us, two are out-standing. Both introduced Arabic stories to the West, where they were stunningly new, fascinating and seminal, each in its own way and time. Closer to our own period is *The Arabian Nights*, first translated into French in 1704 and today familiar to almost everyone; but who has heard of the *Disciplina Clericalis*? Yet, trans-lated into Latin soon after 1106, its stories have had even more influence on European literature than those of the *Nights*.

Its compiler, Petrus Alfunsus, was an exceptional man, many-sided in mind and in circumstances. Circumstances first. He was born in 1062 in Huesca, Aragon, a Jew named originally Moshe Sefardi who was thus educated in both Hebrew and Latin as well as in Spanish and in the flourishing Arab scholarship of Huesca, which had been under Muslim rule until 1035. As a scholar, he had an outstanding place in the learned world, and as a royal physician, first to Alfonso I of Aragon and later to Henry I of England, in courtly circles. At the height of his career (1106), he received Christian baptism, taking the name of his godfather, Alfonso I. Soon afterwards he emigrated to England, where the *Disciplina* was written. He was therefore ideally situated to convey Arab lore to the West in general and to Spain and England in particular, and he accomplished this because his intellectual gifts were equally remarkable.

The Jews were the only people anywhere in Europe who knew both Arabic and Latin, and it was only in Latin, the one general language of the whole continent, that information of any sort could be introduced which through Latin would reach the various vernacular languages. Joseph Bedier[1] and many others after him have pointed out the unique role in this transmission played by Jews in Spanish courts in the era of Arab domination. Thus Petrus Alfunsus was a key man, a polymath who was also a man of the world, erudite in several languages and enjoying as a physician the closest of royal patronage. His knowledge of Arabian sciences led him to bring to the attention of the Latin learned world the then new Arab astronomical tables and to delineate the new cosmography. He himself drew climate maps demonstrating the latter, and discoursed in England on a variety of Arabian discoveries: 'the demarcation of true East and West, the point from which longitudes are to be calculated, the variation of the hour according to the place where the hour is noted, the correspondence between the appearance of the zodiacal signs and the observation of eclipses, and how, contrary to the beliefs of the age, the equatorial regions were habitable'.[2]

Other fields of interest to him were theology and philosophy, which had led to his conversion and which he explicated in his *Dialogi cum Judeo*, a comparison and contrast of Christianity and Judaism. The *Dialogi* also incidentally described the Muslim paradise as a garden of delights and, since this was the earliest account of it in Latin, was the source of later western writings on the subject.

But his greatest fame depends on his 'little book', the *Disciplina Clericalis*, where the scholar, physician, scientist, philosopher and convert is also a succinct and vivid recounter of folktales. For this work he drew, as he tells us in it, 'partly from the stories and warnings of philosophers, partly from Arabic proverbs and admonitions, from tales and poems, and partly from fables about animals and birds'. The stories, chosen from Arab tradition, illustrate the sayings and admonitions, in his expressed hope that by sweetening their lessons with entertainment, readers and hearers would not become bored but would be induced to listen and to retain. In all of these forms in the *Disciplina*, Petrus Alfunsus followed existing Arabic literary patterns, of which more later.

He is, however, original in being the first European writer deliberately to import Arabic culture. Simply by his translating them into Latin, which was the international language of literate Europe, structures and narratives from the Near East became for the first time available to the West. Since cleric could mean an educated layman as well as an ecclesiastic, the *Disciplina* was probably intended for both. The one received a connoisseur's collection of good stories, the other a resource-book of precepts illustrated by brief tales or *exempla*, which priests might use in sermons. The word *disciplina* can be variously translated. 'Discipline' is good enough, but 'instruction' and 'guide' have also been used; 'course of study' or 'training' is perhaps best. A course of study for the reader?

The book had tremendous success – at least sixty-three early manuscripts of it still survive. It was rapidly taken up, copied, translated into the vernaculars, preached in the vernaculars, and imitated all over Europe. It is the ancestor of the subsequent long line of exempla-books which became one of the most popular literary types of the Middle Ages, an achievement for canned-sermons less surprising then than now. And since the tales in the *Disciplina* and its successors were secular to begin with, chosen to enliven the morals they explained, they naturally also had far-reaching secular diffusion in writing. Chauvin, the great French Arabist, over a hundred years ago listed some fifty of only the *principal* authors and works which borrowed from Petrus Alfunsus.[3] They include Bandello, Boccaccio, Chaucer, Cinthio, the *fabliaux*, the *Gesta Romanorum*, Giraldi, Gower, Hebbel, *Islandʐk Aeventyri*, *Kaatspel*, Lydgate, *El Conde Lucanor*, Marie de France, the minnesinger, *Il Novellino*, d'Ouville, *Palmblatter*, Pauli, Hans Sachs, the *Scala Coeli*, Sercambi, Straparola, Timoneda, Vincent de Beauvais. To these could be added Cervantes, Gobius and Shakespeare. Gonzales Palencia, who has edited the *Disciplina*, sums it up: 'These names and the number of surviving manuscripts of the *Disciplina* sufficiently prove its influence on the fiction of the world'.[4] Perhaps it is enough to say that narratives used as exempla later became *novelle* in Italy, *fabliaux* in France, and English Literature in England.

The *Disciplina* not only told good stories, it gave them instant respectability. It demonstrated that unreligious nuggets such as these, sometimes comic and sometimes earthy, could be freely told even in churches if they were told as explanations of moral admonitions. But this, too, had been previously discovered in Islamic countries.

Earliest of all in the Near East was what is known as wisdom literature, in which the sayings and instructions of wise men were listed. The Ten Commandments could be called wisdom literature, but apophthegms older by far have been traced to ancient Egypt and Babylonia. Among Muslims, wisdom literature was much admired, ascribed to Islamic figures from the Old Testament such as Solomon, or Islamic figures from Greek philosophy such as Socrates, Diogenes and Aristotle, or to originally pre-Islamic Arab figures such as Idris and Luqman. The form was always didactic, often in brief dialogues of question and answer, master to student or father to son. Then, in the eighth to ninth centuries, there was a movement in Arabic belles-lettres known as *adab*, which liberalized writing away from the purely religious matters (*ilm*). *Adab* was divided into ten parts of which the tenth was held the most excellent – this was 'the knowledge of the stories which people put forward in their friendly gatherings'. So, led by the so-called founder of *adab*, al-Djahiz (776–865), writers have since been free to use the merry stories of oral tradition to amplify wisdom texts. In this sense the Arabs can be credited with having invented tales as literature and thus with having fixed the shape of 'the fiction of the world'.

As well, from the very beginnings of eastern literatures in India, frame-stories had developed. These were extended narratives which provided a continuity throughout a whole work. Into a frame, short tales completely unrelated to each other could be fitted at will, joined only by the fact that each illustrated an admonition. The prototype of this device is found in the *Jataka* tales or 'Birth Stories' of Buddha of the third century B.C. which are used as frame-stories for moralizing verses attributed to the Buddha. To name only its most famous appearances, the frame-story is employed in the great Indian *Panchatantra*, composed some time during the first 500 years A.D., in which the ignorant sons of a king are taught polity by precept and example. The *Panchatantra* was translated from Pehlevi (Middle Persian) to Arabic in the eighth century under the title *Kalila wa-Dimna*; it was in this form that it had extremely wide diffusion east and west, especially in the period of Muslim expansion. At the same time and in the same school, the *Jataka* tales and other works on the legendary life of Buddha, already syncretized from Sanskrit to Pehlevi, were translated into Arabic as *Bilauhar wa Yudasaf* (westernized as *Barlaam and Josaphat*). In this collection, the holy hermit Bilauhar preaches to the king's son in parables. The *Book of Sindibad,* also translated into Arabic in the eighth century, together with its many redactions was a very popular expansion of the Potiphar's Wife motif, in which the prince's advisers and the accusing stepmother argue by illustrations pro and con the perfidy of women. Typically, the narrative of the frame-story is an excuse for a series of good stories and is subordinate to the individual tales.

In this respect, too, the *Disciplina Clericalis* follows the pattern of its eastern predecessors. Its frame is almost negligible: an Arab father or teacher advises his son or pupil about the problems of life and the evils of the world. The son replies, often with a comment, and then asks a question which soon, or later, leads to another precept and another parable – exactly the suspense technique of The Arabian Nights. There can thus be a longish sequence of statements between each exemplum: twenty-six sections of such maxims are to be found, not numbered, while there are thirty-odd numbered stories which make up the body of the book.

But unobtrusive as it is, it was here in the Disciplina that the frame-story was introduced to Europe, a new-to-Europe, far-reaching fictional form. In the fullness of time, the frame-story was to lead to some of our most familiar western narratives – the Decamerone, The Canterbury Tales, the picaresque novel, and all the way to Sherlock Holmes, Poirot, Jeeves and radio and television soap-operas.

Thus we have in the Disciplina not one but four new literary patterns introduced from the East by way of Arabic literature: (1) the exempla-book as a genre; (2) the edifying moral; (3) the entertaining tale as example or illustration of the edifying moral; and (4) the frame-story.

So far we have dealt with form, the novel structural devices that the Disciplina brought from eastern literature to western. But what is even more significant is the content of its stories. Although they too were part of Arabic written works, they had been originally and still continued to be Arabian folktales as well, i.e. stories told by word of mouth. Some of them have been documented as coming from Arabic books known to Petrus Alfunsus. Kalila wa-Dimna, descended from the Sanscrit Panchatantra and translated from Persian to Arabic in the eighth century; the Book of Sindibad (Arabic title The Seven Wazirs), also translated in the eighth century; and the ninth-century adab collection of Hunain b. Ishaq, Kitab Adab al-Falasifa.[5] It is also possible that the prototype of The Arabian Nights based on the Persian Hazar Afsana (A Thousand Tales) was also available to him in Arabic. It is referred to in Spain in the thirteenth century. In the case of others the link with him may have been lost, but earlier Near Eastern sources are known; still others he might not have read but heard, say in his youth from Arab folk in the marketplace at Huesca. For the tales he used, so new to non-Muslim Europe, were from the age-old international folklore of the Indian, Persian, Syriac, Hebrew, Hellenistic and Arabian storehouse. Because they had long circulated orally in the Islamic world, some tales would have passed before Petrus Alfunsus' time into oral tradition at places of contact such as Spain, Provence or Italy. Some narratives from the same store are in fact still current as folktales, both east and west. But by and large this folklore entered western literature through this book, the *Disciplina Clericalis*. It thus became a part of what we have called the 'primitive capital' of European culture, multiplying and spreading over the years in the literature of the westernized world and in European folklore as well. For at the same time that the folktales written down in the *Disciplina* circulated in writing, they were used as parables in countless sermons, and so were also transmitted and multiplied at the folk level. This double front is what makes its effect so gigantic.

Not only the form of the *Disciplina* but also the content is our familiar western property now. Much of what we think of as 'our' heritage, for example the vast influences which originate from the Bible – all the persons in which and the writers of which were eastern – we scarcely accept as coming from the East. It is not surprising that we also do not realize how many of our handed-down mind-sets and traditions, of perceptions we might think fixed only in western genes, have been shaped by eastern folklore. The international folklore of the Near East is in fact the common folk-lore of the civilized world, and Petrus Alfunsus had a lot to do with making it so.

To revert then, although the name of the *Disciplina Clericalis* may be unknown today, its stories on the contrary are old friends. It is just that we know them separately – and separately from it. They are part of the everyday wisdom, fictions and jokes of our western ambience. A glance at the book shows that there is some connection between ourselves and almost all of its parables. For instance, No. I, The Half-Friend, illustrates the still accepted truth that you don't know your friends until you try them. In the *Disciplina*, an Arab father advises his son to test the many friends he claims he has, since 'I am much older than you and have only acquired half a friend'. The son puts the carcase of a calf in a sack and tells his 'friends' that he has killed a man. They all refuse to help him conceal the body. Only the father's half-friend offers to dig a grave and cover up the pretended crime. The frequency of this story in Arabian and other folklore is probably due to its dissemination as one of the *Barlaam and Josaphat* parables, available, as we have seen, to Petrus Alfunsus in Arabic translations made from the eighth century on.

No. II is the exemplum of The Loyal Friend, also drawn from Arab folklore in *adab* collections of popular stories. When a merchant visits his faithful friend in Egypt, he falls in love with the Egyptian's beloved bride-to-be. Out of pure friendship, the Egyptian gives the girl to him. Later the Egyptian loses all his wealth and is so unhappy he gives himself up as a murderer. To save him, the merchant comes and declares himself the guilty party. The real murderer is so moved by their devoted friendship that he confesses. Both the motifs here – the ceded fiancée and the sacrifice of life for a friend – are very common in Arab narrative. The second theme has been traced to Graeco-Roman writing as early as Cicero, the story of Damon and Pythias of Syracuse, the one standing pledge for the other's life: each is so eager to die to save his friend that the tyrant Dionysus spares the offender. But The Loyal Friend became current in the West in its eastern form through the *Disciplina*, rather than as told by and descended from Cicero, because Boccaccio borrowed the story from the *Disciplina* and his treatment was formative. Known as 'Tito and Giuseppe', it is one of the most popular of his tales. At least thirty-five redactions or imitations of his version were cited from European writing in 1910[6]; doubtless many more have appeared since. (This is not to mention early authors other than Boccaccio and their derivatives.) After the Renaissance and the rediscovery of Roman writers, the Damon and Pythias variant became proverbial, and still is. In America, for example, a national fraternal club which has had hundreds of thousands of members is called The Knights of Pythias. And as The Loyal Friend, the tale is a commonplace of European literatures.

But we see even more dramatically the familiarity of Alfunsus' tales when a western descendant of one of them is juxtaposed with its ancestor. Because the need to moralize has of course vanished with the centuries, what was once used as an exemplum is now simply told as an amusing story. But his serious parables, too, often have their current variants.

Here are some versions in modern dress, followed by Petrus Alfunsus' own words.

DREAM BREAD

A Scotsman, an Irishman, and a Jew who were travelling together ran out of food. All they had was one loaf of bread. They decided that whoever dreamed the most wonderful dream should have the loaf to himself, and then went to sleep. When they awoke the Scotsman said, 'I dreamed that

angels led me to the gates of heaven, and the gates opened for me!' The
Irishman said, 'I dreamed that angels took me to the gates of hell and
showed me inside it!' The Jew said, 'Well, when I saw one of you in heaven
and the other in hell, I got up and ate the bread.'

Exemplum XIX
THE TWO CITY DWELLERS AND THE COUNTRY MAN

Once there were two city men and a country man who were going to
Mecca on a pilgrimage. They ate together until they came near Mecca,
where their provisions gave out, and they had nothing left but a little flour
with which they could make one small loaf.

The city men, seeing this, said to each other, 'We have little bread and
our companion eats much; we should think how we can get his share of the
bread and eat it by ourselves.'

They all three agreed to the following plan: that they would make the
loaf and bake it; and while it was cooking, they would go to sleep, and
whoever had the most extraordinary dream should have the bread for
himself. The city dwellers said this as a trick because they thought the
country man was stupid enough to believe such ruses. They made the loaf,
put it on the fire, and then lay down to sleep.

The country man, aware of the trick, took the half-baked loaf from
the fire while his companions were sleeping, ate it, and lay down again.

One of the city dwellers, as if frightened by a dream, awoke and called
to his companion. The second city dweller said, 'What is the matter?'

And the first said, 'I had a wonderful dream: it seemed that two angels
opened the gates of heaven, took me up, and led me before God.'

His companion said to him, 'This dream is wonderful, but I dreamt that
with two angels leading me and opening the earth, I was taken to hell.'

The peasant heard all this and still pretended to be asleep; but the
deceitful city men, who had already been deceived, called the country man
to wake up. And he, slyly, as if he were frightened, answered, 'Who is
calling me?'

They said, 'We, your companions.'

And he said, 'Have you returned already?'

And they said, 'Where did we go, that we should return?'

And the rustic said, 'I dreamed that two angels took one of you and
opened the gates of heaven and took him before God; then two other
angels took the other and opened the earth and took him to hell. When I
saw these things, I thought that neither of you would ever return, and I got
up and ate the bread.'7

WHISTLE THE DOG IN

An old man was sitting in front of the fire one night, and he got to wondering what the weather was like. 'Ma,' he said, 'go out and see if it's raining.' The old woman didn't move. 'No use to going to all that trouble,' she said. 'Just whistle the dog in and feel his back.'

Exemplum XXVII
ANECDOTES OF MAIMUNDUS THE SLAVE

His master ordered him to close the door one night. Maimundus could not get up however because of his laziness, so he said it had already been shut.

When it was morning, the master said to him, 'Maimundus, open the door.'

And the slave answered, 'Master, I knew that you would want it open today, so I did not close it last night.'

Only then did the master realize that, out of laziness, Maimundus had not closed it.

He said to him, 'Get up and do your work, for it is already day, and the sun is high.'

'Master,' replied the slave, 'if the sun is high, give me something to eat.'

The master: 'O worst of slaves, do you want to eat while it is still dark?'

The slave: 'If it is still dark, let me sleep.'

On another occasion, one night the master said to him, 'Maimundus, get up and see whether it is raining or not.'

But Maimundus called the dog, who was lying outside the door, and when the dog came, he felt its feet and found them dry and said, 'Master, it is not raining.'[8]

SORTER LIKE THIS

A long time ago a plantation owner in South Carolina had to go to New York or somewhere else up North on a long visit. As he approached his home on returning, he met one of his hands named Sam. They met in the road in the woods, out of sight of the house.

'Well, Sam,' he asked, 'how are things?'

'Not too good, I reckon,' Sam answered.

'What you mean, not too good?'

'Well, your fine dog, ole Joe, he's daid.'

'Dead. What happened to him?'

'He burned up.'

'How come that?'
'He was in the barn when it burned up.'
'How come the barn to burn up?'
'It caught on fire from the big house.'
'You mean the big house burned down?'
'Yais, sir.'
'How'd it come to burn?'
'Caught on fire from one of them lace curtains.'
'How'd the lace curtain catch on fire?'
'From a candle.'
'What was the candle doing next to lace curtains?'
'Candles was lit on your mother-in-law's coffin and wind blowed lace curtain against one.'
'You mean my mother-in-law's dead?' the plantation owner asked without any marked anxiety.
'Yais, sir.'
'What was the matter with her?'
'Well, it was sorter like this. Your wife she run off with the overseer and then her mother she got so nervous and worked up she jes' died.'[9]

Exemplum XXVII
ANECDOTES OF MAIMUNDUS THE SLAVE

His master was coming from the market happy because he had made a good profit. Maimundus went out to meet him. The master warned him, 'Don't tell me any bad news.'

The servant agreed. 'But our little dog Bispella is dead.'

The master: 'How did it die?'

The slave: 'Our mule got frightened and broke its bridle, and when it ran away, it trampled the dog.'

The master: 'What was done about the mule?'

'He fell into the well – he is dead.'

Master: 'What frightened the mule?'

The slave: 'Your son fell from the balcony and was killed, and this frightened the mule.'

The master: 'What is his mother doing?'

The slave: 'Out of grief for her son, she died.'

The master: 'Who is minding the house?'

The slave: 'No one, because it and everything in it burned to ashes.'

The master: 'How did it catch fire?'

The slave: 'The same night the mistress died, the servant-girl who was sitting with the body forgot about a candle in the bedroom, and so the whole house burned up.'

The master: 'Where is the servant-girl?'

172

The slave: 'She tried to put out the fire and a beam fell on her head and she died.'

The master: 'How did you escape, since you are so lazy?'

The slave: 'When I saw the girl dead, I fled.'

Apropos of the Maimundus stories, which like Dream Bread are still current in western literature and popular jokes, one more version is of interest as evidence of their continued viability in Arabian folklore. Unlike the simpler variants above, this redaction did not come from the *Disciplina* but was recorded in 1800, 700 years afterwards. We can see how our western versions show their derivation from Petrus Alfunsus when they are compared with this more developed, balanced tale of later Arabian provenance.

A half-starving Arab was travelling in the desert when he came on a man eating, his cloth spread by the roadside. The Arab greeted him and sat down, hoping for an invitation to partake, saying he came from the man's village.

'Did'st thou see my house?'

'Yes, and a well-built and handsome one it is.'

'Did'st see my shepherd's dog?'

'Certainly, and he well guards thy herds and flocks.'

'Did'st see my son Khalid?'

'To be sure; he was at school, most cleverly reading the Koran.'

'How is the mother of Khalid?'

'Charmingly, and there is not a more notable manager or better talker in all Arabia, or more celebrated for her charity and goodness.'

'Did'st see my camel?'

'Yes, and he is in great order and strength.'

The man was pleased with all this welcome news and ate with great relish, but did not invite the famished Arab. The Arab said to himself, 'I must address this miserly glutton in another way.' Just then a dog passed.

'Had thy poor dog been alive,' said the hungry man, 'he would have wagged his tail just in this manner.'

'Alas!' said the man, 'is my dog dead? How did he die?'

'From drinking the urine of thy camel.'

'Did my camel die also?'

'No, but they killed him for the mourning repast of Khalid's mother.'

'Alas! is the mother of Khalid dead?'

'Yes.'

'What illness occasioned her death?'

'Why, she so beat her head against the tomb of poor Khalid that she died of the bruises.'

'Ah! Is my son Khalid gone also?'

'Unfortunately so, for a violent earthquake having overthrown thy mansion, he was crushed to death.'

When the surly glutton heard all this, he desisted from eating and leaving all behind him, hastened homeward, while the happy Arab sat down and feasted on his victuals.[10]

Turning to the *Disciplina*'s more serious parables, we find yet another type of medieval European literature, known as *'Ubi sunt . . .?'*, i.e. 'Where are . . . those who have been before us?' Petrus Alfunsus cannot be claimed to have introduced this, since it is a universal theme of Christian philosophy, but in his redaction the special Near Eastern vein of *Ubi sunt* was transplanted, and this afterwards formed the basis of many vernacular renditions. His text is found in Exemplum XXXIV, of The Hermit Who Admonished His Soul: 'Where are the kings? Where are the princes, the rich men who gathered treasures and were proud because of their wealth? Now they are as if they had never existed; now they are dead, as if they had not lived; now they are like the blossom which dropped from the tree and never returned.' Exempla XXXII and XXXIII are related to this. The first tells of a funeral slab on which was written: 'You who pass close by and do not even say "Farewell", stop and retain these my words in your heart. I am what you will be . . .' The second describes the sayings of the philosophers at Alexander's golden sarcophagus, contrasting his power and glory of yesterday with his being mere dust today. Both exempla reflect Semitic tradition: the latter is incorporated via the *Historia de Proeliis* into the Alexander Romance, while the former motif, the inscription at the tomb of a long-dead prince, is found again and again in Arabic writings and folklore, several times in *The Arabian Nights* alone, where the tombs are always in a desert or remote setting. The challenge from a gravestone to a passer-by is familiar in modern English verse from Yeats' sententious 'Epitaph', which is a derivative of Byron's mocking 'Epitaph', Byron of course being aware of both Latin and Levantine patterns.

Metlitski best summarizes the interwoven threads which produced *Ubi sunt* and Petrus Alfunsus' function in transmitting it:

The classical 'ubi sunt' reached the *Disciplina Clericalis* from Arabic sources which, in turn, were affected by the treatment of the theme in the literature of the oriental church. In Arabic poetry variations on the theme have been traced to the pre-Islamic period in the work of 'Adi ibn Zaid (*ca.* 600). 'Ubi sunt reges' with which Petrus Alfunsus begins, is the exact phrasing of a verse on the transitoriness of earthly power which Muslim tradition attributes to Omar b. al-Khattab, the second caliph, and which appears in a sermon of the first caliph, Abu Bakr. The medieval poets who developed this theme in thirteenth-century England were clearly drawing on a meditation on death which had reached them in almost identical language both from classical sources by way of Boethius, and 'ex Arabicis' through Petrus Alfunsus and Muslim Spain.[11]

Translations of the *Disciplina* in medieval French, which closely follow Petrus Alfunsus' words, in turn affected a poem still known throughout the world today, Francois Villon's '*Mais ou sont les neiges d'antan*', while to English-speaking schoolchildren the Arabian message via the *Disciplina* comes today through Shelley's 'Ozymandias':

I met a traveller from an antique land
Who said: Two vast and trunkless legs of stone
Stand in the desert . . . Near them, on the sand,
Half-sunk, a shattered visage lies, whose frown,
And wrinkled lip, and sneer of cold command,
Tell that its sculptor well those passions read
Which yet survive, stamped on these lifeless things,
The hand that mocked them, and the heart that fed:
And on the pedestal these words appear:
'My name is Ozymandias, king of kings:
Look on my works, ye Mighty, and despair!'
Nothing beside remains. Round the decay
Of that colossal wreck, boundless and bare
The lone and level sands stretch far away.

Among the most popular of the *Disciplina* exempla and certainly the most amusing are those about women. As parables they must have fetched reminiscent chuckles from male readers who had heard them before as merry tales. The charm of *adab* lay in just this sort of secret connotation. These stories were part of the *Book of Sindibad* cycle, in other words, anti-women, a subject which if not *the* oldest is one of the oldest and widest-spread in world folklore. Petrus Alfunsus' own humour about women seems to lie in ambiguity over and above the mock-serious freedom allowed by *adab*. He in fact makes a point of saying in his prologue, 'Let the knowledgeable be reminded of what they have forgotten by means of the things which are contained here.' In the following tale he shows delicious skill in punch-line double-entendre which could not be undeliberate.

Exemplum X
THE LINEN SHEET

It is told that a man setting out on a long journey entrusted his wife to his mother-in-law. His wife was in love with another man, and she told her mother. The mother, indulging her daughter, encouraged the affair and invited the suitor. She sat down to eat with him and her daughter. While they were eating, the husband returned and knocked at the door. The wife got up, hid her suitor and went to open the door for her husband.

As soon as he had entered, he demanded that they get the bed ready, for he was tired and wanted to rest. The woman, disturbed, did not know what to do, and her mother, seeing this, said, 'Wait, do not hurry to get the bed ready until we show your husband the linen sheet we have made.'

And the old woman took out a linen sheet and held one end of it as high as she could and gave the other end to the daughter to hold up. Thus, with the outspread sheet, they distracted the husband until the lover who was hidden escaped.

Then the woman said to her daughter, 'Spread this sheet that you and I made with our hands on your husband's bed.'

And he said to the mother-in-law, 'And you, madam, know how to make such linen?'

She answered, 'My son, I have made many like this.'[12]

This tale went from the *Disciplina* to *fabliaux* and to Cervantes. Its popularity in Arab folklore has continued to modern times: a redaction from Egyptian oral tradition dates to the 1880s. In this the wife hides the lover behind one cloth while she ties another over her jealous husband's head, and in gales of laughter tells him the story of a wife who does just this. What with her laughter and his vain shouts and struggles he can neither see nor hear. She continues in her story that the wife calls to the hidden lover, 'Wherever you are, save yourself! By the Prophet, save yourself!' The real lover takes the hint and escapes. When the husband finally gets disentangled, still laughing she asks, 'Did my story please you? Now look behind the cloth – you'll see nothing.'[13]

Deception by means of the truth is a common motif in anti-women folktales from the Near East. In one type, the wife tells the true story as fiction, as in this Egyptian example, but while the lover is hidden in a chest. An example of another type is found paired in the *Disciplina* with The Linen Sheet; it is about a grape harvester (Exemplum IX) who comes home unexpectedly because he has injured one eye. His wife covers the good eye on the pretext that it must be protected lest it too lose vision. Her lover is thus able to leave unseen. These two similar tricks are in a sense combined in the Egyptian story – the wife covers the eyes as in the one, but by a cloth as in the other – and were perhaps originally the same folk-story.

The Linen Sheet would have been known to Petrus Alfunsus from an Arabic translation of the *Hitopadesa*, a book also incorporated in the *Panchatantra*; both works were available to him in Arabic.

From the *Book of Sindibad* collections which include derivatives such as *The Seven Sages*, *The Forty Wazirs*, etc., come his other parables of women: The Sword (No. XI), The Well (No. XIV) and The Weeping Bitch (No. XIII). The source of No. XXXV, about the blind husband and the lovers in the pear tree, has not been determined but is of the Levantine rather than the Indian branch of this story. All of these, transmitted by the *Disciplina*, became as popular in western writing as in the East. The tale of The Sword we will meet anew in *The Arabian Nights*. Both it and The Well were retold in the *Decamerone* (1353) from Petrus Alfunsus' rendition and thus early entered the mainstream of European literature. The Weeping Bitch, although part of the original *Disciplina*, had an independent history in England as *Dame Sirith*, the oldest *fabliau* in Middle English.

The next three stories show how Alfunsus' concise and concrete little parables developed into our familiar western classics. First, The Well, Exemplum XIV, and then Boccaccio's retelling, to which one could add many parallels, including a nineteenth-century newspaper account told as a true incident in Lewes, Sussex, England;[14] next The Weeping Bitch (Exemplum XIII) and *Dame Sirith*; and lastly, The Blind Man and the Adulterous Youth (Exemplum XXXV), the lovers in the pear tree, from which Chaucer's famous analogue, 'The Merchant's Tale', descends.

Exemplum XIV
THE WELL

There was a young man who applied all his efforts and thoughts and time to learning the many wiles of women; and having done this, he decided to get married. But first he went to seek advice from the wisest man in that region, and he asked him how he could guard the woman he wanted to marry.

When he heard the question, the wise man advised him to build a house with high stone walls, to put his wife inside, to give her enough to eat and not too many clothes, and to build the house with only one door and one window through which she might look; and the window should be so high and of such a design that no one could enter or leave by it. The young man, when he had heard the advice, did all that the wise man instructed him. When he left his house in the morning, he locked the door; when he entered, he did the same; and when he slept, he hid the keys under his pillow. He did this for a long time.

But one day, when the young man went to the market place, his wife went up to the window as she usually did to watch the people coming and going. While she was at the window she saw a young man, handsome of body and countenance, and immediately fell in love with him. The woman, because she was burning with love for the young man, as I have said, because she was so closely guarded, began to think how and by what ruse she could talk to the young man she loved. Being clever and deceitful, she decided to steal the keys from her husband while he slept; and so she did.

And every night, she would give wine to her husband to get him drunk so that she could safely go to her lover and do as she wished. The husband, who had learned from philosophers that all the actions of women conceal some deceit, began to wonder why his wife gave him something to drink every night; and in order to observe her he pretended to be drunk. The wife, unaware of this, got up out of the bed, went to the door, opened it, and went out to meet her lover.

The husband got up silently in the dark and went to the door, closed it and locked it, and went up to the window and stood until he saw his wife coming back in her nightgown. When she returned and saw the door closed, she was very disturbed, but she nevertheless knocked on the door. And he, who could hear and see her (as if he did not know anything), asked who it was. She begged him to forgive her and promised never to do such a thing again, but she got nowhere, because the husband angrily said that he would not let her in but would tell her parents about her behaviour. But she, crying louder and louder, said that if he did not open the door, she would throw herself into a well that was near the house and end her life, and he would have to give account to her friends and relatives for her death. He, ignoring her threats, did not let her in.

The clever, deceitful woman picked up a stone and threw it in the well so that her husband hearing the sound of the stone falling into the well would think that she had thrown herself into the well. And when she had done this she hid herself behind the well.

The husband, innocent and unwary, when he heard the splash of the stone in the well, thought he had really heard his wife fall in, and immediately he ran out of the house and went to the well. The wife, when she saw the door open, slyly entered the house, locked the door, and went up to the window.

He, seeing himself duped, said, 'O deceitful woman, full of the devil's tricks, let me in and I will forgive you whatever you have done to me.'

Insulting him and swearing, she refused to let him in, saying, 'O wicked deceiver, since every night you sneak out and leave me so as to visit prostitutes, I will declare your wickedness to your parents.' And so she did. And they believing these things greatly reproached him. And thus she with her guile caused blame which *she* deserved to fall on her husband, who gained little by carefully guarding his wife. In fact, he lost much by it; because a series of misfortunes happened to him: in the opinion of many, he was believed to have deserved what he suffered; and so, deprived of wealth, stripped of dignities, his reputation ruined by his wife's slander, he was punished for adultery.[15]

DECAMERONE (VII, 4)

There was once, then, in Arezzo, a rich man called Tofano and he was given to wife a very fair lady, by name Madam Ghita, of whom, without knowing why, he quickly waxed jealous. The lady, becoming aware of this, was despited thereat and questioned him once and again of the reason of his jealousy; but he was able to assign her none, save such as were general and naught; wherefore it occurred to her mind to cause him to die of the disease whereof he stood without reason in fear. Accordingly, perceiving that a young man, who was much to her taste, sighed for her, she proceeded discreetly to come to an understanding with him and things being so far advanced between them that there lacked but with deeds to give effect to words, she cast about for a means of bringing this also to pass; wherefore, having already remarked, amongst her husband's other ill usances, that he delighted in drinking, she began not only to commend this to him, but would often artfully incite him thereto. This became so much his wont that, well nigh whensoever it pleased her, she led him to drink even to intoxication, and putting him to bed whenas she saw him well drunken, she a first time foregathered with her lover, with whom many a time thereafter she continued to do so in all security. Indeed, she grew to put such trust in her husband's drunkenness that not only did she make bold to bring her gallant into the house, but went whiles to pass a great part of the night with him in his own house, which was not very far distant.

The enamoured lady continuing on this wise, it befell that the wretched husband came to perceive that she, whilst encouraging him to drink, natheless herself drank never; wherefore suspicion took him that it might be as in truth it was, to wit, that she made him drunken, so she might after do her pleasure what while he slept, and wishing to make proof of this, an it were so, he one evening, not having drunken that day, feigned himself, both in words and fashions, the drunkenest man that was aye. The lady put him to bed and betook herself to the house of her lover. As for Tofano, no sooner did he know the lady to have left the house than he straightway arose and going to the doors, locked them from within; after which he posted himself at the window, so he might see her return and show her that he had gotten wind of her fashions; and there he abode till such time as she came back. The lady, returning home and finding herself locked out, was beyond measure woeful and began to essay an she might avail to open the door by force, which, after Tofano had awhile suffered, 'Wife,' quoth he, 'thou weariest thyself in vain, for thou canst nowise come in here again. Go, get thee back whereas thou hast been till now and be assured that thou shalt never return thither till such time as I shall have done thee, in respect of this affair, such honour as beseemeth thee in the presence of thy kinsfolk and of the neighbours.'

The lady fell to beseeching him for the love of God that it would please him open to her, for that she came not whence he supposed, but from keeping vigil with a she-neighbour of hers, for that the nights were long and she could not sleep them all out nor watch at home alone. However, prayers profited her nought, for that her brute of a husband was minded to have all the Aretines know their shame, whereas none as yet knew it; wherefore, seeing that prayers availed her not, she had recourse to threats and said, 'An thou open not to me, I will make thee the woefullest man alive.' 'And what canst thou do to me?' asked Tofano, and Mistress Tessa, whose wits Love had already whetted with his counsels, replied, 'Rather than brook the shame which thou wouldst wrongfully cause me suffer, I will cast myself into this well that is herenigh, where when I am found dead, there is none will believe otherwise than that thou, for very drunkenness, hast cast me therein; wherefore it will behove thee flee and lose all thou hast and abide in banishment or have thy head cut off for my murderer, as thou wilt in truth have been.'

Tofano was nowise moved by these words from his besotted intent; wherefore quoth she to him, 'Harkye now, I can no longer brook this thy fashery; God pardon it thee! Look thou cause lay up this distaff of mine that I leave here.' So saying, the night being so dark that one might scarce see other by the way, she went up to the well and taking a great stone that lay thereby, cried out, 'God pardon me!' and let it drop into the water. The stone, striking the water, made a very great noise, which when Tofano heard, he verily believed that she had cast herself in; wherefore, snatching up the bucket and the rope, he rushed out of the house and ran to the well to succour her. The lady, who had hidden herself near the door, no sooner saw him run to the well than she slipped into the house and locked herself in; then, getting her to the window, 'You should water your wine, whenas you drink it,' quoth she, 'and not after and by night.' Tofano, hearing this, knew himself to have been fooled and returned to the door, but could get no admission and proceeded to bid her open to him; but she left speaking softly, as she had done till then, and began, well nigh at a scream, to say, 'By Christ His Cross, tiresome sot that thou art, thou shalt not enter here tonight; I cannot brook these thy fashions any longer; needs must I let every one see what manner of man thou art and at what hour thou comest home anights.' Tofano, on his side, flying into a rage, began to rail at her and bawl; whereupon the neighbours, hearing the clamour, arose, both men and women, and coming to the windows, asked what was to do. The lady answered, weeping, 'It is this wretch of a man, who still returneth to me of an evening, drunken, or falleth asleep about the taverns and after cometh home at this hour; the which I have long suffered, but, it availing me not and I being unable to put up with it longer, I have bethought me to shame him therefor by locking him out of doors, to see and he will mend himself thereof.'

Tofano, on the other hand, told them, like an ass as he was, how the case stood and threatened her sore; but she said to the neighbours, 'Look you now what a man he is! What would you say, were I in the street, as he is, and he in the house, as am I? By God His faith, I doubt me you would believe he said sooth. By this you may judge of his wits; he saith I have done just what methinketh he hath himself done. He thought to fear me by casting I know not what into the well; but would God he had cast himself there in good sooth and drowned himself, so he might have well watered the wine which he hath drunken to excess.' The neighbours, both men and women, all fell to blaming Tofano, holding him at fault, and chid him for that which he said against the lady; and in a short time the report was so noised abroad from neighbour to neighbour that it reached the ears of the lady's kinsfolk, who came thither and hearing the thing from one and another of the neighbours, took Tofano and gave him such a drubbing that they broke every bone in his body. Then, entering the house, they took the lady's gear and carried her off home with them, threatening Tofano with worse. The latter, finding himself in ill case and seeing that his jealousy had brought him to a sorry pass, for that he still loved his wife heartily, procured certain friends to intercede for him and so wrought that he made his peace with the lady and had her home again with him, promising her that he would never be jealous again. Moreover, he gave her leave to do her every pleasure, provided she wrought so discreetly that he should know nothing thereof; and on this wise, like a crack-brained churl as he was, he made peace after suffering damage. So long live Love and death to war and all its company![16]

Exemplum XIII
THE WEEPING BITCH

It is related that a nobleman had a very chaste and beautiful wife. He wanted to go to Rome to pray in the holy places, and he did not want to leave any other guardian for his wife but herself, trusting in her chaste habits and the honour of her uprightness. When the retinue was ready, he departed and the wife remained, living chastely and acting prudently in all things.

It happened that she needed something, and she left her own house and went to a neighbouring house. As she came home after transacting her business, a young man saw her and fell madly in love with her. He, desiring to be loved by her for whom he burned so ardently, sent many messages to her. But she refused his messages and rejected him completely.

The young man seeing himself utterly scorned, grief-stricken, fell gravely ill; but nevertheless he would often go where he had seen his lady leave, hoping to meet her; but he was not able to effect it at all. Weeping for sorrow, he met an old woman wearing the habit of a nun, and she asked the cause of his unhappiness; but the young man was not very anxious to reveal what was going on in his mind.

The old woman said to him, 'The longer a sick man delays in revealing his illness to the doctor, the more he will suffer from the illness.'

Hearing this, he told her what had happened to him and his secret.

The old lady said to him, 'With God's help I'll find a remedy for what you have told me.'

And she left him and returned to her own house. She forced a little dog which she had at home to go without food for two days. On the third day she gave the hungry dog bread made with mustard, and as the dog ate the bread, its eyes began to water with the sharpness of the mustard. The old woman brought the little dog to the house of the chaste woman whom the young man loved, and the woman received her respectfully because of her very religious appearance. The little bitch was following the old woman. When the woman saw it weeping, she asked what was wrong with it and why it was crying.

The old woman said to her, 'Dear friend, do not ask what is wrong, because the sorrow is so great that I can hardly talk about it.'

And the woman begged her even more earnestly to tell her.

The old woman: 'This little dog which you see was my daughter, who was very chaste and modest and was loved by a young man; but she was so chaste that she spurned him and rejected his love. The young man, pining away, became very ill. For her sin, my wretched daughter was turned into a little bitch.' And so saying, the old lady burst into tears.

The decent woman said at this, 'O dear lady, what shall I do? I am guilty of a similar crime; for a young man loves me, but because of my love of chastity I have disdained him, and he has also fallen ill.'

'Dear friend, I advise you to have pity on him as quickly as possible and do what he asks, so that you may not be turned into a dog just as my daughter was. If I had known of the love between my daughter and the young man, my daughter would never have been transformed.'

The chaste woman said to her, 'I beg you to give me good advice, so that I may not be turned into a little bitch, deprived of my own form.'

'Willingly,' said the old woman, 'For the love of God and the health of my soul and because I feel sorry for you, I will seek the young man, and if he can be found, I will bring him back to you.'

The woman thanked her, and the wily old woman kept her word and brought back the young man as she had promised, and thus brought them together.[17]

DAME SIRITH

As I came along the road I heard a story about a fine, lively man, who was clever, learned, handsome, and well-dressed. He began to love a married woman – he shouldn't have done that. His heart belonged entirely to her, so that he had no rest: the love was so severe.

He thought very hard about how he could get her. One day it happened that the husband went off on a business trip. The other man went to the house which she lived in, which was a fine place. He came into the hall where she was standing in her expensive clothes, and he began like this:

'May God Almighty be here!'

'Welcome, as ever I hope for joy' said this wife. 'If you would like to, come in and sit down, my dear, and tell me what you want. By Our Lord, the King of Heaven, if I can do anything to please you, you could find me very generous. I'll very gladly do what I can for you, with no sorrow!'

'Lady, may God reward you. If you won't give me away, or be angry, I'll tell you my business. But I'd hate to make you angry for anything I did.'

'No, not at all, Willikin, not for anything that has ever been mine, though you want it ever so much, will I be rude. I don't know anything about meanness, and I don't intend to learn. You can say anything you like, and I shall listen and sit still while you tell it. And if you tell me what is right, I shall do what you want – you can be sure of that. And though you say anything shameful, I shan't blame you for what you say.'

'Now I have got permission, it would be wrong if I should be unhappy. Certainly, lady, you speak very graciously, and I shall come to the point and tell you everything I want, and why I have come. I am not one to tell lies, and I won't. I've loved you for many years – though I haven't been here to show my love. While your husband is at home nobody can have a quiet word with you with any grace. Yesterday, as I came along the road, I heard about your husband and heard that he'd gone to the fair at Boston in Lincolnshire. And because I knew he was out, I took the trouble to speak to you. His life must be very pleasant who could possess such a woman, in privacy. Lady, if you agree, I'll love you both quietly and secretly.'

'By our Lord, the King of Heaven, who is above us, I won't do that on any account! I have my lord, as my husband, who brought me with great honour to this house as a maiden. He loves me, and I love him well. Our love is as true as steel, without a doubt. Though he's away from home on business, I'd be a fool if I learned to be a whore. That will never happen, for me to do such a false thing, in bed or anywhere else in the house. Not while he's alive, though he's a hundred miles beyond Rome, not for anything would I take any man on earth as my mate, before he came home!'

'Lady, lady, change your attitude. You were always gracious, and will be still. For the Lord's sake who created us, alter your attitude, change your mind, and have pity on me.'

'Oh dear! Oh dear! Do you think I'm a fool? As sure as Christmas, you *are* silly. You'll never change my mind. My husband is a gracious courteous man, and a man of substance. And I am a good and faithful wife. No one can know a more faithful woman than I am. That time will never come when either by persuasion or through pride I shall do anything shameful.'

'Sweet darling, have mercy! I'm not offering you shame or disgrace, but secret love as a man who wants to do well in love and find happiness!'

'As ever I hope to eat or drink, you're losing all your labour here. You may just as well go home, dear brother, for I don't want your love or anyone else's but my wedded husband's, and I don't hesitate to tell you so.'

'Certainly, lady, I'm sorry for that. And sad is the man who works hard and fails at last. He's no choice but to complain. That's certainly my situation, who love the love that I must lose. And lady, now, good-day! And may that Lord, that can rule all, grant that your mind may so change, that I may no longer mourn for you!'

He went away gloomily, and thought both night and day how he might change her. A friend advised him to leave his great sorrow, and go and see gracious Dame Sirith. Straightaway he went there as fast as he could, meeting no one on the way. He was full of misery and grief. He greeted her politely with gentle and also cunning words.

'God bless you, Dame Sirith. I've come to speak with you from great need. If you can help me, you shall have, as you shall see, a great reward.'

'Welcome to you, dear son; and if I know or am able to do something for you in any way I shall do my very best. So, dear son, tell me what you want me to do.'

'A cure, dear old lady; I'm getting on very badly; I live a life of misery and care:

> With much unease I lead my life
> And all because of a sweet wife
> Whose name is Margery.
> I have loved her many a day
> And of her love she says me nay
> So here I come to thee.
> Unless she change and be more kind,
> For sorrow must I lose my mind,
> Or to my death to go.
> I had bethought myself to slay
> But then a friend showed me the way
> To you, my grief to show.

'He told me that without fail you could help and assist and bring me out of my misery through your trickery and devices. And I will give you a rich reward when that is done.'

'God's blessing be here! In this, my son, you have great sin. Lord, for his sweet name, let there be no shame to you for it! You're going to earn God's anger when you put such blame on me, for I'm old and ill and crippled. Illness has made me quite tame. Bless you, bless you, dear boy! – that you may not get into trouble because of this lie that is invented about me, who am so hard pressed. I'm a holy woman, I know nothing about witchcraft, only about alms given by good men. I keep going day by day, and say my *pater-noster* and creed so that God may help them when they need it; God grant that they may succeed who have helped me to keep going. His life and soul deserve to be disgraced who sent you to me on this business. And may I be avenged on him who spoke this shame about me.'

'Dear old lady, leave all this: it seems to me you're being silly. The man who directed me to you knew that you could bring people together. Dame Sirith, help me if you can to be reconciled to my sweetheart, and I will give you a really big gift, lots of pounds and pence, warm clothes, warm shoes, if my business is well done. You will be able to boast of a regular fortune if you will help me!'

'Don't lie to me, Willikin. By your loyalty, are you really being sincere? Do you really love Dame Margery?'

'Yes, old lady, I really do: I love her: it could do me harm if I don't get her to do what I want.'

'Well, good Willikin, I'm sorry for your harm. May our Lord send you help soon. If I could be sure it wouldn't be known, it would seem a good thing if I could get you what you wanted on your own. Promise me for certain, with raised hand, that you'll keep it quiet, and I will see if I can tell her. I wouldn't want for all the world to be brought before the Chapter for any such affairs. I'd be straightaway sentenced to ride shamefully on an ass, driven by priests and clerks.'

'Certainly, old lady, I don't want you to have any ill-treatment or shame for doing me a good turn. I promise you my truth here that I shall do everything I can to keep it quiet, by the holy cross.'

'You're very welcome here, Willikin! Here you've made a promise that may please you very well. You can bless this moment, for you can make yourself very happy. There's no need to sigh any more. It's your good fortune that you ever came here, for I'll go there straightaway and make her understand. I'll teach her such a lesson that she shall love you much more than any man in the country.'

'As I hope to have the peace of God, you've said well, Dame Sirith, and you shall have good fortune. Here is twenty shillings. I give it to you as a reward, to buy sheep and pigs for yourself.'

'As ever I hope to enjoy a roof over my head or a floor under my feet, pennies were never better laid out than these shall be, for I'll do the business, and a wonderful trick, as you shall see very well.

[To the dog] – Now I'm going to make you eat pepper and mustard – that will make your eyes run! I know very well where and when I shall tell a lie about your running eyes.'

'What on earth are you up to now? You must have gone mad! Are you giving the dog mustard?'

'Be quiet you fool! With this trick I'll get her love to be all yours. I shall get no rest nor peace till I have told how you will do. Wait for me here till I come back home.'

'Right, by the summer flower, nothing will take me from here, till you come back.'

Dame Sirith went off, like a miserable wretch, until she came to the house where this wife lived. When she came to the door, she began very pitifully.

'Lord' she said, 'how miserable these old women are who always live in poverty. No man knows so much trouble as a poor woman who falls into want. Any man can tell that by me, for I can't either walk or sit. I wish I were dead. Hunger and thirst have already killed me. I can hardly stir a limb for great hunger and thirst and cold. What can such a wretch live for? Why won't God fetch my soul?'

'Good woman, may God release you! I'll find you food today, for the love of God. I am so sorry for your misery, for I see how badly clothed and shod you are. Come in here. I'll feed you.'

'God Almighty reward you, and the lord who was set on the cross, and fasted forty days to noon, and has power over heaven and earth. May that lord repay you.'

'Have this meat and bread too, and cheer up, I tell you; and have this cup of drink.'

'May God reward you for your efforts,' then said that old woman –

God curse her life. 'Alas, alas, that I'm still alive! I'd forgive all the sin to the man who'd cut off my head! I wish someone would take my life!'

'What's the matter, good woman?'

'But I can easily be sorry. I had a lovely noble daughter – you couldn't ever see a more beautiful girl. She had a courteous husband – you couldn't find a more generous man. My daughter loved him all too well, which is why I'm so heartbroken. He went out one day, and that's the reason that my daughter was disgraced. He made a trip out of town, and a fine scholar in orders came and offered his love to my daughter and she wouldn't do what he wanted. He couldn't get his way for anything he asked for. So he began to do magic and he turned my daughter into a bitch. This bitch here is my daughter I'm telling you about. My heart is breaking for sorrow about her. See how her eyes run, the tears run together on her cheek. So it's no wonder, lady, if my heart's breaking. And any young housewife there may be has very little liking for her life, if any scholar offers her his love, unless she gives way and lets him succeed.'

'O Lord Christ, what can I do! Only the other day a scholar came to me and offered me his love after his own fashion, and I wouldn't pay any attention to him. I think he'll transform me. How do you think, old woman, that I can escape?'

'God Almighty help you that you don't become bitch or pup! Dear lady, if any scholar offers you that love-business, I advise you to give him what he wants, and become his lover straightaway. And if you don't do that, you're taking up a worse plan.'

'Lord Christ, how sorry I am that the scholar went away before he had taken me. I'd give anything for him to have once slept with me and done it immediately. I'll be yours for evermore, old woman, if you'll fetch me Willikin, the scholar I've told you about. I'll give you presents you'll always be better off for, by God's own bell!'

'For sure, my sweet lady, if I can do it without being blamed I'll be glad to try. If I can meet him anywhere, I'll not hesitate. Good day, lady: I'm off!'

'See you do what I asked you, at all events. Unless you bring me Willikin, I'll never be able to laugh or sing or be glad!'

'Certainly, lady, I'll bring him even today if I can by my efforts.'

She went home and found Willikin, by our Lord!

'Sweet Willikin, don't worry, I've done very well with her. Come on quickly with me there, for she's sent for you. You can be glad now for sure!'

'May God who rules heaven and earth reward you, dear old woman!'

This fine man immediately went with Sirith to his sweetheart that very minute.

Dame Sirith began to tell [the girl] and swore by God's own bell she had found him. – 'Lady, I've so looked for Willikin that now I've brought him to you.'

'Welcome, Willikin, sweet man, you're more welcome than the king!

Sweet Willikin, I promise you my love, to do all you want to. I've changed my mind, for I don't want at all that you should die!'

'Lady, as sure as I expect noon, so I'm ready and eager to do everything you say. Old woman, by God, you must go away, while she and I amuse ourselves.'

'God knows, so I will. And see you plough her and stretch out her thighs! God give you sorrow if you spare her while you're with her. And if there's anyone who is foolish and can't get his sweetheart for any price, I'll make him succeed – if he will pay me – for I know very well how!'[18]

Exemplum XXXV[19]
THE BLIND MAN AND THE ADULTEROUS YOUTH

There was once a blind man who had a very beautiful wife. With great diligence he guarded her chastity, so jealous was he. And it happened one day, when they were both in an orchard in the shade of a pear tree, that she with his consent climbed the tree to pick pears. The blind man, being very suspicious, embraced the trunk while his wife was in the tree, so that no one else could climb up.

But as the tree had many branches, a lad who had previously climbed it was hidden in them, waiting for the blind man's wife. He joined her with great joy and they began to play the game of Venus. While they were at this, the blind man heard the noise and put two and two together, and with great anguish began to cry out, 'O most damned woman! Even if I can't see, I can feel and hear! My other senses are more acute and strong. I know that you have a lover with you. I plead to Jupiter, sovereign god, who can fill with delight the hearts of the sad and give sight to the blind!'

With these words, sight and the light of nature were restored to the blind man. And looking up, he saw the adulterous lad with his wife. He cried at once, 'O false and deceitful wife! Why do you trick and deceive me when I believed you faithful and good? Woe is me, for from now on I don't expect anything good from you.' But she, hearing how her husband was shouting at her, although she had at first been frightened suddenly took on a deceitful trick and with a cheerful face replied in a loud voice, 'I thank all the gods who have heard my prayers and restored my beloved husband's sight. For know, my dear lord, that the sight which you have received was given to you through my wishes and actions. For until now I have been working in vain, with medicines and in many other ways. Finally I turned to beseeching the gods and sending them pleas and prayers for your sight to be restored. The god Mercury, sent by Jupiter the king, appeared to me in my dreams and told me to climb into a pear tree and to play there the game of Venus with a young man, and that this would restore the light to your eyes. I did this for your good and your health. So you must give thanks to the gods and above all you must give thanks to me, for you have recovered your sight through me.'

The blind man believed his wife's deceitful words. He was reconciled to her and accepted her as virtuous, recognizing that his reproaches were not necessary. So he thanked her and rewarded her with great gifts, as if for an important service.[20]

Two more exempla from the *Disciplina* are of special interest as old favourites of western tradition: No. XII, The King and his Storyteller and No. XXIII, The Oxen Promised to the Wolf and the Fox's Judgment. The first is one of the 'endless tale' type, the counting of sheep to fall asleep, and may well be the source of this still current western habit. The second is the best of the fables used in the *Disciplina* where actually there are only four fables: the mule who boasts of his ancestry; the three teachings of the bird; the ungrateful serpent who kills the man who rescues him (Exempla IV, XXII and V) – and this one.

Exemplum XII
THE KING AND HIS STORYTELLER

A king had a storyteller who usually told him five tales each night. It happened finally that the king, troubled with cares, could not sleep, and he ordered the storyteller to tell him more tales. The storyteller told him three more, but they were short, and the king asked for more. The storyteller demurred because, as it seemed to him, he had already told a good many.

The king replied, 'You have already told many, but they were very short. I want you to tell me a long one, and then I will let you go to bed.'

The storyteller agreed and began thus:

A peasant who had a thousand silver coins went to market and bought two thousand sheep at six denarii each. And when he was returning, it happened that the river was swollen with flood waters, and he was not able to cross by the bridge or the tord. Worried, he began looking for a place where he could cross with his sheep. He finally found a small boat which would only hold two sheep and the shepherd at the same time. But driven by necessity, he put two sheep in the boat and crossed . . .

When the storyteller had told this, he fell asleep.

The king woke him up so that he could finish the story that he had begun, and he said, 'The river is very wide, the boat is very small, and the sheep are very numerous. Let the peasant ferry his sheep across first, and then I will finish the story.'

And thus the storyteller silenced the king who was eager to hear long tales.[21]

As for fables, the name we all know is Aesop. In the many mixtures of parables ascribed to him from late antiquity onwards, there is one which tells of a fox and a goat in a well. The fox frees himself by jumping on the goat, whom he had agreed to help in turn. Instead, he skips away with an admonition to the goat that before one goes in anywhere, one should think how to get out.

Petrus Alfunsus' story may belong to this same large general class of tales about animals in wells, but it is different in these respects: its moral instead is, Don't give up a sure thing for a promise, and its 'plot' is more complicated, having as preliminary the element of the hasty promise, followed by the cheese of the moon's reflection in the well, and then the trick of the buckets. In folklore terms these are three separate motifs. Interestingly enough, the Aesop version is distributed chiefly in eastern Europe and the East, while the cheese and the bucket types are chiefly in western Europe. This must reflect, at least in part, the geographical impact of the *Disciplina*.

Exemplum XXIII
THE OXEN PROMISED TO THE WOLF AND THE FOX'S JUDGMENT

They tell about a ploughman who, because his oxen would not make a straight furrow, said to them, 'The wolves can eat you!'

A wolf heard him and was delighted. When the sun was setting and the villager had unhitched his oxen from the plough, the wolf came to him and said, 'Give me the oxen you promised me.'

The ploughman said, 'Although I said it, I did not swear to it.'

The wolf argued, 'I should have them, because you promised.'

Finally they agreed to go to court, and on the way they met a fox who said to them, 'Where are you going?' And they told him what had happened.

'There is no need to seek another judge,' he said, 'because I will give you a fair judgement; but first let me speak privately with each of you.

The fox first spoke privately with the ploughman and said to him, 'Give one hen to me and one to my wife, and you shall have your oxen.

The ploughman agreed. Having done this, the fox spoke with the wolf saying, 'Listen, my friend I have spoken with this villager and he agreed that if you leave his oxen in peace, he will give you a cheese as large as a shield.' The wolf agreed and the fox said to him, 'Let the ploughman lead his oxen away. I will take you to the place where his cheeses are made.'

The wolf, deceived by the clever words of the fox, let the villager go. The fox led the wolf astray, and as dark night approached, he led him to a deep well and showed him, as he stood on the edge, the form of the half-moon shining in the bottom of the well. 'This is the cheese I promised you;' he said, 'go down, if you like, and eat it.'

The wolf said: 'You go down first, and if you cannot bring it up alone, call me to help you, and I will do what you say.'

As they talked, they saw a rope hanging into the well; on each end of the rope was a bucket, and they hung in such a way that when one was raised, the other one was lowered. The fox, as soon as he saw it, as if following the wolf's instructions, got in one bucket and went to the bottom. The wolf, pleased because of this, said, 'Why do you not bring the cheese up to me?'

And the fox answered, 'I cannot because of its size. Get into the other bucket and come help me, as you promised.'

The wolf got into the other bucket, and since he was heavy, his bucket went straight to the bottom, while the other one containing the fox, who was light, rose up. When the fox reached the edge of the well, he jumped out and left the wolf in the well. And thus because the wolf relinquished what was present for what was to come, he lost the oxen and the cheese. [22]

Exemplum XXIII is another one from the store of international folklore. Its continuous dissemination in Arabian tradition is attested by Chauvin[23] and by Gonzales Palencia, who reports having heard it in Rabat in 1948, as it was told by Petrus Alfunsus.[24] It became a classic in France, thanks to a line of borrowing which originated with the *Disciplina* and which was popularized by Marie de France and La Fontaine in turn. The story has lasted in English-speaking oral lore too. In Caxton's *The Fables of Aphonce* (1484), it is given *in toto*, including this conversation between the fox in the bucket going up and the wolf going fast down. Wolf: 'My godsip, ye go hence?' Fox: 'Thou sayest true . . . For thus it is of the world. For when one cometh down, the other goeth upward.' Without the cheese motif the story appears in Joel Chandler Harris' *Uncle Remus* as 'Old Mr Rabbit, He's a Good Fisherman,' – a rabbit is now in the fox's place as 'hero', and the fox is in the wolf's.[25] This was still current in Michigan, again among Blacks, in the 1950s. The latter preserves almost intact the verse ending the Uncle Remus tale which began at least with Caxton:

Good-by, Brer Fox, take keer yo' cloze
For dis-is de way de worril goes;
Some goes up en some goes down,
You'll git ter de bottom all safe en soun'.

Get Up and Bar the Door

There lived a man in yonder glen,
    And John Blunt was his name O.
He maks gude maut and he brews gude ale
    And he bears a wondrous fame O.

The wind blew in the hallan ae night,
    Fu snell out oer the moor.
'Rise up, rise up, auld Luckie,' he says,
    'Rise up, and bar the door.'

They made a paction tween them twa,
    They made it firm and sure,
Whaeer sud speak the foremost word
    Should rise and bar the door.

Three travellers that had tint their gate,
    As thro the hills they foor,
They airted by the line o light
    Fu straught to Johnie Blunt's door.

They haurld auld Luckie out o her bed
    And laid her on the floor,
But never a word auld Luckie was say,
    For barrin o the door.

'Ye've eaten my bread, ye hae drinken my ale,
    And ye'll mak my auld wife a whore!'
'A ha, Johnie Blunt! ye hae spoke the first word,
    Get up and bar the door.'[1]

The Silent Couple

A man of infamous character one night told his wife to make haste and get supper ready; she accordingly brought to the table some dry stale bread. 'Why my dear,' said he, 'who the devil can eat such dry, hard bread as that?' 'Get up and moisten it,' said she. 'No, do you;' returned the husband; 'I'll be hanged if I do,' replied the wife; 'I'm fatigued, and won't stir an inch.' Thus they went on, each growing more and more obstinate, till at length it was determined by the consent of both, that whoever should speak the first word, should instantly get up and moisten the bread. In this interesting situation they remained for a considerable time, when one of the neighbours accidentally came in, who had a sneaking attachment to the lady; they both looked at him attentively, but said nothing; 'Good evening:' said the visitor – they said nothing, 'what's the matter,' continued he, 'why are you silent?' – they said nothing – Whence he conjectured that they had laid a wager to preserve silence. 'You are a man,' said he to the husband, 'why don't you speak?' – He said nothing; – he kissed his wife – but the man said nothing; – he disgraced her – but the man said nothing; – his facetious neighbour gave him a blow on the cheek – but the man said nothing; – irritated, he at length went to the justice, and complained that he could not make the man speak; – he was committed to prison – still he said nothing. The next morning he was again brought before the judge – but still said nothing. The judge ordered him to be hanged for contumacy. When the sentence was on the point of being executed, the wife appeared, and in a most pitiable tone exclaimed; 'Alas my unfortunate husband!' 'You devil,' said he, 'go home and moisten the bread.'[2]

VI

THE ARABIAN NIGHTS

Nothing can say more for the world-wide diffusion of *The Arabian Nights* than a passage from *Huckleberry Finn*. Here, gliding downstream on the Mississippi in the 1840s, the unlettered Huck is explaining to the slave Jim how it is that kings are mostly rapscallions:

> My, you ought to seen old Henry the Eight when he was in bloom. He *was* a blossom. He used to marry a new wife every day, and chop off her head next morning. And he would do it just as indifferent as if he was ordering up eggs. 'Fetch up Nell Gwynn,' he says. They fetch her up. Next morning, 'Chop off her head' – and they chop it off. 'Fetch up Jane Shire,' he says; and up she comes. Next morning, 'Chop off her head' – and they chop it off. 'Ring up Fair Rosamun.' Fair Rosamun answers the bell. Next morning, 'Chop off her head.' And he made every one of them tell him a tale every night; and he kept that up till he had hogged a thousand and one tales that way, and then he put them all in a book, and called it Domesday Book – which was a good name and stated the case.

So much for Scheherazade, so much for English history. The fact none the less is that the frame-story of the *Nights* and the knowledge that its tales were made into a book penetrated to non-literate people where hearsay of few books did. And if on the American frontier, then elsewhere too.

For readers, *The Arabian Nights* has been known since 1704 when Antoine Galland's translation was published in French and in English. Ever since, it has been for the West *the* introduction to the

Arab world. Generations of readers have formed their notion of the East from it. It took Europe by storm from the very start, went through four editions in English before 1713, and was serialized in the *London News* – it took three years – beginning in 1723. Speaking for England, James Beattie could say in 1783 that it was 'a book which most young people in this country are acquainted with', and some 200 years later it has been published more than 400 times in the languages of western Europe. The *Nights* contributed in the eighteenth century to the growth of interest in oriental studies, to the development of folklore and of narrative as fields of study, and to fiction in the rise of a whole school of pseudo-oriental novels and tales, and its influence on the romantic movement in the nineteenth century can only be described as immense. All this while Arabs looked down on the *Nights* as unworthy and untypical of Arab writing, colloquial and decadent, not literature at all but a hodge-podge of street folklore in vulgar language. And folklore is of course what it is; even in this century its stories continue to be told to rapt audiences in cafés and marketplaces in Cairo and Baghdad. But to the West, translation has eliminated the vulgarity, and *The Arabian Nights* has become not only literature and not only *our* literature, but actually one of our classics. It is reproduced in print and as plays, ballets, films, puppet shows and pantomimes, especially for the young. Thanks to the early translators who preferred its fairytales and strange voyages and adventures to its more realistic stories, the work has become a synonym for the marvellous and romantic. But the whole collection contains many other kinds of material: love stories, travel tales, tales of rogues and criminals, anecdotes, animal fables, instructive illustrations, pious tales, stories of demons, a cycle of anecdotes about Harun al-Rashid, *novelle* about husbands and wives, stories based on the Crusades, long epic-like romances of dynasties and battles, brief commentaries, frame-stories containing other frame-stories, even an entire book – the *Book of Sindibad* (here *The Seven Wazirs*) – with a previous and later separate history of its own. In addition, poems, sometimes of considerable length and complication, are inserted in many tales.

The term 'whole collection' needs qualifying, since like all collections of folklore the *Nights* has no single, final form. The stories are printed in varying number and order, depending on the translator, and 1001 is taken to mean any large number rather than an exact figure. Galland, who was an officer in the French diplomatic service, used first a Syrian manuscript of the *Nights* and then other written sources, but his chief supplement was a Syrian living in Paris who told him Arabian folktales including the two gems, 'Aladdin' and 'Ali Baba'. It is revealing that a hundred years later (1812) the Grimm Brothers' *Kinder und Hausmarchen,* which is accepted as the beginning of modern folktale collecting directly from the folk, contained German versions of these two stories. Galland's was the formative standard European edition for over a hundred years, parts of it even being translated back into Arabic. By the nineteenth century, other manuscripts had been found and published in Arabic. The basis for subsequent European texts was the Egyptian (Bulaq) recension; E. W. Lane's English translation of this appeared as early as 1838–40. The best translation in English is that of John Payne, published in the 1880s, which Richard Burton copied sometimes verbatim in his more famous but inferior work, and the best modern one is by E. Littman in German (1920s). Burton's corresponds to some extent with its prototype, Payne's; otherwise no two of the six or so standard scholarly editions are alike. But taken all together – inclusive of Payne's and Burton's additional volumes which add material from the late-discovered Calcutta (1814–18) and Breslau (1825–43) texts – they constitute the corpus of the *Nights* now generally accepted. None the less, because in the West the entire work in any version is hard to come by, while selections are continually published, very few people today know the extraordinary variety of the book as a whole.

The wide geographic diversity of origin of its contents adds to its complexity. Narrative elements have been traced to India of the fifth century B.C. and the third century A.D., to Iran, Iraq, Egypt, Turkey and Greece as well as to Jewish and pre-Islamic Arab sources, but all have been assimilated into an Islamic background. The Scheherazade frame-story may be Indian with Iranian personal names, or it may be derived from a Persian variant of the biblical Book of Esther dating from the third century A.D. The first reference to the *Nights* by name, then simply *A Thousand Tales (Hazar Afsana),* is in a ninth-century fragment in Persian, followed in the tenth century by mention of the frame-story characters by the famous al-Mas'udi in his *Golden Meadows.* In the work itself, scholars detect several layers beginning with an eighth-century Arabic translation of *Hazar Afsana,* which was augmented in the ninth century by other stories including those of Sindbad the Sailor; in the tenth century all of these were made part of a compilation of 480 narratives by a certain Ibu 'Abdus; in the twelfth century Egyptian tales were added; and the latest form of the work extended into the sixteenth century with elements from the Crusades, the Mongols' taking of Baghdad, the Baibars cycle, and the Turks' conquest of Egypt. Since the *Nights* are a composite work of separate tales, told orally originally and over the course of many centuries, they have been – in Vance Randolph's immortal words – 'shaped and polished by the natural hazards of oral transmission'. Material is added or subtracted by chance and circumstance, but to survive, a story must have the approval of audiences, who thus keep it and its teller on the rails. Millions of listeners over the years have thus supplied the shaping while the tellers provided the polish.

But these normal changes, inherent in folklore, which brought about the differing contents of the basic manuscripts of the *Nights*, must be kept distinct from arbitrary editorial changes made once it became part of the literature of the West. Since 1704, editors or translators have expurgated many stories, or added others which do not belong, or exaggerated the erotic element, or mistranslated, or given inaccurate notes, or rearranged tale-groups. Because each reader accepts what he reads as the real thing, there must be a number of different impressions of the *Nights*. We have mentioned its early image as the marvellous and romantic. But it also reintroduced to Europe several cynical exempla which had appeared in the *Disciplina Clericalis*. These include The Sword, The Weeping Bitch, The Unjust Banker, The Four Depositors and The Barrels of Oil. Reintroduction is perhaps however the wrong word, because these tales had made their own way in the West in the 600 years since the *Disciplina*. As far as realistic *contes* go, anecdotal, *novelle*-like and humorous, many in the *Nights* were already known to Europe before 1704, say from Boccaccio onwards, if not in literature then in folklore. In fact, the great attraction of its fairytales for its first translators in the eighteenth century may have been that these were new to them, while the *novelle* type were familiar merry or bawdy stories, heard rather than read.

The plan here is to present narratives from the *Nights* which also survive in western tradition because they were either adopted from the *Nights* or from a common reservoir on which the *Nights* drew as well. This common reservoir was the international folklore of the Middle and Near East, referred to before, with which the West lost contact after the Middle Ages. But there is in fact so much commonality that selection becomes a problem. Many conspicuous parallels must be overlooked altogether: motifs from folklore such as the magicians' contest in shape-changing, the two trees from lovers' graves growing into one, the witch on a broomstick, the awakened sleeper (which the West knows from *Vida es Sueno*, *Schluck und Jau* or *The Taming of the Shrew*), the swan maiden who is won by hiding her feathers and who escapes by finding them, the spirit tricked into going back into a bottle, the Polyphemus story from the *Odyssey*, the *inclusa* or Miles Gloriosus type in which lovers use a secret tunnel to trick the husband, the Peeping Tom motif, the patient calumniated wife, the fox who feigns death, the magic flights and flying carpets, the sword between two lovers as symbol of their chastity, the two sisters who envy the youngest sister, the Angel of Death, the ogre's heart in an egg, the Barbara Allen motif of the disdainful girl who lets her lover die and then dies on his grave, the island which is a huge fish as in St Brendan's voyage, the castles with forbidden rooms as in Bluebeard, the many, many magic objects.

Since Sindbad's voyages, Aladdin and Ali Baba are too familiar to need recall, tales of marvels will not be represented. The selections are instead from the shorter, more realistic genres. One or two stories are included even though they do not have direct western variants because they strike a congeniality of spirit with us today, and also because they show different phases of the encyclopaedic variety we are dealing with.

1   THE BARBER'S STORY OF HIS FIFTH BROTHER

My fifth brother was cropped of his ears, O Prince of the Faithful. He was a pauper, who begged alms by night, and subsisted upon what he thus acquired by day: and our father was a very old man, and he fell sick and died, leaving to us seven hundred pieces of silver, of which each of us took his portion; namely, a hundred pieces. Now my fifth brother, when he had received his share, was perplexed, not knowing what to do with it; but while he was in this state, it occurred to his mind to buy with it all kinds of articles of glass, and to sell them and make profit: so he bought glass with his hundred pieces of silver, and put it in a large tray, and sat upon an elevated place, to sell it, leaning his back against a wall. And as he sat, he meditated, and said within himself, Verily my whole stock consisteth of this glass: I will sell it for two hundred pieces of silver; and with the two hundred I will buy other glass, which I will sell for four hundred; and thus I will continue buying and selling until I have acquired great wealth. Then with this I will purchase all kinds of merchandise and essences and jewels, and so obtain vast gain. After that, I will buy a handsome house, and memlooks, and horses, and gilded saddles; and I will eat and drink; and I will not leave in the city a single female singer but I will have her brought to my house that I may hear her songs. – All this he calculated with the tray of glass lying before him. – Then, said he, I will send all the female betrothers to seek in marriage for me the daughters of Kings and Wezeers; and I will demand as my wife the daughter of the chief Wezeer; for I have heard that she is endowed with perfect beauty and surprising loveliness; and I will give as her dowry a thousand pieces of gold. If her father consent, my wish is attained; and if he consent not, I will take her by force, in spite of him: and when I have come back to my house, I will buy ten young eunuchs, and I will purchase the apparel of Kings and Sultans, and cause to be made for me a saddle of gold set with jewels; after which I will ride every day upon a horse, with slaves behind me and before me, and go about through the streets and markets to amuse myself, while the people will salute me and pray for me. Then I will pay a visit to the Wezeer, who is the father of the maiden, with memlooks behind me and before me, and on my right hand and on my left; and when he seeth me, he will rise to me, in humility, and seat me in his own place; and he himself will sit down below me, because I am his son-in-law. I will then order one of the servants to bring a purse containing the pieces of gold which compose the dowry; and he will place it before the Wezeer; and I will add to it another purse, that he may know my manly spirit and excessive generosity, and that the world is contemptible in my eye: and when he addresseth me with ten words, I will answer him with two. And I will return to my house; and when any person cometh to me from the house of the Wezeer, I will clothe him with a rich dress: but if any come with a present, I will return it: I will certainly not accept it. Then, on the night of the bridal display, I will attire myself in the most magnificent of my dresses, and sit upon a mattress covered with silk; and when my wife cometh to me, like the full moon, decked with her ornaments and apparel, I will command her to stand before me as stands the timid and the abject; and I will not look at her, on account of the haughtiness of my spirit and the gravity of my wisdom; so that the maids will say, O our master and our lord, may we be thy sacrifice! This thy wife, or rather thy handmaid, awaiteth thy kind regard, and is standing before thee: then graciously bestow on her one glance; for the posture hath become painful to her. – Upon this, I will raise my head, and look at her with one glance, and again incline my head downwards; and thus I will do until the ceremony of displaying her is finished; whereupon they will conduct her to the sleeping-chamber; and I will rise from my place, and go to another apartment, and put on my night-dress, and go to the chamber in which she is sitting, where I will seat myself upon the deewan; but I will not look towards her. The tire-women will urge me to approach her; but I will not hear their words, and will order some of the attendants to bring a purse containing five hundred pieces of gold for them, and command them to retire from the chamber. And when they have gone, I will seat myself by the side of the bride; but with averted countenance, that she may say, Verily this is a man of a haughty spirit. Then her mother will come to me, and will kiss my hands, and say to me, O my master, look upon thy handmaid with the eye of mercy; for she is submissively standing before thee. But I will return her no answer. And she will kiss my feet, again and again, and will say, O my master, my daughter is young, and hath seen no man but thee; and if she experience from thee repugnance, her heart will break: incline to her, therefore, and speak to her, and calm her mind. And upon this I will look at her through the corner of my eye, and command her to remain standing before me, that she may taste the savour of humiliation, and know that I am the Sultan of the age. Then her mother will say to me, O my master, this is thy handmaid: have compassion upon her, and be gracious to her: – and she will order her to fill a cup with wine, and to put it to my mouth. So her daughter will say, O my lord, I conjure thee by the requisitions of God, that thou reject not the cup from thy slave; for verily I am thy slave. But I will make her no reply; and she will urge me to take it and will say, It must be drunk: – and will put it to my mouth: and upon this, I will shake my hand in her face, and spurn her with my foot, and do thus. – So saying, he kicked the tray of glass, which, being upon a place elevated above the ground, fell, and all that was in it broke: there escaped nothing: and he cried out and said, All this is the result of my pride! And he slapped his face, and tore his clothes; the passengers gazing at him, while he wept, and exclaimed, Ah! O my grief![1]

The great comparative mythologist, Max Muller, marvelled that when far more serious matters had been forgotten, this simple story-type had persisted through the centuries, still being told in nurseries and schools East and West. As we know it best in the West it is usually ascribed to Aesop but actually derived from La Fontaine's 'La Laitière et le Pot au Lait', published in 1678.[2] A typical version of 'The Milkmaid and her Pail' comes from a third-grade school-text for American children: A milkmaid was walking along with a pail of milk on her head, singing merrily. She was thinking of the money which the milk would bring, for she was carrying it to town to sell. 'Let me see,' she said to herself, 'here are eight quarts of milk, and with the money I can get for it I can buy thirty eggs. From thirty eggs I can safely say that twenty-five chicks will be hatched. They will be big enough to take to market at Christmas, and they will bring a good price then. They will come to fifteen or twenty dollars, at least, and with that I will buy a new dress and a new hat. Then I will wear them to church, and all the young fellows will want to walk home with me. But I won't look at any of them – no, not I!' She tossed her head proudly, and the pail, which she had altogether forgotten, tipped over and fell, and all the milk was spilled on the ground.[3]

Known to folklorists as one of the 'Air Castle' tale-types and to people in general as 'Don't count your chickens before they're hatched', this has been much studied. There are two versions of it in the Nights. In the one not included here, a poor fakir collects a pot of butter and dreams of a series of profitable sales which will enable him to marry and have a son, whom one day his wife will forget to watch, at which he, the fakir, will kick her. He kicks and shatters the pot.

The man as the central figure follows the oldest written forms of the story, derived from Kalila wa-Dimna, which was translated from Sanskrit into Arabic in the eighth century. In Kalila wa-Dimna, a brahman has a jar of honey. When the tale appeared in the

Directorium Vitae Humanae of Jacques de Vitry, despite the fact that Vitry had been Bishop of Acre from 1216 to 1227, the central figure was a woman, an indication that it was already established in this form in western tradition. In the Spanish *El Conde Lucanor* (by Don Juan Manual, 1282–1347) a woman is carrying honey; in Rabelais (c. 1532) a shoemaker has a pot of milk; in later German accounts it is often both a man and wife who daydream. In England, the milkmaid variant was a household word as early as the first part of the fifteenth century when it was referred to in the Wakefield *First Shepherds' Play*. Despite all this, and despite the fact that the Arabic *Kalila wa-Dimna* is among the world's most prolific books, its fables having been translated into European (and other) languages many, many times (Hans Sachs, John of Capua, etc.), for the modern West, La Fontaine's retelling of this tale is the formative one.

The prior history of *Kalila wa-Dimna* is of interest as an example of what is meant by the international folklore of the Middle East. We are dealing here with documents and are thus entering literary history as well, but we must remember that these early manuscripts are simply written-down folklore. The progenitor was the *Panchatantra* (the *Five Books*), in England sometimes also called *The Fables of Bidpai*, a third-century tale-collection in Sanskrit. The original and its third through fifth-century descendants have been lost. According to legend, one of these was translated into Persian in the fourth century. The just King Anushirwan of Persia whom we have met with 'Antar, and about whom more anecdotes are coming later, sent his greatest scholar, Burzoe, to India to learn Indian wisdom. After many years of wasted effort, Burzoe asked the king of India if he might see the *Panchatantra*. Only one copy existed and it was kept under lock and key. The king said he was not to take it nor to copy it, but he could come every day and read it. Burzoe memorized what he read, every night wrote it down, and when he had finished, returned to Persia. Whether through Burzoe or not, it was from the Pehlevi, i.e. Middle Persian, that a Syrian translation was made in the sixth century, and one in Arabic in the eighth. The one in Arabic is the one important to the West. The title, *Kalila wa-Dimna*, is so named from the jackals which tell the stories in the *Panchatantra*.

With the spread of Islam this redaction was carried both east where it mingled with existing forms and west where it was translated into Latin in the twelfth century by Baldo, into Spanish in the thirteenth, and in the thirteenth again into Latin by John of Capua as the *Directorium Vitae Humanae*, which put it into the mainstream of

THE PAST WE SHARE

exempla circulation and folk diffusion. And after that, everywhere! – at least in Europe, in both folklore and literature.

Borrowers from *Kalila wa-Dimna* of special interest to us include Planudes' Greek collection of *Aesop's Fables* (thirteenth century), the *Decamerone* which is of course fourteenth-century Italian, the Turkish *History of the Forty Wazirs* (fifteenth century) and the Latin *Gesta Romanorum*, fifteenth century. The English *Moral Philosophy of Doni* (sixteenth century) and *Lights of Canopus* (nineteenth), which are descendants rather than borrowers, reflect its continuity in English and its puzzling changes of name.

2 A DREAM

It is related also, that a man in Baghdad was possessed of ample riches and great wealth; but his wealth passed away and his state changed, and he became utterly destitute and could not obtain his sustenance save by laborious exertion. And he slept one night, overwhelmed and oppressed, and saw in his sleep a person who said to him, Verily thy fortune is in Cairo: therefore seek it and repair to it. So he journeyed to Cairo; and when he arrived there, the evening overtook him, and he slept in a mosque.

Now there was adjacent to the mosque a house; and as God (whose name be exalted!) had decreed, a party of robbers entered the mosque and thence passed to that house; and the people of the house, awaking at the disturbance, raised cries, whereupon the Walee came to their aid with his followers, and the robbers fled. The Walee then entered the mosque and found the man of Baghdad sleeping there: so he laid hold upon him and inflicted upon him a painful beating until he was on the point of death, and imprisoned him.

And he remained three days in the prison, after which the Walee caused him to be brought and said to him, From what country art thou? He answered, From Baghdad. And what affair, said the Walee, was the cause of thy coming to Cairo? He answered, I saw in my sleep a person who said to me, Verily thy fortune is in Cairo: therefore repair to it. And when I came to Cairo, I found the fortune to be those blows that I have received from thee.

And upon this the Walee laughed so that his teeth showed, and said to him, O thou of little sense, I saw three times in my sleep a person who said to me, Verily a house in Baghdad, in such a district and of such a description, hath in its court a garden at the lower end of which is a fountain, wherein is wealth of great amount: therefore repair to it and take it. But I went not. And thou, through the smallness of thy sense, hast journeyed from city to city on account of a thing thou hast seen in sleep, when it was only an effect of confused dreams.

Then he gave him some money and said to him, Help thyself with this to return to thy city. So he took it and returned to Baghdad. Now the house which the Walee had described, in Baghdad, was the house of that man. Therefore when he arrived at his abode, he dug beneath the fountain and beheld abundant wealth. Thus God enriched and sustained him, and this was a wonderful coincidence.[4]

This is a well-known and widespread folktale, found in Europe long before Galland and his translation of the *Nights* and collected in the British Isles down to modern times. English versions tell of a pedlar named John Chapman or John Rolle who dreams of a treasure to be found on London Bridge. When he goes there, a shopkeeper relates his (the shopkeeper's) dream of a treasure located in the pedlar's own garden, which is variously placed in Swaffham in Norfolk, Launceston in Cornwall, or Upsall in Yorkshire. The pedlar goes home and digs it up. Another bit is added: the treasure is in a box that has an inscription in Latin which when translated reads, 'Under me doth lie, Another much richer than I', or words to that effect. The pedlar digs again and finds a bigger fortune than before.

In a recension told in County Kerry around 1950 the hero is again named John, that is, Sean, but known as Jack, Poor Jack of the Thorn, and the bridge is in Limerick. There, a man asks him why he is walking up and down on the bridge for three days. Sean/Jack explains. The man says, 'Ah, poor silly man, don't be wasting your time. I also dreamt of a treasure supposed to be hidden in a little farm in County Kerry at the back of the house of a man named Poor Jack of the Thorn, under a whitethorn bush. And I suppose the man does not exist.' Sean/Jack goes home and digs up the treasure, and a poor scholar later translates the Latin, which leads to the second find. Sean becomes the richest man in County Kerry.[5]

Here is Levantine philosophy, that man goes where the will of God sends him; what appears to be the wrong place is in fact a step to the right place – the appointment in Samarra. In 'A Dream', the know-all lecture of the official is especially relished since at the end the laugh is on him.

3 THE MERCHANT AND THE TWO SHARPERS

There was once in a city called Sendeh a very wealthy merchant, who made ready merchandise and set out with it for such a city, thinking to sell it there. There followed him two sharpers, who had made up into bales what goods they could get and giving out to him that they also were merchants, companied with him by the way. At the first halting-place, they agreed to play him false and take his goods; but, at the same time, each purposed inwardly foul play to the other, saying in himself, 'If I can cheat my comrade, it will be well for me and I shall have all to myself.' So each took food and putting therein poison, brought it to his fellow; and they both ate of the poisoned mess and died. Now they had been sitting talking with the merchant; so when they left him and were long absent from him, he sought for them and found them both dead; whereby he knew that they were sharpers, who had plotted to play him foul, but their treachery had recoiled upon themselves; so the merchant was preserved and took what they had.[6]

The classic parallel here is Chaucer's 'The Pardoner's Tale', but the earliest written example is in the *Jatakas* or birth-tales of Buddha, third century B.C. Thus the story early entered the Middle Eastern float of folktales and thence made its way to Europe. Modern treatments are to be found in Kipling's *Second Jungle Book* (The King's Ankus), in Jack London's *When God Laughs*[7] (Just Meat), and in Robert M. Coates' 'Winter Fishing' where the life insurance policies of two partners, each the other's beneficiary, replace the goods, and ice-axe and shotgun replace the poison.[8] Much more widely known of course is the 1948 film version, *The Treasure of the Sierra Madre*, based on the novel published in 1927 by B. Traven, a Pole who wrote in German. In it three adventurers find gold; when one is captured by the Indians, the other two plan to keep his share. Of the two the villainous one shoots his companion but is himself killed by bandits. Thinking it sand, the bandits throw away the gold dust. In all these cases, whether there are two or three or more characters, it takes only two to make the story; the third party, when he is innocent and even when he reaps the reward, is *de trop* as is the reward.

Chaucer's redaction, however, includes yet another character, an old man. The three roisterers, who are looking to slay Death in order to end a plague, demand that the old man lead them to him. He does this by directing them to an oak tree under which lie the fatal gold florins. Chaucer in this detail is very close to Muslim analogues in which Isa (Jesus) warns his disciples that gold found in a lonely place will cause the death of three travellers. The mutual murders follow, but Isa restores the men to life. The particular element of a holy man leading to gold but warning that it is death was taken up in Italy in books of *novelle* and in an old miracle-play of St Anthony.[9] Chaucer may have drawn on oral sources of this very popular story, but at least one Italian collection, the *Cento Novelle Antiche*, is believed to have been made in the thirteenth century and is therefore old enough to have been a literary bridge from the Levant to 'The Pardoner's Tale'.

4 THE JOINT DEPOSITORS

Four merchants were sharers in a sum of a thousand pieces of gold, which they had mixed together, and put into one purse; and they went with it to purchase merchandise, and, finding in their way a beautiful garden, they entered it, and left the purse with a woman who was the keeper of that garden. Having entered, they diverted themselves in a tract of the garden, and ate and drank and were happy; and one of them said, I have with me some perfume. Come, let us wash our heads with this running water; and perfume ourselves. – Another said, We want a comb. And another said, We will ask the keeper: perhaps she hath with her a comb. And upon this, one of them arose and went to the keeper, and said to her, Give me the purse. She replied, When ye all present yourselves, or thy companions order me to give it thee. Now his companions were in a place where the keeper could see them, and she could hear their words. And the man said to his companions, She is not willing to give me aught. So they said to her, Give him. And when she heard their words, she gave him the purse; and he went forth fleeing from them. Therefore when he had wearied them by the length of his absence, they came to the keeper, and said to her, Wherefore didst thou not give him the comb? And she replied, He demanded of me nothing but the purse, and I gave it not to him save with your permission, and he hath departed hence and gone his way. And when they heard the words of the keeper, they slapped their faces, and seized her with their hands, saying to her, We gave thee not permission save to give the comb. She replied, He did not mention to me a comb. And they seized her and took her up to the Kadee; and when they presented themselves before him, they stated to him the case; whereupon he bound the keeper to restore the purse, and bound a number of her debtors to be answerable for her.

So she went forth perplexed, not knowing her way; and there met her a boy, whose age was five years; and when the boy saw her, thus perplexed, he said to her, What is the matter, O my mother? But she returned him not an answer, despising him on account of the smallness of his age. And he repeated his question to her a first and a second and a third time. So at length she told him what had happened to her. And the boy said to her, Give me a piece of silver that I may buy some sweetmeat with it, and I will tell thee something by which thine acquittance may be effected. The keeper therefore gave him a piece of silver, asking him, What hast thou to say? And the boy answered her, Return to the Kadee, and say to him, It was agreed between me and them that I should not give them the purse save in the presence of the four. So the keeper returned to the Kadee, and said to him as the boy had told her; upon which the Kadee said to the three men, Was it thus agreed between you and her? They answered, Yes. And the Kadee said to them, Bring to me your companion and take the purse. Thus the keeper went forth free, no injury befalling her; and she went her way.*[10]

* It is singular enough that this story is told of the Attorney-General Noy, in the reign of James II. For merchants we have graziers, and for a guardian of a garden a keeper of an inn, and the little boy, five years old, is the lawyer, William Noy, beginning his learned labours, and much advanced in reputation, it is said, by this story. It may or may not be true, and we have no higher authority for it than a collection of anecdotes; but it is something to find it thus wandering – seeking an owner so far from its native soil. (Asiatic Journal, N. S. vol. xxx. p. 230.)

5   THE RIGHTEOUSNESS OF KING ANUSHIRWAN

It is told of the just King Anushirwan that he once feigned himself sick and bade his stewards and attendants go round about the provinces of his empire and the quarters of his realm and seek him out a rotten brick from some ruined village, that he might use it as medicine, avouching that the physicians had prescribed this to him. So they went the round of the provinces of his realm and of all the lands under his dominion and returned and said to him, 'In all the realm we have found no ruined place nor old rotten brick.' At this he rejoiced and returned thanks to God, saying, 'I was but minded to prove my kingdom and try my empire, that I might know if there were therein any ruined [or deserted] place, so I might rebuild [or repeople] it; but, since there is no place in it but is inhabited, the affairs of the realm are well ordered and accomplished and [its] prosperity hath reached the pitch of perfection.'[11]

Another western 'everyday classic' is an analogue of this. A good king (not named) is looking for a wife. He proclaims that his servant will lead the royal horse through the country, asking each maiden he meets for left-over dough to feed it. Excited by the prospect of marrying the king, each girl vies with the others to produce the fullest bowl of scraps. Eventually the servant comes to a lowly farmhouse where the blushing maid confesses that she has no scraps; she uses up all the dough when she bakes. 'That one is the bride for me,' says the king. In a variant from North Carolina (1928) called 'Searching for a Wife', the king is replaced by an ordinary man.[12]

It is noteworthy that a second Anushirwan story in the Nights is somewhat related to this one. On his way to a hunt, he asks for water at a house. A damsel gives it mixed with the juice from one sugar cane. Since these villagers get so much juice from one cane, Anushirwan privately decides to increase their tax. At the end of the day he stops at the same house and asks for another drink. This time it takes three canes. The king asks why. 'Because the king's mind is changed.' 'How knewest thou that?' 'When a king's mind is changed against a folk, their prosperity ceaseth.' Anushirwan takes the damsel to wife.[13]

The point in all of these is the identification of the king with his realm, as is indeed stated in the last example. The rotten brick and the scraps of dough are signs of weakness. Thus despite the pretence that they are needed by the king or his horse, their absence is a matter for rejoicing and reward.

6   KHUSRAU AND SHIRIN WITH THE FISHERMAN

King Khusrau of Persia loved fish; and one day, as he sat in his saloon, he and Shirin his wife, there came a fisherman, with a great fish, and presented it to the King, who was pleased and ordered the man four thousand dirhems. When he was gone, Shirin said to the King, 'Thou hast done ill.' 'Wherefore?' asked he; and she answered, 'Because if, after this, thou give one of thy courtiers a like sum, he will disdain it and say, "He hath but given me the like of what he gave the fisherman." And if thou give him less, he will say, "He makes light of me and gives me less than he gave the fisherman." ' 'Thou art right,' rejoined Khusrau; 'but the thing is done and it ill becomes a king to go back on his gift.' Quoth Shirin, 'An thou wilt, I will contrive thee a means to get it back from him.' 'How so?' asked he; and she said, 'Call back the fisherman and ask him if the fish be male or female. If he say, "Male", say thou, "We want a female", and if he say, "Female", say, "We want a male".'

So he sent for the fisherman, who was a man of wit and discernment, and said to him, 'Is this fish male or female?' The fisherman kissed the ground and answered, 'It is of the neuter gender, neither male nor female.' The King laughed and ordered him another four thousand dirhems. So the fisherman went to the treasurer and taking his eight thousand dirhems, put them in a bag he had with him. Then, throwing the bag over his shoulder, he was going away, when he dropped a dirhem; so he laid the bag off his back and stooped down to pick it up. Now the King and Shirin were looking on and the latter said, 'O King, didst thou note the meanness and greediness of yon man, in that he must needs stoop down, pick up the one dirhem. and could not bring himself to leave it for one of the King's servants?' When the King heard this, he was wroth with the fisherman and said, 'Thou art right, O Shirin!' So he called the man back and said to him, 'Thou low-minded fellow! Thou art no man! How couldst thou put the bag off thy shoulder and stoop to pick up the one dirhem and grudge to leave it where it fell?' The fisherman kissed the earth before him and answered, 'May God prolong the King's life! Indeed, I did not pick up the dirhem, because of its value in my eyes; but because on one of its faces is the likeness of the King and on the other his name; and I feared lest any should unwittingly set his foot upon it, thus dishonouring the name and presentment of the King, and I be blamed for the offence.' The King wondered at his wit and shrewdness and ordered him yet other four thousand dirhems. Moreover, he let cry abroad in his kingdom, saying, 'It behoveth none to order himself by women's counsel; for whoso followeth their advice, loseth, with his one dirhem, other two.'[14]

King Khusrau was the grandson of Anushirwan, our friend the just king who ruled when Muhammad was born. Anushirwan was 'Le Roi Soleil' of the Levant, synonymous with all that is grand and good in a monarch. Khusrau's uncle usurped the throne, but with the help of Maurice, the Greek Emperor of the East, Khusrau regained it and married Maurice's daughter. Her name was Irene, but in Persia she was known as Shirin ('sweet') and was celebrated for her beauty by the poet Nizami. Here this very exalted couple is presented in a hard-fisted ordinary light, complete with traditional moral. In fact the story is commonly called 'Don't Take the Advice of Women'.

The honour due to the king's image on coins has a modern parallel in England where all stamps bear the sovereign's head. Out of respect for the monarch, to affix a stamp upside-down is 'not done'.

As for not taking the advice of women, it is a very common eastern admonition and is attached to many illustrative stories of which this is just one. Another, more widely distributed, involves a man who hopes to ingratiate himself with a local potentate by bringing him a basket of fruit. Which fruit? He asks his wife, who suggests pomegranates. On the principle of never taking advice from a woman, he brings figs instead. Figs being cheap, the potentate's retinue mock him and pelt him with them. The man comforts himself with, 'At least they weren't pomegranates'.

7 THE TALE OF THE FATHER OF FARTS

During the reign of the khalifat Haroun al-Rachid there was a kadi in the city of Trablus in Syria who exercised the functions of his office with a notorious severity. His only servant, and the only woman in his harem, was an old negress like a Nile buffalo; for the man's parsimony equalled the rigour of his judgments. Allah curse him! Though he was abundantly rich, he lived on stale bread and onions. Also his avarice went hand in hand with an ostentation of generosity. When a neighbour called about meal time, the kadi would cry to the negress: 'Lay the gold-fringed cloth!' No one was ever invited to the repast which followed, and the show of the cloth, instead of being taken as an indication of bounty, passed into a proverb; so that a man who had been ill-served at any feast would say: 'I ate at the kadi's gold-fringed cloth.' It will be seen that this wretched old man, to whom Allah had given both riches and honour, lived a life which would have sickened a starving dog. May he burn in Hell!

One day, certain folk who wished to influence the kadi to give a favourable judgment, said to him: 'O our master, why do you not take a wife? That old negress is not worthy of you.' 'Who would find me a wife?' asked the kadi; and one of them answered: 'I have a very beautiful daughter; your slave would be highly honoured if you would take her to your house.' The kadi promptly accepted this offer, and the marriage took place at once. The girl was conducted to her husband's house in the evening and, being most discreet and amiable, refused to show her surprise when no food was produced and no mention made of it. The guests and witnesses stayed on in hope for some time and then, as the kitchen fire was not even lighted, returned to their own homes, cursing the bridegroom's meanness.

The young wife had begun to starve before she heard her husband tell the negress to lay the gold-fringed cloth. As she was accustomed to plenty of excellent food in her father's house, she went forward eagerly as soon as the cloth was laid, but only to discover that the sole dish was a basin containing three bits of brown bread and three onions. As she sat in amaze, the kadi took one of the pieces of bread himself, gave the like to the negress, and invited the girl to devour her share, saying: 'Do not fear to abuse the gifts of Allah!' He swallowed his portion with great gusto, and the negress made but one mouthful of hers, for it was the first meal of the day; but for all her good will the unfortunate wife could not swallow a mouthful of the horrible stuff. She left the table, fasting and bitterly resenting the darkness of her destiny. Three days passed and, on each, the gold-fringed cloth was set with brown bread and sorrowful onions. But on the fourth day, the kadi, hearing cries from his harem, went to investigate and was met by the negress who told him that her mistress had revolted against the house and had sent to fetch her father.

The kadi sought his wife with furious flaming eyes, heaped curses upon her, accused her of all debauchery, cut away her hair by force, and repudiated her by the third divorce. Casting her forth into the street, he shut the door violently behind her. May Allah damn the foul old knave!

A few days afterwards, this avaricious son of avarice found another wife in the person of the daughter of certain folk who wished to stand well with him. He married again; but the poor child, after three days of onions, revolted and was divorced. Yet this served as no lesson to others who needed the good graces of that horrible old man, and he married several other daughters on the same terms, casting them forth after a day or so, because they could not abide the onions.

But a time came when the multitude of his divorces was noised abroad and grew to be the general subject of conversation in the harems; the matrons banded together and decreed that henceforth the miser was to be considered unmarriageable.

Now that no woman would have it, the kadi began to be tormented by his father's inheritance and took long walks to cool its importunity. One evening, he saw a woman approaching him mounted upon a grey mule, and was very much affected by the richness of her clothes and possibility of her figure. He gave a twist to the sad ends of his moustaches and bowed before her respectfully, saying: 'Whence come you, noble lady?' 'Along this road,' she answered. 'I know that, I know that,' answered the kadi with a chuckle, 'but from what city?' 'From Mosul,' she answered. 'Are you married or single?' said he. 'Single,' said she, 'If you would like to be a wife,' said he, 'I will bind the bargain by becoming your husband.' 'Tell me where you live,' said she 'and I will let you know tomorrow.' The kadi told her where he lived; but she knew already, she knew. She left him with charming glances out of the corners of her eyes.

Next morning, she sent a a message to the kadi saying that she would marry him if she received a dowry of fifty dinars. The miser had a violent struggle with himself, but he sent the fifty dinars, bidding the negress to bring back the bride. As soon as the girl arrived at his house, the marriage contract was written out, and the witnesses went away unfed.

Soon the kadi called to the negress, saying: 'Lay the gold-fringed cloth.' When the basin was brought in, holding three dry crusts and three onions, the new bride took her portion and ate it with relish, saying: 'I thank Allah for an excellent repast.' She smiled gratefully at the kadi, and he cried: 'I also thank Him that He has sent me, out of His generosity, a wife who is all perfection, who takes today's little and tomorrow's much with equal mind!' But the blind pig did not know the destiny which lay in wait for him in the cunning brain of that delightful woman.

Next morning, when her husband was away at the diwan, the girl inspected all the rooms of the house and came at last to a cabinet whose door was closed with three enormous locks and strengthened by three strong iron bars. She walked about and about this cabinet with the liveliest curiosity, until she found a hole in one of the mouldings which would almost admit the passage of a finger. Setting her eye to it, she was overjoyed to see all the kadi's accumulated treasure of gold and silver set in open copper jars upon the floor inside. Being determined to profit by this discovery, she procured a long palm stalk and, smearing the end of it with a sticky paste, passed it through the hole in the moulding; by twisting it about in the mouth of one of the jars, she caused several gold pieces to adhere to it, and triumphantly withdrew them. Returning to her own apartment, she gave the money to the negress, saying: 'Go out to the market and buy fresh rolls sprinkled with sesame, some saffron rice, some tender lamb, and the finest fruits and pastries which you can find.' The negress went forth in eager astonishment and brought back all these excellent things to her mistress, who made her partake of them in equal shares. 'Light of my head,' the poor old woman cried, 'may this succulent generosity turn to fair white fat upon you! I have never eaten such a meal!' 'You may feed thus every day if you will only keep silence and say nothing to the kadi,' answered the girl; so the negress kissed her hand and promised absolute discretion.

'Lay the gold-fringed cloth!' cried the kadi when he returned at noon; but his wife served him with the remains of her own excellent meal. He ate greedily until he could hold no more, and then asked the source of the provision. 'Dear master,' replied the girl, 'I have many relations in this city; one of them sent these dishes to me. I would have thought nothing of them, had it not been for the joy it gives me to share them with you.' And the kadi rejoiced in his soul that he had married such a wife.

Next morning the palm stalk was no less successful, so that the wife was able to purchase a lamb stuffed with pistachios, and other admirable matters. She invited some of her neighbours to eat with her, and all the women feasted pleasantly until the hour of the kadi's return. Soon after the guests had departed, carrying with them the promise that these joyful mornings should often be repeated, the kadi entered and bade the negress spread the gold-fringed cloth. But when he was served with even more delicate and numerous viands than the day before, he became a little anxious and asked his wife how she had come by such costly things. The girl, who was herself waiting upon him, answered without hesitation: 'Dear master, you must take no more thought for our nourishment. One of my aunts sent me these few trifling dishes. Oh, I am happy if my master is satisfied.' The kadi congratulated himself on having married so thoughtful and well-related a damsel, and set about stuffing himself to the supreme limit of his capacity.

At the end of a year of such living the kadi had become so fat and had developed so notorious a belly that the people used the thing as a proverb, saying: 'As large as the kadi's belly!' 'As stupendous as the kadi's belly!' The poor fool did not know that his wife had sworn to avenge all those unfortunate girls whom he had starved and shorn and cast aside; but you shall now hear how thoroughly she carried out her intention.

Among the neighbours whom she fed daily was a pregnant woman, the wife of a necessitous porter and already the mother of five children. One day her hostess said to her: 'Dear neighbour, as Allah has given you a numerous family and very little else, would you like to hand over your baby to me when it is born, that I, who am barren, may care for it and rear it as my own? If you agree and promise to keep absolute silence, I will see that you and yours never feel the pinch of poverty again.' The porter's wife accepted this offer and promised absolute secrecy. On the day appointed by Allah, she gave birth to a boy who was twice the size of an ordinary infant, and the kadi's wife received him.

That morning the girl prepared a dish consisting of beans, peas, white haricots, cabbage, lentils, onions, cloves of garlic, various heavy grains and powdered spices. The kadi's enormous belly was quite empty when he returned for the midday meal, so he took helping after helping of this mixture, until all was finished. 'Make me such a dish every day,' he said. 'It slips most pleasantly and easily down the throat.' 'May it be both delicious and digestible!' answered his wife.

The kadi congratulated himself, as he had so often done before, on his excellent choice of a wife; but an hour afterwards his belly began visibly to swell. A noise as of a far-off tempest made itself heard inside him; low grumblings and far thunders shook the walls of his being and brought in their train sharp colics, spasms, and a final agony. He grew yellow in the face and began to roll groaning about the floor, holding his belly in his two hands. 'Allah, Allah!' he cried, 'I have a terrible storm within! Who will deliver me?' Soon his paunch became as tight as a gourd and his cries brought his wife running. She made him swallow a powder of anise and fennel, which was soon to have its effect, and, at the same time, to console and encourage him, began rubbing and patting the afflicted part, as if he had been a little sick child. Suddenly she ceased the movement of her hand and uttered a piercing cry: 'Yuh, yuh, a miracle, a prodigy! O my master, my master!' In violent contortions, the kadi stammered forth: 'What is the matter, what is the miracle?' But she only answered: 'Yuh, yuh! O my master, my master!' 'Tell me what the matter is!' he yelled; and she passed her hand afresh over that tempestuous belly, as she replied: 'Exalted be the name of the Highest! He says, and it is done! Who shall discover His secret purposes, my master?' Between two howls, the kadi gasped: 'May Allah curse you for torturing me so! What is the matter? Tell me at once!' Then said his wife: 'Master, dear master, His will be done! You are with child! And your time is close at hand!'

The kadi rose up at these incredible words, and cried: 'Have you gone mad? How can a man be pregnant?' 'As Allah lives I do not know,' she answered, 'but the child is moving in your belly; I have felt it kicking and touched its head. Allah scatters increase where He will, may His name be exalted! Pray for the Prophet, my husband!' So the kadi groaned out in the midst of his convulsion: 'May the blessing of Allah be upon him!' Then his pains increased and he fell howling to the floor in a crisis of agony. Suddenly came relief. A long and thunderous fart broke from him, shaking the foundations of the house and throwing him violently forward, so that he swooned. Then followed a multitude of other escapes, gradually diminishing in sound but rolling and re-echoing through the troubled air. Last came a single deafening explosion and all was still.

As the kadi came gradually to himself, he saw a little mattress by his side, on which a new-born baby, swaddled in linens, lay squalling and grimacing. His wife bent over him, saying: 'Praise be to Allah and to His Prophet for this happy deliverance!' Then she went on murmuring the sacred names over her husband and the child, until the kadi did not know whether he dreamed or whether his recent sufferings had turned his head. But when he came to consider the matter calmly, the sight of the child, the cessation of his pain, and the memory of the tempest which had escaped from his belly, forced him to believe in this miraculous birth. Also maternal love caused him to accept the infant. 'Surely Allah may bring forth His people according to His will!' he said. 'Even a man, if he is fated to do so, may bear a child in due season! Get me a nurse, dear wife, for I cannot feed the child myself.' 'I had already thought of that; I have one waiting in the harem,' she replied. 'But a mother's milk is best of all. Are you sure that your breasts have not swelled?' The kadi felt anxiously, and answered, 'No, there is nothing there.'

The young wife rejoiced at the success of her strategy and, after telling the kadi that he must keep his bed for forty days and forty nights, gave him such medicines as are usual and petted him till he fell into a doze. Being worn out by his colic, the old man slept for a long time and, when he woke, found his body as well as his mind was ill at ease.

His first care was to enjoin secrecy on his wife, saying: 'I am lost for ever if folk get to know that the kadi has given birth to a veritable child.' Instead of reassuring him, his wife answered: 'We are not the only folk who know of the fortunate miracle. All our neighbours have already heard about it from the nurse. And I am afraid that it will be as difficult to prevent the news from spreading through the city, as it would have been to stay the tongue of the nurse in the first place. They are all babblers.'

The kadi spent the forty days upon his bed in deep mortification, not daring to move for fear of complications and internal bleeding, and brooding all the time over his monstrous accident. 'Surely my foes will accuse me of many ridiculous things,' he said to himself. 'They will say that I have let myself be buggered in some extraordinary fashion, and that it is all very well for me to be severe in my judgments when I have given myself up to such strange immoralities that I can bear a child. As Allah lives I am sure that they will accuse me of having been buggered; me, their virtuous kadi; and I have almost forgotten what it feels like!'

Thus he reflected, little knowing that his avarice was the cause of all his woes; and the more he thought, the blacker and more pitiable his case appeared to him. When his wife told him at last that he might rise without fear of complications, he bathed in the house, because he did not dare to go to the hammam. Finally he resolved to quit the city of Trablus, rather than run the risk of being recognized in the streets. He informed his wife of his intention and she, while pretending deep grief that he would be obliged to abandon his great office, only made him the more fixed on flight, by saying: 'Evil tongues are certainly wagging about you now; but your adventure will soon be forgotten. Then you can return and devote yourself to rearing your child . . . I think that we had better call him Miracle.' 'Call him what you like,' answered the kadi. That night he departed from the city by stealth, leaving his wife in charge of the house and child, and journeyed in the direction of Damascus.

He came to Damascus weary, but happy in the thought that no one knew his name or story. Yet, in the next few hours, he heard the tale of his exploit repeated countless times in all the public places of that city. Also, as he had feared, each new tale-teller added some fresh detail to tickle the laughter of his hearers, attributing extraordinary organs to the kadi and bestowing on him every variety of that name which he dared not formulate even to himself. But happily no one knew his face and he was able to go on his way unrecognized. Towards night he even grew so hardened that he would pause and listen to his own story. In fact, when he heard himself accused not of one child but of a whole family, he could not help laughing a little, and murmuring: 'They may say what they like, as long as they do not recognize me.'

Though he lived in Damascus even more miserly than before, his provision of money at length ran out and he was obliged to sell his clothes for bread. Finally, rather than send a message to his wife in which he would have to tell her where his treasure lay, he hired himself out to a mason as a mortar-carrier.

Years went by, and the old kadi, round whom the curses of the people of Trablus swarmed at night, became as thin as a cat locked in a barn. At last, feeling certain that the years would have effaced the memory of his misfortune, he left Damascus and came, a mere wraith of skin and bone, to his native city. As he went through the gate, he saw a group of children playing together and heard one of them say to another: 'How do you expect to win when you were born in the kadi's year, the year of the Father of Farts?' 'I thank Allah,' murmured the delighted kadi, 'that he has caused my tale to be forgotten! Behold, some other kadi has become a proverb in the mouths of the children!' He went up to the boy who had spoken, saying: 'What kadi is this whom you call the Father of Farts?' 'He was given that name,' answered the child, 'because once, when he had broken wind enormously, his wife made him think . . .', but nothing is to be gained by repeating the sorry story here.

Realizing for the first time that he had been fooled by his wife, the kadi left the children and ran in all haste to his own house; but the doors were open to the wind, the floor was broken, and the walls had crumbled away. In the remains of the treasure cabinet, there was no gold piece or silver piece, nor hint nor smell that such had been. His neighbours, hearing him lament, told him, as well as they could for laughter, how his wife had given him up for dead and departed with all his goods into a far country. Without answering a word, he turned and left that city. Nor was anything ever heard of him again.[15]

It is still told today.

THE MAN THAT HAD A BABY

One time there was a man that thought women always make too much fuss about having a baby. He says it's just natural for a female to shell out young-uns, and don't hurt no more than getting rid of a tape-worm. This crack made the man's wife pretty mad, and she says, 'All right, I'll fix it with the doctor so you can have our next baby, and see how you like it.' The fellow just laughed, and he says that's fair enough, and we will take turn about from now on.

Next time the fellow got drunk they put him to bed with bandages, and some croton oil for a physic, and the doctor fastened a big stout plaster over his ass-hole. So next morning the man's belly was swelled up like a balloon, and you could hear him hollering all over town. Doc says just take it easy, as these pains will only last four or five hours. Then the fellow begun to kick and raise hell, so it took the whole family to hold him in the bed. Finally the doctor brought a little pet monkey and slipped it under the quilt, and then he cut the big plaster loose. The patient give a whoop and shit all over himself. The bed was plumb full, and running over on the carpet besides. Just then the little monkey showed up, a-wiping hockey out of its eyes, and chattering. Soon as the fellow seen the monkey he begun to holler worse than ever. 'What does the little bastard mean, laughing like a fool when his poor mother is a-dying?' he yelled. Even Doc had to grin when he heard that one, and the man's wife pretty near had a fit.

After Doc left with his monkey, it took the folks all day to clean up the house, and get things a-running orderly again. When the fellow sobered up everybody says he must have dreamed the whole thing, and Doc advised him to go easy on the applejack. The man didn't drink no liquor at all for a long time after that, and he give up talking about how it ain't no trouble for a woman to have a baby.[16]

The most common European form of this folktale is as a joke on a parson or priest, 'The Priest and the Calf ', Russian variant 'The Pope Who Begot a Calf ', etc., with varying circumstances for the priest's becoming pregnant. As for literature, Boccaccio in the *Decamerone*, IX, 3, deals not with a priest but with a stupid man tricked first into believing he is pregnant and later that he has miscarried. Imitated by Hans Sachs, Nicolas de Troyes and Straparola, this nevertheless is one instance where the *Decamerone* form of a tale-type did not become the dominant.one. The fart as the birth seems to have reached western writing in the *Pentamerone* of Giambattista Basile in Naples in 1634 (Day II, Tale 3), when in the telling of a quite different story a foolish ogre thinks he has given birth to a young girl. Humour of this sort is of course universal.

Classical Greece knew it too but more subtly, as when in Aristophanes' *Parliament of Women*, a constipated man prays for relief to the goddess of childbirth.

8   WOMEN'S WILES

On the following night Dunyazad said to her sister Shahrazad, 'O sister mine, an thou incline not unto sleep, prithee tell us a tale which shall beguile our watching through the dark hours.' She replied: With love and gladness. It hath reached me, O magnificent King, that whilome there was in the city of Baghdad, a comely youth and a well-bred, fair of favour, tall of stature, and slender of shape. His name was Ala al-Din, and he was of the chiefs of the sons of the merchants and had a shop wherein he sold and bought. One day, as he sat in his shop, there passed by him a merry girl who raised her head and, casting a glance at the young merchant, saw written in a flowing hand on the forehead of his shop door these words, 'THERE BE NO CRAFT SAVE MEN'S CRAFT, FORASMUCH AS IT OVERCOMETH WOMEN'S CRAFT'. When she beheld this, she was wroth and took counsel with herself, saying, 'As my head liveth, there is no help but I show him a marvel-trick of the wiles of women and put to naught this his inscription!' Thereupon she hied her home; and on the morrow she made her ready and donning the finest of dress, adorned herself with the costliest of ornaments and the highest of price and stained her hands with Henna. Then she let down her tresses upon her shoulders and went forth, walking with coquettish gait and amorous grace, followed by her slave-girl carrying a parcel, till she came to the young merchant's shop and, sitting down under pretext of seeking stuffs, saluted him with the salam and demanded of him somewhat of cloths. So he brought out to her various kinds, and she took them and turned them over, talking with him the while. Then said she to him, 'Look at the shapeliness of my shape and my semblance! Seest thou in me aught of default?' He replied, 'No, O my lady'; and she continued, 'Is it lawful in anyone that he should slander me and say that I am humpbacked?' Then she discovered to him a part of her bosom, and when he saw her breasts his reason took flight from his head and his heart clave to her and he cried, 'Cover it up, so may Allah veil thee!' Quoth she, 'Is it fair of anyone to decry my charms?' and quoth he, 'How shall any decry thy charms, and thou the sun of loveliness?' Then said she, 'Hath any the right to say of me that I am lophanded?' and tucking up her sleeves, she showed him forearms as they were crystal; after which she unveiled to him a face, as it were a full moon breaking forth on its fourteenth night, and said to him, 'Is it lawful and right for any to decry me and declare that my face is pitted with small-pox or that I am one-eyed or crop-eared?' and said he, 'O my lady, what is it moveth thee to discover unto me that lovely face and those fair limbs, wont to be so jealously veiled and guarded? Tell me the truth of the matter, may I be thy ransom!' And he began to improvise:

White Fair now drawn from sheath of parted hair, * Then in the
blackest tresses hid from sight,
Flasheth like day irradiating Earth * While round her glooms the
murk of nightliest night.

Then the girl said to the young merchant, 'Know, O my lord, that I
am a maid oppressed of my sire, who speaketh at me and saith to me, Thou
art loathly of looks and semblance, and it besitteth not that thou wear rich
raiment; for thou and the slave girls are like in rank, there is no distinguish-
ing thee from them. Now he is a richard, having a mighty great store of
money, and saith not thus save because he is a pinchpenny, and grudgeth
the spending of a farthing; wherefore he is loath to marry me, lest he be put
to somewhat of expense in my marriage, albeit Almighty Allah hath been
bounteous to him and he is a man puissant in his time and lacking naught
of worldly weal.' The youth asked, 'Who is thy father and what is his
condition?' and she answered, 'He is the Chief Kazi of the well-known
Supreme Court, under whose hands are all the Kazis who administer
justice in this city.' The merchant believed her and she farewelled him and
fared away, leaving in his heart a thousand regrets, for that the love of her
had prevailed over him, and he knew not how he should win to her;
wherefore he woned enamoured, love-distracted, unknowing if he were
alive or dead. As soon as she was gone, he shut up shop and walked
straightway to the Court, where he went in to the Chief Kazi and saluted
him. The magistrate returned his salam and treated him with distinction
and seated him by his side. Then said Ala al-Din to him, 'I come to thee
seeking thine alliance and desiring the hand of thy noble daughter.' Quoth
the Kazi, 'O my lord merchant, welcome to thee and fair welcome; but
indeed my daughter befitteth not the like of thee, neither beseemeth she
the goodliness of thy youth, and the pleasantness of thy composition, and
the sweetness of thy speech'; but Ala al-Din replied, 'This talk becometh
thee not, neither is it seemly in thee; if I be content with her, how should
this vex thee?' So the Kazi was satisfied, and they came to an accord and
concluded the marriage contract at a dower precedent of five purses ready
money and a dower contingent of fifteen purses, so it might be hard for
him to put her away, her father having given him fair warning, but he
would not be warned. Then they wrote out the contract-document, and
the merchant said, 'I desire to go in to her this night.' Accordingly they
carried her to him in procession that very evening, and he prayed the
night-prayer and entered the private chamber prepared for him; but, when
he lifted the head-gear from the bride's head and the veil from her face, and
looked, he saw a foul face and a favour right fulsome; indeed he beheld
somewhat whereof may Allah never show thee the like! loathly, dispens-
ing from description, inasmuch as there were reckoned in her all legal
defects. So he repented, when repentance availed him naught, and knew
that the girl had cheated him.

The unhappy merchant carnally knew the loathly bride, sore against the grain, and abode that night troubled in mind, as he were in the prison of Al-Daylam. Hardly had the day dawned when he arose from her side, and betaking himself to one of the Hammams, dozed there awhile, after which he made the Ghusl-ablution of ceremonial impurity and donned his everyday dress. Then he went out to the coffee house and drank a cup of coffee; after which he returned to his shop and, opening the door, sat down, with concern and chagrin manifest on his countenance. After an hour or so, his friends and intimates among the merchants and people of the market began to come up to him, by ones and twos, to give him joy, and said to him, laughing, 'A blessing! a blessing! Where be the sweet-meats? Where be the coffee? 'Twould seem thou hast forgotten us; and nothing made thee oblivious save that the charms of the bride have disordered thy wit and taken thy reason, Allah help thee! We give thee joy, we give thee joy.' And they mocked at him whilst he kept silence before them, being like to rend his raiment and shed tears for rage. Then they went away from him, and when it was the hour of noon, up came his mistress, the crafty girl, trailing her skirts and swaying to and fro in her gait, as she were a branch of Ban in a garden of bloom. She was yet more richly dressed and adorned, and more striking and cutting in her sym-metry and grace than on the previous day, so that she made the passers stop and stand in espalier to gaze upon her. When she came to Ala al-Din's shop, she sat down thereon and said to him, 'Blessed be the day to thee, O my lord Ala al-Din! Allah prosper thee and be good to thee, and perfect thy gladness and make it a wedding of weal and welfare!' He knitted his brows and frowned in answer to her; then asked her, 'Wherein have I failed of thy due, or what have I done to harm thee, that thou shouldst require me after this fashion?' She answered, 'Thou hast been no wise in default; but 'tis yonder inscription written on the door of thy shop that irketh me and vexeth my heart. An thou have the courage to change it and write up the contrary thereof, I will deliver thee from thine evil plight.' And he answered, 'Thy requirement is right easy: on my head and eyes!' So saying he brought out a sequin, and summoning one of his Mamelukes, said to him, 'Get thee to Such-an-one the Scribe, and bid him write us an epi-graph, adorned with gold and lapis lazuli, in these words, THERE BE NO CRAFT SAVE WOMEN'S CRAFT, FOR INDEED THEIR CRAFT IS A MIGHTY CRAFT AND OVERCOMETH AND HUMBLETH THE FALSES OF MEN.' And she said to the white slave, 'Fare thee forthright.' So he repaired to the Scribe, who wrote him the scroll, and he brought it to his master, who set it on the door and asked the damsel, 'Is thy heart satisfied?' She answered, 'Yes! Arise forth-with and get thee to the place before the citadel, where do thou foregather with all the mountebanks and ape-dancers, and bear-leaders, and drum-mers and pipers, and bid them come to thee tomorrow early, with their kettle-drums and flageolets, whilst thou art drinking coffee with thy father-in-law the Kazi, and congratulate thee and wish thee joy, saying: A blessing, O son of our uncle! Indeed, thou art the vein of our eye! We rejoice for thee, and if thou be ashamed of us, verily we pride ourselves upon thee; so, although thou banish us from thee, know that we will not forsake thee, albeit thou forsake us. And do thou fall to throwing dinars and dirhams amongst them; whereupon the Kazi will question thee, and do thou answer him, saying: My father was an ape-dancer, and this is our original condition; but our Lord opened on us the gate of fortune, and we have gotten us a name amongst the merchants and with their provost. Upon this he will say to thee, Then thou art an ape-leader of the tribe of the mountebanks? and do thou rejoin, I may in nowise deny my origin for the sake of thy daughter and in her honour. The Kazi will say, It may not be that thou shalt be given the daughter of a Shaykh who sitteth upon the carpet of the Law, and whose descent is traceable by genealogy to the loins of the Apostle of Allah, nor is it meet that his daughter be in the power of a man who is an ape-dancer, a minstrel. Then do thou reply, Nay, O Efendi, she is my lawful wife, and every hair of her is worth a thousand lives, and I will not put her away though I be given the kingship of the world. At last be thou persuaded to speak the word of divorce, and so shall the marriage be voided and ye be saved each from other.' Quoth Ala al-Din, 'Right is thy rede,' and locking up his shop, betook himself to the place before the citadel, where he foregathered with the dancers, the drummers and pipers, and instructed them how they should do, promising them a mighty fine reward. They received his word with 'Hearing and obeying'; and he betook himself on the morrow, after the morning prayer, to the presence of the Judge, who received him with humble courtesy and seated him by his side. Then he addressed him and began questioning him of matters of selling and buying and of the price current of the various commodities which were carried to Baghdad from all quarters, whilst his son-in-law replied to all whereof he was questioned. As they were thus conversing, behold, up came the dancers and drummers with their drums and pipers with their pipes, whilst one of their number preceded them, with a long pennon-like banner in his hand, and played all manner antics with voice and limbs. When they came to the Court-house, the Kazi cried, 'I seek refuge with Allah from yonder Satans!' and the young merchant laughed but said naught. Then they entered and saluting his worship the Kazi, kissed Ala al-Din's hands and said, 'A blessing on thee, O son of our uncle! Indeed, thou coolest our eyes in whatso thou doest, and we beseech Allah for the enduring greatness of our lord the Kazi, who hath honoured us by admitting thee to his connection, and hath allotted to us a portion in his high rank and degree.' When the Judge heard this talk, it bewildered his wit and he was dazed and his face flushed with rage, and quoth he to his son-in-law, 'What words are these?' Quoth the merchant, 'Knowest thou not, O my lord, that I am of this tribe? Indeed, this man is the son of my maternal uncle and that other the son of my paternal uncle, and if I be reckoned of the merchants, 'tis but by courtesy!' When the Kazi heard these words his colour changed – And he was troubled and waxed wroth with exceeding wrath, and was like to burst for stress of rage. Then said he to the young merchant, 'Allah forfend that this should last! How shall it be permitted that the daughter of the Kazi of the Moslems cohabit with a man of the dancers and vile of origin? By Allah, unless thou repudiate her forthright, I will bid beat thee and cast thee into prison and there confine thee till thou die. Had I foreknown that thou wast of them, I had not suffered thee near me, but had spat in thy face, for that thou art more ill-omened than a dog or a hog.' Then he kicked him down from his place and commanded him to divorce; but he said, 'Be ruthful to me, O Efendi, for that Allah is ruthful, and hasten not: I will not divorce my wife, though thou give me the kingdom of Al-Irak.' The Judge was perplexed and knew that compulsion was not permitted of Holy Law; so he bespake the young merchant fair and said to him, 'Veil me, so may Allah veil thee. An thou divorce her not, this dishonour shall cleave to me till the end of time.' Then his fury got the better of his wit and he cried, 'An thou divorce her not of thine own will, I will forthright bid strike off thy head and slay myself; Hell-flame but not shame.' The merchant bethought himself awhile, then divorced her with a manifest divorce and a public, and on this wise he won free from that unwelcome worry. Then he returned to his shop and presently sought in marriage of her father her who had done with him what she did and who was the daughter of the Shaykh of the guild of the blacksmiths. So he took her to wife and they abode each with other and lived the pleasantest of lives and the most delightsome, till the day of death: and praise be to Allah the Lord of the Three Worlds.[17]

This tale has been found in the fifteenth-century *Fakihat al-Khalifa* by 'Arab-Shah. From there it made its way into the Breslau Arabic text of the *Nights*. But it was printed, again from 'Arab-Shah, by Lescallier in his *Voyages de Sindbad* in 1814, long before the Breslau text was known to exist. (The Breslau edition was the one used by Burton for his *Supplemental Nights*.)

9   THE MAN WHO SAW THE NIGHT OF POWER

A certain man had longed all his life to look upon the Night of Power,* and

---

* One of the last nights of Ramazan (supposed, on the authority of a tradition of the Prophet, to be either the 20th, 22nd, 24th or 28th of the month) on which the Koran is said to have been revealed *en bloc* to Gabriel, who communicated it piece-meal to Muhammad, beginning at once with chapter xcvi (or, according to some, chapter lxxiv). On this night the Muslims believe that the affairs of the universe are settled for the ensuing year, that all created things prostrate themselves in adoration to Allah (cf. the medieval legend of Christmas Eve, when the cattle were fabled to worship God in the stalls, etc.), salt water becomes sweet, the angels descend to bless the faithful and all prayers, prayed in cognizance of the fact, are granted. 'Verily we sent it [the Koran] down on the Night of Power, and what giveth thee to

it befell that, one night, he looked up at the sky and saw the angels and Heaven's gates opened and beheld all things in the act of prostration before their Lord, each in its several room. So he said to his wife, 'Harkye, such an one, God hath shown me the Night of Power, and it hath been proclaimed to me, from the invisible world, that three prayers will be granted unto me; so do thou counsel me what I shall ask.' Quoth she, 'O man, the perfection of man and his delight is in his yard; so do thou pray God to greaten thy yard and magnify it.' So he lifted up his hands to heaven and said, 'O my God, greaten my yard and magnify it.' Hardly had he spoken when his yard became as big as a calabash and he could neither sit nor stand nor move; and when he would have lain with his wife, she fled before him from place to place. So he said to her, 'O accursed woman, what is to be done? This is thy wish, by reason of thy lust.' 'Nay, by Allah,' answered she; 'I did not ask for this huge bulk, for which the gate of a street were too strait. Pray God to make it less.' So he raised his eyes to heaven and said, 'O my God, rid me of this thing and deliver me therefrom.' And immediately his yard disappeared altogether and he became smooth [like a woman]. When his wife saw this, she said, 'I have no occasion for thee, now thou art become yardless;' and he answered her, saying, 'All this comes of thine ill-omened counsel and the infirmity of thy judgment. I had three prayers accepted of God, wherewith I might have gotten me my good, both in this world and the next, and now two are gone in pure waste, by thy lewd wish, and there remaineth but one.' Quoth she, 'Pray God the Most High to restore thee thy yard as it was.' So he prayed to his Lord and his yard was restored to its first case. Thus the man lost his three wishes by the ill counsel and lack of sense of the woman.[18]

A very versatile story, this, found everywhere and over a long period. It hangs on foolish wishes or wishes granted in unacceptable forms which must be cancelled by further wishes. An analogue is in the Panchatantra and it is generally believed to be of ultimate Indian origin, but it was first recorded by Phaedrus, the first century A.D. Roman redactor of Aesop, as 'Mercurious et Mulieres Duae', in which the god Mercury gives a wish to each of two women. One has an infant son; her wish is to see him when he is bearded. The other wishes that whatever she touches will follow her. Result, the baby grows a beard, and the woman inadvertently touches her nose which proceeds to follow her and hits the ground. Like other fables 'of Aesop', the tale of wishes foolishly wasted would have been in

know what is the Night of Power? The Night of Power is better than a thousand months; the angels and the Spirit (Gabriel) descend therein, by leave of their Lord, with every commandment. Peace is it till the breaking of the dawn.' – Koran xcvii. 'By the Manifest Book, we sent it down on a blessed night . . . whereon is apportioned each determined decree, as a commandment from us.' – Koran xliv. 1, 2 and 3.

the international reservoir of Near Eastern folklore long before Phaedrus, and would have developed into 'The Night of Power' long before the *Nights*, but this story is distinguished by the many variations on its basic idea. There can be one wish each to one person, two persons or three persons, or three wishes to one person, or, most usual, three wishes to a married couple. The wife spoils the first wish, an angry husband spoils the second, and the third goes to restore the *status quo ante*.

A fairly consistent theme is the granting of the wishes by a deity or supernatural creature of some sort, fairy-queen, wood-spirit, elf, devil, etc. In Europe a common form was of Christ and Peter giving the wishes to a poor peasant who entertained them hospitably. Payne's note explains the divine element in the Muslim Night of Power. A modern Arabic version recently collected among the folk in Tunis is of a husband to whom God gives three wishes. He gives one to his wife, who promptly asks to be the most beautiful woman in the world in the hope that she can then leave her husband. He asks that she be changed into a dog, but his sons protest and ask him to wish her back as she was.[19] In modern western variants, the influence of the story as given in the *Nights* is obvious, but it is typically modified to something like the following. The pudding motif dates at least from Perrault.

THE THREE WISHES

An old couple fell on bad times and at last were without food. But when a little man knocked at the door and said he was hungry, they gave him their last bit of bread. When he left he thanked them and said, 'I'm a king in a far-off land. You can make three wishes and they will come true.'

The old people laughed. 'Wouldn't it be nice if wishes came true!' said the wife. 'I wish we had a black pudding.' Whoosh, down the chimney, and there was a black pudding in front of them. 'You fool,' cried the husband. 'You could have wished for anything and all you asked for was a pudding! I wish it were stuck on your nose!' Whoosh, and the pudding was on her nose. The third wish had to be used to get it off.

There wasn't much they could do then, except eat the pudding, and that they did.

William W. Jacobs' short story, 'The Monkey's Paw', gave this tale a new circulation and fame in the West. But its note is tragic and macabre; the father's wish for money is brought about by the death of the only son, who is insured. The mother's wish for his return, a corpse from the grave, is cancelled by the father's wish to let him be in peace. In this Jacobs may have been influenced by the old English ballad, 'The Wife of Usher's Well', in which a mother's wish reclaims for one night as if alive the bodies of her three drowned sons. The motif of ghastly return from the dead occurs in many European ballads and legends, but it is not part of our essential type, which is a merry tale in both senses of the word.

10 THE MERCHANT'S WIFE AND THE PARROT

There was once a merchant who travelled much, and he had a fair wife, whom he loved, and was jealous over her, by reason of the greatness of his love. So he bought her for a hundred dinars a green parrot, which talked like a man and used to tell him all that passed in his absence. Whilst he was abroad on one of his voyages, his wife fell in love with a young Turk, who used to visit her, and she entertained him and lay with him whilst her husband was away. When the latter returned, the parrot told him what had happened, whereat he was sore enraged and offered to kill his wife; but she said, 'O man, fear God and return to thy wits. How can a bird have sense or understanding? If thou wilt that I make this manifest to thee, so thou mayst know its truth from its leasing, go this night and lie with one of thy friends, and in the morning come back and question the parrot [of what passed during the night,] and thou wilt see if it speak truth or not.'

The husband accordingly went forth and passed the night with one of his friends, whilst, as soon as it was dark, the wife covered the parrot's cage with a piece of leather and fell to sprinkling water on it from above. Moreover, she fanned it sharply with a fan and flashed light on it from the lantern, as it were the glancing lightning, grinding the while at the hand-mill. Thus she did, without ceasing, till daybreak; and the parrot thought that the sprinkling of the water on its cage was rain and the fanning a stormy wind and the flashing of the lantern lightning and the noise of the hand-mill thunder. When her husband returned, she bade him question the parrot; so he went up to the cage and began to talk with the bird and question it of the past night. Quoth it, 'O my lord, who could see or hear aught last night?' 'And why so?' asked he. 'Because,' replied it, 'of the much rain and wind and thunder and lightning.' 'Thou liest,' said the merchant. 'There was nothing of all this last night.' Quoth the bird, 'I tell thee but what I saw and heard.' Then was he certified that the parrot had lied in all it had told him of his wife and would have made his peace with the latter; but she said, 'By Allah, I will not be friends with thee, till thou kill this parrot that lied to thee of me.' So he rose and killed the parrot; but, a few days after, he saw the young Turk come forth of his house and knew that the parrot had spoken the truth and repented of having slain it. Then he went in at once to his wife and cut her throat and casting her into the river, vowed never to take another wife.[20]

The Book of Sindibad seems to epitomize male chauvinism. First, it is based on the lustful stepmother and the chaste youth, of all folktales the oldest, widest-spread, and most damaging to women. For details of the lustful stepmother motif, see the chapter on Joseph and Potiphar's Wife. Secondly, baleful as that was by itself, in the *Book of Sindibad* — perhaps as early as the fifth century B.C. in India — it became a frame-story. In this way not only was the diffusion of the lustful stepmother motif continued and multiplied, but also marshalled and carried along with it were other anti-women exempla which thus reached maximum distribution as well. And then to cap it all, the *Sindibad* frame and its tales were, as the *Seven Wazirs*, included and perpetuated in *The Arabian Nights*, thus joining in the *Nights'* vast circulation. Probably no other book, or rather family of books, has done as much harm.

There were two branches of the *Book of Sindibad*, eastern and western, the western being known as *The Seven Wise Masters*, *Les Sept Sages de Rome* or *The Seven Sages of Rome*. Both branches reached Europe. In the eastern, Sindibad is the counsellor of the prince who has been falsely accused by his stepmother. In the western, the prince has seven counsellors. The adviser or advisers tell stories showing the perfidy of women, while the stepmother retaliates with accounts of wicked men. Needless to say, the men have most of the better stories. The number of tales varies with each version and the individual tales vary too; only four are found in both eastern and western groups: the boar ourwitted by a shepherd or monkey; the seneschal; the dog who saves a baby and is wrongly killed (see also *Beth Gelert*); and the man, his wife and the tell-tale bird, our 'Merchant's Wife and the Parrot'. This last appearrs in almost every important book of medieval narratives, in all countries of Europe a favourable illustration of the deception of women.

To take only one example, *The Canterbury Tales*, we find that Chaucer knew it in two forms. In his chief retelling of it in 'The Manciple's Tale' the bird is a white crow and the husband is Phoebus, who slays his wife and then turns the crow black to punish him. Thus the future blackness of crows. In 'The Wife of Bath's Prologue' Chaucer refers to 'a wise wife, if she knows her own good' who will convince her husband that the bird is mad and use her maid as witness – in other words, to the standard story.

11 THE KING AND HIS VIZIER'S WIFE

There was once a king, who was given to the love of women, and one day, being alone in his palace, he espied a beautiful woman on the roof of her house and could not contain himself from falling in love with her. He asked his servants to whom the house belonged and they said, 'To thy vizier such an one'. So he called the vizier in question and despatched him on an errand to a distant part of the kingdom; then, as soon as he was gone, he made an excuse to gain access to his house. When the vizier's wife saw him, she knew him and springing up, kissed his hands and feet and welcomed him. Then she stood afar off, busying herself in his service, and said to him, 'O our lord, what is the cause of thy gracious visit? Such an honour is not for the like of me.' Quoth he, 'Love of thee and desire of thee have moved me to this.' Whereupon she kissed the earth before him a second time and said, 'O our lord, indeed I am not worthy to be the handmaid of one of the king's servants; whence then have I the great good fortune to be in such favour with thee?' Then the king put out his hand to her, but she said, 'This thing shall not escape us; but take patience, O king, and abide with me all this day, that I may make ready for thee somewhat of victual.' So the king sat down on his vizier's couch and the lady brought him a book wherein he might read, whilst she made ready the food. He took the book and beginning to read, found therein moral instances and exhortations, such as restrained him from adultery and broke his intent to commit sin.

After a while, she returned and set before him a collation of ninety dishes of different kinds and colours, and he ate a spoonful of each and found that the taste of them was one. At this, he marvelled exceedingly and said to the lady, 'O damsel, I see these meats to be many and various of hue, but the taste of them is one.' 'God prosper the king!' replied she. 'This is a parable I have set for thee, that thou mayst be admonished thereby.' 'And what is its meaning?' asked he. 'May God amend the case of our lord the king!' answered she. 'In thy palace are ninety concubines of various colours, but their taste is one.' When the king heard this, he was ashamed and rising hastily, went out and returned to his palace, without offering her any affront; but, in his haste and confusion, he forgot his signet-ring and left it under the cushion where he had been sitting.

Presently the vizier returned and presenting himself before the king, kissed the earth and made his report to him of the state of the province in question. Then he repaired to his own house and sat down on his couch, and chancing to put his hand under the cushion, found the king's seal-ring. So he looked at it and knew it and taking the matter to heart, held aloof from his wife nor spoke with her for a whole year, whilst she knew not the reason of his anger. At last, being weary of estrangement, she sent for her father and told him the case, whereupon quoth he, 'I will complain of him to the king, some day when he is in presence.'

So, one day, he went in to the king and finding the vizier and the cadi of the army before him, made his complaint in the following words: 'May God the Most High amend the king's case! I had a fair garden, which I planted with my own hand and spent my substance thereon, till it bore fruit and its fruit was ripe, when I gave it to this thy vizier, who ate of it what seemed good to him, then forsook it and watered it not, so that its flowers withered and its beauty departed and it became waste.' Then said the vizier, 'O king, what this man says is true. I did indeed care for the garden and ate thereof, till, one day, going thither, I saw the track of the lion there, wherefore I feared him and withdrew from the garden.' The king understood the parable and knew that, by the track of the lion, he meant his own seal-ring, which he had forgotten in his house; so he said, 'Return to thy garden, O vizier, and fear nothing, for the lion came not near it. It hath been told me that he went thither, but by the honour of my fathers and forefathers, he offered it no hurt.' 'I hear and obey,' answered the vizier, and returning home, made his peace with his wife and thenceforth put faith in her chastity.[21]

VINEYARD I WAS AND VINEYARD I AM

From Giuseppe Bernoni, *Tradizioni Populari Veneziana, 1875-77*

A king, averse to marriage, commanded his steward to remain single. The latter, however, one day saw a beautiful girl named Vigna, and married her secretly. Although he kept her closely confined in her chamber, the king became suspicious and sent the steward off on an embassy. After his departure the king entered the apartment occupied by him and saw his officer's wife sleeping. He did not disturb her, but in leaving the room, dropped one of his gloves accidentally on the bed. When the husband returned he found it, but kept a discreet silence, ceasing however all demonstrations of affection, believing his wife had been faithless.

The king, anxious to see again the beautiful woman, made a feast and ordered the steward to bring his wife. He denied in vain that he had one, but brought her at last, and while everyone else was talking gaily at the feast she was silent. The king observed it and asked her the cause of her silence; and she answered with a pun on her name: 'Vineyard I was and Vineyard I am, I was loved and no longer am: I know not for what reason the Vineyard has lost its season.'

Her husband, who heard this, replied: 'Vineyard thou wast and Vineyard thou art, loved thou wast and no longer art: the Vineyard has lost its season for the lion's claw.' The king, who understood what he meant, answered: 'I entered the Vineyard, I touched the leaves, but I swear by my crown that I have not tasted the fruit.' Then the steward understood that his wife was innocent, and the two made peace and always after lived happy and contented.[22]

Both of these tales derive ultimately from the *Sindibad* group; so does another version of the story in *El Conde Lucanor*, one which includes the monotonous feast as well as the lion's track of The King and his Vizier's Wife. The *Decamerone* (I, 5) retains the 'all women are the same' theme, but not the lion. What is noteworthy is that the tale is in eastern versions of *The Seven Wise Masters* (in Arabic *The Seven Wazirs*) but not to be found in western collections stemming, like them, from the *Book of Sindibad*. The only surviving *Seven Wazirs*, in fact, is the one incorporated into the *Nights*. There is evidence that the *Nights* was known in Arabian Spain as early as the thirteenth century and could thus have been used by the Infante Don Juan Manuel in *El Conde Lucanor*, since Don Juan, who could read Arabic, drew on Arab *exempla*. The Italian variants imply folk diffusion of the Levantine form in Venice and Florence, both points of contact for trade with the East.

12   THE LADY AND HER TWO LOVERS

There was once a man, who was swordbearer to one of the kings, and he loved a certain woman of the common people. One day, he sent his page to her with a message, as of wont between them, and the latter sat down with her and toyed with her. She inclined to him and pressed him to her bosom, whereupon he sought to lie with her and she consented unto him; but, as they were thus, the swordbearer knocked at the door. So she clapped the young man into an underground chamber there and opened the door to his master, who came in, sword in hand, and sat down on her bed. Then she came to him and sported and toyed with him, kissing him and pressing him to her bosom, and he took her and lay with her.

Presently, her husband knocked at the door and he said to her, 'Who is that?' 'My husband,' replied she. Quoth he, 'How shall I do?' And she, 'Draw thy sword and stand in the vestibule and rail at me and revile me; and when my husband comes in to thee, do thou go forth and go thy ways.' He did as she bade him, and when the husband entered, he saw the king's swordbearer standing with his drawn sword in his hand, reviling and threatening his wife; but, when the other saw him, he was ashamed and sheathing his sword, went forth the house. Quoth the man to his wife, 'What means this?' And she answered, saying, 'O man, how blessed is the hour of thy coming! Thou hast saved a true-believer from death; and it was on this wise. I was on the housetop, spinning, when there came up to me a youth, panting and distracted for fear of death, fleeing from yonder man, who followed hard upon him with his drawn sword. The young man fell down before me, and kissed my hands and feet, saying, "O my lady, save me from him who would kill me without just cause!" So I hid him in the underground chamber there and presently in came yonder man to me with his naked sword in his hand, demanding the youth. But I denied him to him, whereupon he fell to reviling and threatening me as thou sawest. And praised be God who sent thee to me, for I was at my wits' end and had none to deliver me!'

'Well hast thou done, O woman!' answered the husband. 'Thy reward is with God and may He abundantly requite thee!' Then he went to the trapdoor and called to the page, saying, 'Come forth and fear not; no harm shall befall thee.' So he came out, trembling for fear, and the husband condoled with him on what had befallen him, saying, 'Be of good cheer: none shall hurt thee'; whilst the page called down blessings on his head. Then they both went forth, nor was either aware of that which the woman had contrived.[23]

In the genealogy of stories, this classic is known as The Sword or *De Gladio* from its first written appearance in the West as Exemplum XI of the *Disciplina Clericalis*. That the tale is contained in the anti-women *Book of Sindibad* scarcely needs stating. It is also in the *Hitopadesa*, and in the *Sukasaptati* and parrot-stories group. Interestingly, although found in all eastern versions of the *Sindibad* cycle, like 'The King and his Vizier's Wife', The Sword is not found in western ones. It was the *Disciplina* which brought it to the *Decamerone*, VII, 6 and thus into the mainstream. The *fabliau* 'Le Lai de l'Épervier' is a version close to Arab tradition which was also very popular, and there are many folk examples, European as well as eastern ones; in the latter the lady is sometimes the wife of a simpleton such as the Hoja Nasr al-Din.

Basset cites '*L'Amant et le Mari Trompés*', a Turkish variant which is fairly representative of western folktales too:

A man loved the wife of the Hoja. He had a young page, beardless and pretty. One day he said to him, 'Go to her and tell her to prepare for my visit.' The page went. She could not keep from embracing him and clasping him to her breast, so well that she accomplished what she wished. While the page was with her, his master noticed that he was late; he went to look for him and entered the Hoja's house. When the wife saw this, she hid the page under the bed and received the master as usual. At this moment the Hoja knocked on the door. She said to her lover, 'Get up, go out into the court with a drawn sword.' He did. When the Hoja entered he asked his wife, 'What was that man doing here?' 'My husband,' she replied, 'that is our neighbour; his servant escaped and took refuge with us. His master rushed after him to kill him, but I hid him under the bed.' The Hoja said to the youth, 'Come out, my child, and pray to God for this honourable lady who has done you such a great service, that God will recompense her.'[24]

13 THE TALE OF THE SAGE AND HIS THREE SONS

There was once a Sage of the sages, who had three sons and sons' sons and when they waxed many and their seed multiplied, there befell dissension between them. So he assembled them and said to them, 'Be ye single-handed against all others and despise not one another lest the folk despise you, and know that your case is the case of the man and the rope which he cut easily, when it was single; then he doubled it and could not cut it: on this wise is division and union. And beware lest ye seek help of others against your own selves or ye will fall into perdition, for by what means soever ye win your wish at his hand, his word will rank higher than your word. Now I have money which I will presently bury in a certain place, that it may be a store for you against the time of your need.' Then they left him and dispersed and one of the sons fell to spying upon his sire, so that he saw him hide the hoard outside the city. When he had made an end of burying it, the Sage returned to his house; and as soon as the morning morrowed, his son repaired to the place where he had seen his father bury the treasure and dug and took all the wealth he found and fared forth. When the old man felt that his death drew nigh, he called his sons to him and acquainted them with the place where he had hidden his hoard. As soon as he was dead, they went and dug up the treasure and came upon much wealth, for that the money, which the first son had taken singly and by stealth, was on the surface and he knew not that under it were other monies. So they carried it off and divided it and the first son claimed his share with the rest and added it to that which he had before taken, behind the backs of his father and his brethren. Then he married his cousin, the daughter of his father's brother and was blessed through her with a male-child, who was the goodliest of the folk of his time. When the boy grew up, his father feared for him poverty and decline of case, so he said to him, 'Dear my son, know that during my green days I wronged my brothers in the matter of our father's good, and I see thee in weal; but, an thou come to want, ask not one of them nor any other than they, for I have laid up for thee in yonder chamber a treasure; but do not thou open it until thou come to lack thy daily bread.' Then the man died, and his money, which was a great matter, fell to his son. The young man had not patience to wait till he had made an end of that which was with him, but rose and opened the chamber, and behold, it was empty and its walls were whitened, and in its midst was a rope hanging down as for a bucket and ten bricks, one upon other, and a scroll, wherein was written, 'There is no help against death; so hang thyself and beg not of any, but kick away the bricks with thy toes, that there may be no escape for thy life, and thou shalt be at rest from the exultation of enemies and enviers and the bitterness of beggary.' Now when the youth saw this, he marvelled at that which his father had done and said, 'This is an ill treasure.' Then he went forth and fell to eating and drinking with the folk, till naught was left him and he passed two days without tasting food, at the end of which time he took a handkerchief and selling it for two dirhams, bought bread and milk with the price and left it on the shelf and went out. Whilst he was gone, a dog came and seized the bread and polluted the milk, and when the young man returned and saw this, he beat his face, and fared forth distraught. Presently, he met a friend, to whom he discovered his case, and the other said to him, 'Art thou not ashamed to talk thus? How hast thou wasted all this wealth and now comest telling lies and saying, The dog hath mounted on the shelf, and talking such nonsense?' And he reviled him. So the youth returned to his house, and verily the world had waxed black in his eyes and he cried, 'My sire said sooth.' Then he opened the chamber door and piling up the bricks under his feet, put the rope about his neck and kicked away the bricks and swung himself off; whereupon the rope gave way with him and he fell to the ground and the ceiling clave asunder and there poured down on him a world of wealth. So he knew that his sire meant to chasten him by means of this and he invoked Allah's mercy on him. Then he got him again that which he had sold of lands and houses and what not else and became once more in good case; his friends also returned to him and he entertained them for some time. Then said he to them one day 'There was with us bread and the locusts ate it; so we set in its place a stone, one cubit long and the like broad, and the locusts came and nibbled away the stone, because of the smell of the bread.' Quoth one of his friends (and it was he who had given him the lie concerning the dog and the bread and milk), 'Marvel not at this, for rats and mice do more than that.' Thereupon he said, 'Get ye home! In the days of my poverty I was a liar when I told you of the dogs jumping upon the shelf and eating the bread and defiling the milk; and today, because I am rich again, I say sooth when I tell you that locusts devoured a stone one cubit long and one cubit broad.' They were abashed by his speech and departed from him; and the youth's good prospered and his case was amended. [25]

Francis James Child's definitive collection of traditional ballads in English, *The English and Scottish Popular Ballads* (Boston, 1884–98), includes this narrative type which in folklore studies is often called Treasure from the Ceiling. As No. 267, 'The Heir of Linne', the verse versions printed by Child are similar only in general to the story in the *Nights*: having squandered his fortune and estate, the 'unthrifty' heir at last remembers his father's message and so finds new treasure and buys back his estate and status. But Child also includes an inferior sentimental broadside which is much closer to our tale. This is the eighteenth-century 'The Drunkard's Legacy'. Clouston had a chapbook redaction of the same in prose, also of the eighteenth century, from which he quoted 'the elaborate title' that serves as a summary: 'The Drunkard's Legacy. In four parts. Giving an account, First, of a Gentleman having a wild Son, and foreseeing he would come to poverty, had a cottage built with one door to it, always kept fast. His father, on his dying bed, charged him not to open it 'till he was poor and slighted, which the young man promised he would perform. Secondly, of this young man's pawning his estate to a Vintner, who, when poor, kicked him out of doors. Thinking it time to see his Legacy, he broke open the door, when, instead of money, he found a Gibbet and Halter, which he put round his Neck, and jumping off the Stool, the Gibbet broke, and a Thousand Pounds came down upon his head, which lay in the Ceiling. Thirdly, of his redeeming the Estate, and fooling the Vintner out of Two Hundred Pounds, who, for being jeered by his neighbours, cut his own throat. And Lastly, of the young man's Reformation.'[26]

'The Drunkard's Legacy' was widely popular, as were analogues in France, Germany, Italy and Greece. Child mentions references to sixteenth-century English storybooks and French fabulists. Ultimately, this tale too is to be traced to the *Sindibad* cycle.

14 THE LADY AND HER FIVE SUITORS

A certain woman of the daughters of the merchants was married to a man who was a great traveller. It chanced once that he set out for a far country and was absent so long that his wife, for pure weariness, fell in love with a handsome young man of the sons of the merchants, who returned her passion, and they loved each other with an exceeding love. One day, the youth fell out with another man, who lodged a complaint against him with the chief of the police, and he cast him into prison. When the news came to his mistress, she well-nigh lost her wits and rising, donned her richest clothes and repaired to the house of the chief of the police, whom she saluted and presented with a petition to the effect that the prisoner was her brother, who had been unjustly accused and condemned on false witness, and that she had none other to come in to her nor to provide for her support and beseeching him of his grace to release him.

When the magistrate had read the petition, he cast his eyes on her and fell in love with her; so he said to her, 'Go into the house, till I bring him before me; then will I send for thee and thou shalt take him.' 'O my lord,' answered she, 'I have none save God the Most High. Indeed, I am a stranger and may not enter any one's house.' Quoth the chief of the police, 'I will not let him go, except thou enter my house and I take my will of thee.' 'If it must be so,' rejoined she, 'thou must come to my house and sit and sleep and rest the whole day there.' 'And where is thy house?' asked he. 'In such a place,' answered she and appointed him for such a time.

Then she went out from him, leaving his heart taken with love of her, and repaired to the Cadi of the city, to whom said she, 'O my lord the Cadi, look into my case, and thy reward be with God the Most High!' Quoth he, 'Who hath wronged thee?' And she answered, saying, 'O my lord, I have a brother and I have none but him and it is on his account that I come to thee; for that the chief of the police hath imprisoned him for a wrong-doer, on the evidence of false witnesses, and I beseech thee to intercede for him with the chief of the police.' When the Cadi looked on her, he fell in love with her and said to her, 'Enter the house and rest awhile with my women, whilst I send to the chief of the police to release thy brother. If I knew the forfeit that is upon him, I would pay it out of my own monies, so I may have my desire of thee, for thou pleasest me with thy sweet speech.' Quoth she, 'If thou, O my lord, do thus, we must not blame others.' But the Cadi answered, saying, 'An thou wilt not come in, go thy ways.' Then said she, 'If thou wilt have it so, O my lord, it will be safer and better in my house than in thine, for here are slave-girls and servants and goers-in and comers-out, and indeed I am a woman who knows nought of this fashion; but necessity compels.' 'And where is thy house?' asked the Cadi. 'In such a place,' answered she and appointed him for the same time as the chief of the police.

Then she went to the Vizier, to whom she preferred her petition for the release of her pretended brother from prison: but he also required her of herself, saying, 'Suffer me to have my desire of thee and I will set thy brother free.' Quoth she, 'If thou wilt have it so, be it in my house, for there it will be safer both for me and for thee. It is not far distant and thou knowest that which behoveth us women of cleanliness and elegance.' 'Where is thy house?' asked he. 'In such a place,' answered she and appointed him for the same time as the two others.

Then she went out from him to the King of the city and told him her story and sought of him her brother's release. 'Who imprisoned him?' asked he; and she replied, 'The chief of the police.' When the King heard her speech, it transfixed his heart with the arrows of love and he bade her enter the palace with him, that he might send to the Cadi and release her brother. 'O King,' answered she, 'this thing is easy to thee, whether I will or not; and if the King will indeed have this of me, it is of my good fortune; but, if he will come to my house, he will do me the more honour, even as saith the poet: Friends, have ye seen or heard o' the visit of a wight Whose virtues are indeed illustrious in my sight?'

Quoth the King, 'We will not cross thee in this.' So she told him where her house was and appointed him for the same time as the three others.

Then she left him and betaking herself to a carpenter, said to him, 'I would have thee make me a cabinet with four compartments, one above another, each with its door to lock up. Let me know thy hire and I will give it thee.' 'My hire will be four dinars,' replied the man; 'but, O noble lady, if thou wilt vouchsafe me thy favours, I will ask nothing else of thee.' 'If thou wilt have it so,' rejoined she, 'then make the cabinet with five compartments, each to lock up.' 'It is well,' said he; 'sit down, O my lady, and I will make it for thee forthright, and after I will come to thee at my leisure.' So she sat down whilst he fell to work on the cabinet, and when he had made an end of it, she carried it home and set it up in the sitting-chamber. Then she took four gowns and carried them to the dyer, who dyed them each of a different colour; after which she busied herself in making ready meat and drink and fruits and flowers and perfumes.

When it was the appointed time, she donned her costliest apparel and scented and adorned herself, then spread the room with various kinds of rich carpets and sat down to await who should come. The Cadi was the first to appear, and when she saw him, she rose and kissed the earth before him, then made him sit down by her on the couch and fell to jesting and toying with him. By and by, he would have her do his desire, but she said, 'O my Lord, put off thy clothes and turban and don this yellow cassock and this kerchief, whilst I bring thee meat and drink; and after thou shalt do thy desire.' So saying, she took his clothes and turban and clad him in the yellow cassock and the kerchief; but hardly had she done this, when there came a knocking at the door. Quoth he, 'Who is that at the door?' And she answered, 'My husband.' 'What is to be done?' said the Cadi; 'and where shall I go?' 'Fear nothing,' replied she; 'I will hide thee in this cabinet.' Quoth he, 'Do as seemeth good to thee.' So she took him by the hand and pushing him into the lowest compartment, locked the door on him.

Then she went to the door, where she found the chief of the police; so she kissed the earth before him and brought him into the saloon, where she made him sit down and said to him, 'O my lord, this is thy house and I am thy handmaid, and thou shalt pass all this day with me; wherefore do thou doff thy clothes and don this red gown, for it is a sleeping gown.' So she took away his clothes and made him don the red gown and set on his head an old patched rag she had by her; after which she sat down by him on the couch and they sported awhile, till he put out his hand to her; but she said to him, 'O lord, this day is thine, all of it, and none shall share in it with thee; but first, of thy favour and grace, write me an order for my brother's release, that my heart may be at ease.' 'I hear and obey,' answered he; 'on my head and eyes be it,' and wrote a letter to his treasurer, to the following effect: 'As soon as this letter reaches thee, do thou, without delay and without fail, set such an one free, neither answer the bearer a word.' Then he sealed it and she took it from him, after which she began to toy with him

235

on the couch, when, behold, some one knocked at the door. Quoth he, 'Who is that?' 'My husband,' answered she. 'What shall I do?' asked he, and she said, 'Enter this cabinet, till I send him away and return to thee.' So she clapped him into the second compartment and locked the door on him; and all this time the Cadi heard what they said and did.

Then she went to the door and opened it, whereupon the Vizier entered. She kissed the earth before him and received him with all worship, saying, 'O my lord, thou honourest us by thy coming to our house; may God never deprive us of the light of thy countenance!' Then she seated him on the couch and said to him, 'O my lord, these thy clothes and turban are the apparel of the vizierate; so leave them to their own time and don this light gown, which is better fitted for carousing and making merry and sleep.' So he put off his clothes and turban and she dressed him in a blue cassock and a tall red cap, after which she began to toy with him and he with her, and he would have done his desire of her; but she put him off, saying, 'O my lord, this shall not escape us.' Presently there came a knocking at the door, and the Vizier said to her, 'Who is that?' 'My husband,' answered she. Quoth he, 'What is to be done?' 'Fear nothing,' said she, 'but enter this cabinet, till I get rid of him and come back to thee.' So she put him in the third compartment and locked the door on him, after which she went out and opened the door and in came the King.

When she saw him, she kissed the earth before him, and taking him by the hand, led him into the saloon and seated him on the couch at the upper end. Then said she to him, 'Verily, O King, thou dost us honour, and if we brought thee the whole world and all that therein is as a gift, it would not equal a single one of thy steps towards us; but give me leave to speak one word.' 'Say what thou wilt' answered he, and she said,' 'O my lord, take thine ease and put off thy clothes and turban.' So he put off his clothes, which were worth a thousand dinars, and she clad him in a patched gown, not worth ten dirhems, and fell to talking and jesting with him, whilst the folk in the cabinet heard all that passed, but dared not say a word. Presently, the King put his hand to her neck and sought to do his desire of her; but she said, 'This thing shall not escape us; but, first, I had promised myself to entertain thee in this sitting-chamber, and I have that which shall content thee.' At that moment, some one knocked at the door and he said to her, 'Who is that?' 'My husband,' answered she, and he, 'Make him go away of his own accord, or I will go forth to him and send him away perforce.' 'Nay, O my lord,' replied she; 'have patience till I send him away by my skilful contrivance.' 'And how shall I do?' asked the King; whereupon she took him by the hand and making him enter the fourth compartment of the cabinet, locked it upon him.

Then she went out and opened the door, when the carpenter entered and saluted her. Quoth she, 'What manner of thing is this cabinet thou hast made me?' 'What ails it, O my lady?' asked he, and she said, 'The top compartment is too strait.' 'Not so,' answered he; and she, 'Go in thyself and see; it is not wide enough for thee.' Quoth he, 'It is wide enough for four,' and entered the fifth compartment, whereupon she locked the door on him. Then she took the letter of the chief of the police and carried it to the treasurer, who kissed it and delivered her lover to her. She told him all that had passed and he said, 'And how shall we do now?' Quoth she, 'We will remove hence to another city, for there is no tarrying for us here after this.' So they packed up their goods and loading them on camels, set out forthright for another city.

Meanwhile, the five abode in the cabinet three whole days, without eating or drinking, until at last the carpenter could retain his water no longer; so he made water on the King's head, and the King made water on the Vizier's head, and the Vizier on the Chief of the Police, who did the like with the Cadi; whereupon the latter cried out and said, 'What filth is this? Doth not this strait that we are in suffice us, but you must make water upon us?' The Chief of the Police recognized the Cadi's voice and answered, saying, 'God increase thy reward, O Cadi!' And when the Cadi heard him, he knew him for the Chief of the Police. Then the latter lifted up his voice and said, 'What means this nastiness?' and the Vizier answered, saying, 'God increase thy reward, O Chief of the Police!' whereupon he knew him to be the Vizier. Then the Vizier lifted up his voice and said, 'What means this nastiness?' But when the King heard his Vizier's voice, he held his peace and concealed his affair. Then said the Vizier, 'May God curse the woman for her dealing with us! She hath brought hither all the chiefs of the state, except the King.' Quoth the King, 'Hold thy peace, for I was the first to fall into the toils of this lewd baggage,' 'And I,' cried the carpenter, 'what have I done? I made her a cabinet for four dinars, and when I came to seek my hire, she tricked me into entering this compartment and locked the door on me.' And they fell to talking with one another, to divert the King and do away his chagrin.

Presently the neighbours came up to the house and seeing it deserted, said to one another, 'But yesterday our neighbour the wife of such an one was in it; but now there is no sound to be heard therein nor soul to be seen. Let us break open the doors and see how the case stands, lest it come to the ears of the King or the Chief of the Police and we be cast into prison and regret that we did not this thing before.' So they broke open the doors and entered the saloon, where they saw the cabinet and heard the men within groaning for hunger and thirst. Then said one of them, 'Is there a genie in the cabinet?' 'Let us heap faggots about it,' quoth another, 'and burn it with fire.' When the Cadi heard this, he cried out at them, saying, 'Do it not!' And they said to one another, 'Verily, the Jinn make believe to be mortals and speak with men's voices.' Thereupon the Cadi repeated some verses of the sublime Koran and said to the neighbours, 'Draw near to the cabinet.' So they drew near, and he said, 'I am so and so the Cadi, and ye are such an one and such an one, and we are here a company.' Quoth the neighbours, 'And how came ye here?' And he told them the whole case from beginning to end.

Then they fetched a carpenter, who opened the five doors and let out the Cadi and the Vizier and the Chief of the Police and the King and the Carpenter; and when they saw how they were accoutred, each fell a-laughing at the others. Now she had taken away all their clothes; so each of them sent to his people for fresh clothes and put them on and went out, covering himself therewith from the sight of the folk.[27]

This story appears twice in the *Nights*. The other version involves four men pursuing a virtuous wife who, with her husband, works out a way to be rid of them. She invites them *seriatim* to the house. Each brings a gift and is then stripped and dressed in a coloured shift. At this point the next arrival interrupts, and the preceding gallant is locked in a room. The last to arrive is the husband. The wife tells him that she met four clowns at the bazaar, and the victims, one by one, have to caper and tell a story to entertain the husband, and are then dismissed.[28]

Like so many of our *contes*, this tale-type has a rich genealogy. It appears in the Sanskrit *Kathasaritsagara* or *Ocean of the Streams of Story* compiled by Somadeva, which is a huge collection of tales current at about A.D. 1000 but – a familiar refrain by now – containing narratives much, much older. A bas-relief of the third century B.C. at Barhut suggests that this story is depicted there, which reinforces other arguments for its Buddhist origin. Variants are found in the Persian *Tuti-Nameh*, *Bahar-i-Danish* and *The 1001 Days*, in the Arabian text of the *Book of Sindibad* called the *Seven Wazirs*, as well as in the Turkish *History of the Forty Vezirs*, the French *fabliau* of *Constant du Hamel*, the Latin *Gesta Romanorum*, etc. The best English version, thought to be based on 'De Castitate' in the *Gesta* (which was probably written in England), is *The Wright's Chaste Wife* by Adam of Cobsam, written *c.* 1462.

In this, the wright's wife brings no dowry except a garland of roses that will keep its colour as long as she is true. The wright builds a room in a tower so that no one can corrupt her. It has a trapdoor which leads to a pit. He is sent for by a lord to build a hall and will thus be absent for two or three months. The lord asks him about the garland, which the wright explains. Secretly the lord goes to make trial of the wife. He declares his love and offers her forty marks. She takes the money and sends him to the secret chamber where he falls into the pit. Despite his pleas, she will not let him out until her husband has seen him, and in order to get food, he has to spin flax. The lord's steward asks the wright where the lord has gone and notices the garland. He too decides to try out the wife and meets the same fate at the cost of twenty marks. The proctor of the parish church next inquires, and the same thing happens to him (twenty marks). When the wright returns, the wife says they are three workmen who have come to help them. She will not let them out until the lord's lady comes and hears the story. The lady laughs, and takes her husband and the others off, after giving the money collected from the three to the wife.

A comparison with the earlier story in the *Gesta Romanorum* is enlightening as a demonstration of the use of such stories as exempla in sermons. Here the carpenter is given a shirt instead of a garland; the shirt will never need washing unless he or his wife is unfaithful. The suitors are three knights who are kept on bread and water but not made to work, and the lord's lady is not introduced. But the morality is explained in full detail: the wife is holy Mother Church, the carpenter the good Christian, the shirt the Faith, the knights pride of life, lust of the eyes, and lust of the flesh. 'These you must shut up in the chamber of penance till you get an eternal reward . . . Let us therefore pray God,' etc.[29]

The *Gesta* example and *The Wright's Chaste Wife* hang on the chastity-token, which of course does not appear in either of the texts in the *Nights*, and which distinguishes a separate division of this tale-type, the other being known by the incident common to the type as a whole, that of the entrapped suitors. Both forms in fact are included in the *Kathasaritsagara*. For the motif of the chastity-token, there is the story of Devasmita, in which the god Siva gives to her and her husband two red lotuses when the husband, a merchant, has to go to another country on business. There, four young merchants, hearing the story of the lotus, resolve to corrupt Devasmita. They go to the city where she lives and bribe a female ascetic, who uses the device of the weeping bitch to persuade her that she is over-chaste. But Devasmita sees through this and arranges to have each man drugged and branded when, in turn, they visit her. She then goes to join her husband and, because of the brands, is able to claim the four men as her escaped slaves. The truth then comes out, a ransom is paid for the merchants, and the husband and wife return home in great honour.

The source in the *Kathasaritsagara* of the narrative without the chastity-token is the account of the virtuous wife Upakosa. In this, the three suitors are stripped, anointed with lamp-black and locked in a basket. The fourth appointment is with a banker who holds money belonging to Upakosa's husband but has said he will deny it unless she yields to him. He now promises Upakosa that he will deliver the money to her after the visit. He is stripped in his turn and, since dawn is breaking, put out in the street. Upakosa goes immediately to the king and claims against the banker for her money. When he denies having it, she says that her household gods are in the basket and will bear witness for her. Rather than be exposed, the three testify from within the basket, and the banker acknowledges the debt. The king asks to see the household gods, the culprits are revealed and ridiculed, and the whole story is told.

While the Persian *Tuti-Nameh* perpetuated the chastity-token, the Arabian *Seven Wazirs* handed on the entrapped-suitors motif by itself, which expanded into the two versions in the *Nights*. The compartmented cabinet was already in the *Seven Wazirs*; so was the fact that the lady acts to rescue a lover from prison, not to protect a husband's rights. The scatological element in the cabinet incident may perhaps survive in current folk humour such as the American anecdote 'Senator Banks', about the initiation rites of men's clubs.[30] The chastity-token has of course a separate history in other stories. It is most popular in its form of a shirt or mantle, as in the English ballad 'The Boy and the Mantle', the *fabliau Cort Mantel,* and in Norse, German, Irish and other analogues.[31]

It is in character that the *Nights*, representative of Arabian folklore and thus of the diverse ways of life assimilated by the Arabs – different in details of material culture and in views of social classes, of shame, humour, etc. – should develop two striking variants from one popular story.

For a modern version we turn again to ballads. Child regards 'The Friar in the Well' as derivative of the entrapped suitors type, saying that the story:

> is not beyond the 'imaginary forces' of any Western people, but an open well inside of an English house is at least of unusual occurrence, and if we find something of the kind . . . in an Eastern tale of similar character, a borrowing seems more plausible than an invention. There is a considerable class of tales, mostly Oriental, in which a chaste wife discomfits two or three would-be seducers . . . In the Persian *Tuti Nama* . . . the wife lays a bed over a dry well, her suitors are invited to sit on it, and they fall in; and here, it is not unreasonable to suppose, we may have the remote source of the trick in our ballad.[32]

THE FRIAR IN THE WELL

As I lay musing all alone, fa, la, la, la, la
A pretty jest I thought upon, fa, la, la, la, la
Then listen a while, and I will you tell
Of a friar that loved a bonny lass well.
Fa, la, la, la, la, fa, la, la, lang-tre-down-dilly.

He came to the maid when she went to bed,
Desiring to have her maidenhead,
But she denied his desire,
And told him that she feared hell-fire.

'Tush,' quoth the friar, 'thou needst not doubt
If thou wert in hell I could sing thee out.'
'Then,' quoth the maid, 'thou shalt have thy request.'
The friar was glad as a fox in his nest.

'But one thing,' quoth she, 'I do desire,
Before you have what you require,
Before that you shall do the thing,
An angel of money thou shalt me bring.'

'Tush,' quoth the friar, 'we shall agree,
No money shall part my love and me.
Before that I will see thee lack,
I'll pawn the grey gown from my back.'

The maid bethought her of a wile
How she the friar might beguile.
While he was gone, the truth to tell,
She hung a cloth before the well.

The friar came, as his cogenant was,
With money to his bonny lass,
'Good morrow, fair maid!' 'Good morrow!' quoth she.
'Here is the money I promised thee.'

She thanked the man, and she took his money.
'Now let us go to it,' quoth he, 'sweet honey.'
'O stay,' quoth she, 'some respite make,
My father comes, he will me take.'

'Alas!' quoth the friar, 'where shall I run,
To hide me till that he be gone?'
'Behind the cloth run thou,' quoth she,
'And there my father cannot thee see.'

Behind the cloth the friar crept,
And into the well on the sudden he lept.
'Alas,' quoth he, 'I am in the well!'
'No matter,' quoth she, 'if thou wert in hell.

Thou sayst thou couldst sing me out of hell,
Now prithee sing thyself out of the well.'
The friar sung with a pitiful sound,
'Oh help me out, or I shall be drowned!'

Quoth he, 'For sweet Saint Francis sake
On his disciple some pity take.'
Quoth she, 'Saint Francis never taught
His scholars to tempt young maids to naught.'

The friar did entreat her still
That she should help him out of the well.
She heard him make such piteous moan
She helped him out and bid him be gone.

Quoth he, 'Shall I have my money again,
Which thou from me hast beforehand ta'en?'
'Good sir,' said she, 'there's no such matter.
I'll make you pay for fouling my water.'

The friar went all along the street,
Dripping wet like a new-washed sheep.
Both old and young commended the maid
That such a witty prank had played.

Beth Gelert or
The Grave of the Greyhound[1]

The spearman heard the bugle sound,
   And cheerly smil'd the morn,
And many a brach, and many a hound Obey'd
   Llewelyn's horn.

'Oh where does faithful Gelert roam,
   The flower of all his race;
So true, so brave, a lamb at home,
   A lion in the chase?'

In sooth he was a peerless hound,
   The gift of royal John,
But, now no Gelert could be found,
   And all the chase rode on.

Unpleas'd Llewelyn homeward hied,
   When near the portal-seat,
His traunt Gelert he espied
   Bounding his Lord to greet.

But, when he gain'd his castle-door
   Aghast the chieftain stood;
The hound all o'er was smear'd with gore,
   His lips, his fangs, ran blood.

Onwards, in haste, Llewelyn pass'd,
   And on went Gelert too;
And still, where'er his eyes he cast,
   Fresh blood-gouts shock'd his view.

O'erturn'd his infant's bed he found,
   With blood-stain'd covert rent;
And all around the walls the ground
   With recent blood besprent.

He call'd his child – no voice replied –
   He search'd with terror wild;
Blood, blood he found on every side,
   But nowhere found his child.

'Hell-bound! my child's by thee devour'd,'
   The frantic father cried;
And to the hilt his vengeful sword
   He plung'd in Gelert's side.

His suppliant looks, as prone he fell,
   No pity could impart;
But still his Gelert's dying yell
   Pass'd heavy o'er his heart.

Arous'd by Gelert's dying yell,
   Some slumb'rer waken'd nigh: –
What words the parent's joy could tell
   To hear his infant's cry!

Conceal'd beneath a tumbled heap
   His hurried search had missed,
All glowing from his rosy sleep,
   The cherub boy he kiss'd.

Nor scath had he, nor harm, nor dread,
   But, the same couch beneath,
Lay a gaunt wolf, all torn and dead,
   Tremendous still in death.

Ah, what was then Llewelyn's pain!
   For now the truth was clear;
His gallant hound the wolf had slain,
   To save Llewelyn's heir.

Vain, vain was all Llewelyn's woe:
   'Best of thy kind, adieu!
The frantic blow, which laid thee low,
   This heart shall ever rue.'

And now a gallant tomb they raise,
   With costly sculture deck'd;
And marbles storied with his praise
   Poor Gelert's bones protect.

There never could the spearman pass,
   Or forester, unmoved;
There, oft the tear-besprinkled grass
   Llewelyn's sorrow proved.

And, till great Snowdon's rocks grow old
   And cease the storm to brave,
The consecrated spot shall hold
   The name of 'Gelert's grave'.[2]

Hasty Action

When the time of birth arrived the brahman's wife brought forth a son bearing the auspicious marks. Then on the tenth day after the birth when he had performed the rite (of name giving) the brahman's wife left the boy in his father's care and went to a near-by river to purify herself and to wash her soiled garments. But the brahman kept watch over the boy, since he was so poor that he could not afford a servant and did his own work. Now as it was a day of the moon's change, the chief queen sent from the king's palace a maid-servant to bring a reader of sacred texts, and she called upon the brahman. When the brahman received the summons he thought: 'If I do not go at once, some one else will get the sacrifice. There is no one to watch the boy. What shall I do?' Under these circumstances he left behind a mongoose that he had raised just like a son, keeping him in his house in the room where the sacred fire was kept and feeding him on kernels of corn and the like, and so the brahman departed. But the mongoose soon saw a cobra coming out of a hole in the ground and going up near the child. And as soon as he saw it his eyes flamed with anger, and his lips, teeth, and paws quivered, and he sprang up at once and fell upon the serpent and tore it to pieces. And when he saw the brahman coming back, he ran forth with great joy to show him (what he had done), with his mouth and paws still stained with blood. Now when that hasty brahman saw the mongoose with his muzzle smeared with blood, he thought: 'What! has he eaten my boy?' and he slew him with his stick. Thereupon, having killed him, as soon as the brahman entered the house, he saw the child lying asleep and unhurt just as he was, and the cobra cut to pieces near him. And he beat his breast, crying out: 'Ah, woe is me, fool that I am! What a wicked thing is this that I have done!'[3]

VII

THE ARABIAN ASTROLOGER

from Washington Irving
The Alhambra, 1832

Washington Irving was American's first and most travelled 'man of letters', who, wherever he went, collected fragments of legends to use in his writings. His interest in all places – from Sleepy Hollow, N.Y., to Bracebridge Hall in England to Granada in Spain – was antiquarian and romantic, especially in Spain where he was fascinated by the Moorish past. He actually lodged in the Alhambra (by permission of its governor) from May to July 1829. In notes kept at the time he writes of listening to storytellers such as Mateo Ximenes who remembered tales told by his grandfather, born a hundred years before, of an Arabic book of magic, of Moorish legacies, buried treasure and an enchanted man who guarded it.

Irving also acknowledged his debt to the *Nafh al-Tib* of al-Maqqari when this huge compilation of historical and literary information written in the early seventeenth century became available in 1840 in English translation. The *Nafh al-Tib* is the only surviving Arab source on Muslim Spain, incorporating letters, poems and quotations from works now lost. Discussing 'The Arabian Astrologer', Irving writes, 'Al Maqqari in his *History of the Mohammadan Dynasties in Spain* cites from another Arab writer an account of a talismanic effigy somewhat similar.' He then gives a résumé of this, to the effect that there formerly stood a square tower in Cadiz surmounted by a statue of a man with a staff in his right hand, while his left pointed to the Straits of Gibraltar. The local Muslims thought it a talisman which exercised a spell over the seas. Under its guidance, swarms of pirates invaded the coast. At length a Muslim admiral, hearing that the statue was of pure gold, had it taken down. When it was broken to pieces, it proved to be only of gilded brass. From then on, however, the pirate raids stopped.

The main motifs in 'The Arabian Astrologer' are in any case recognizably eastern: the astrologer as magician, Egypt as the centre of occult wisdom, the bronze statues pointing to enemy inroads, the City of Irem, the subterranean paradise, the mysterious foreign princess as the cause of discord. We in the West would be conscious of these elements as Arabian even without Irving's notes, because they are also in *The Arabian Nights* as well as in earlier works such as the *Alexander Romance*. In both we hear of the statue of Cadiz, placed by Alexander where the Mediterranean met the Sea of Darkness. The City of Brass, too, lies in the far west near the Dark Sea. Wensinck refers to traditions connected with Alexander which 'speak of a brazen image and a brazen town as the signs of the limits of the West. The town is provided with cupolas and shining pinnacles; it is a place full of all sorts of precious things, but it is a place of death.'[1] We recall too Nectanebos' magic images when he is ruling in Egypt. *The Seven Sages of Rome* also tells of a talisman made by Virgil, a large figure holding a golden apple, surrounded by smaller figures, each for a Roman province. Each has a bell in its hand with which it signals to the central figure when a province rebels.[2] In the Solomon cycle, Solomon appears as a prototype magus of Egypt, who sleeps forever in an underground paradise.

An odd quirk to 'The Arabian Astrologer' is that Alexander Pushkin (1799–1837) recast its plot into Russian verse in 'The Tale of the Golden Cockerel', which led to its spurious circulation as a Russian folktale. Pushkin's version, apart from mentioning once that the astrologer has a Saracen cap, presents the story without a Moorish background. Tsar Dodon is king of an unspecified land. The statue of the horseman has become a golden cockerel (as was an earlier talisman in Irving's tale). The cockerel kills Dodon when he refuses to give the princess to the astrologer. The king, the astrologer, the talisman, the broken promise, and the disappearance of the princess are the same basic story. But modern Soviet critics, opposing the suggestion that Russian writings may derive from foreign sources, have accused the folklorists who documented the connection between Pushkin and Irving of subservience to the West. In any case, westerners today are more familiar with Pushkin than with Irving, especially as regards this work, because in 1910, using Pushkin's story and Russian folk-tunes, Rimsky-Korsakov composed the opera *Le Coq d'Or*. It is this Russian form of the tale that is now best known. But to Irving goes the credit for putting together an amalgam of Arabian folktale motifs in a traditional eastern story-type, that of the enchanter enchanted. If there is no specific Levantine analogue for the story as a whole, there are analogues for it part by part.

By a double irony, Irving winds up representing eastern culture, and *Le Coq d'Or*, western.

The Arabian Astrologer

In old times, many hundreds of years ago, there was a Moorish king named Aben Habuz, who reigned over the kingdom of Granada. He was a retired conqueror; now that he was grown old he desired nothing more than to live at peace and to enjoy in quiet the possessions he had seized from his neighbours.

It so happened, however, that he had young rivals to deal with – princes who had scores to settle with him, and rebellious subjects within his own kingdom. To make the matter worse, as Granada is surrounded by wild and craggy mountains which hide the approach of an enemy, the unfortunate Aben Habuz was kept in a constant state of alarm.

It was in vain that he built watch-towers and stationed guards. His alert foes would baffle every precaution and come breaking out of some unthought-of pass in the mountains – ravage his lands beneath his very nose, and then make off with prisoners and booty. Was ever a retired conqueror in a more uncomfortable predicament!

While he was harassed by these problems, an ancient Arabian physician arrived at his court. His grey beard descended to his girdle and he had every mark of extreme age, yet he had travelled almost the whole way from Egypt on foot. His fame had preceded him. His name was Ibrahim Ebn Abu Ayub; he was said to have lived ever since the days of Mahomet and to be the son of Abu Ayeb, the last of the companions of the prophet. As a child, he had followed the conquering army into Egypt, where he had remained many years studying the dark sciences, particularly magic, among the Egyptian priests. It was moreover said that he had found out the secret of prolonging life, by means of which he had arrived to the great age of upward of two centuries; though, as he did not discover the secret until well stricken in years, he could only perpetuate his grey hairs and wrinkles.

This wonderful old man was very honourably entertained by the king. He would have given him an apartment in his palace, but the astrologer preferred a cave in the side of the hill which rises above the city of Granada, being the same on which the Alhambra has since been built. He caused the cave to be enlarged so as to form a spacious and lofty hall with a circular hole at the top, through which, as through a well, he could see the heavens and behold the stars even at midday. The walls of this hall were covered with Egyptian hieroglyphics and with the figures of the stars in their signs. This hall he furnished with many implements, made under his direction by cunning workers of Granada, but the magic properties of which were known only to himself. In a little while the sage Ibrahim became the bosom counsellor of the king, to whom he applied for advice in every emergency. Aben Habuz was once inveighing against his neighbours and bewailing the vigilance he had to observe to guard against invasions. When he had finished the astrologer remained silent for a moment, and then replied, 'Know, O king, that when I was in Egypt I beheld a great marvel devised by a pagan priestess of old. On a mountain overlooking the great valley of the Nile was a figure of a ram and above it a figure of a cock, both of molten brass and turning on a pivot. Whenever the country was threatened with invasion, the ram would turn in the direction of the enemy and the cock would crow; upon this the people knew of the danger and could guard against it in time.'

'God is great!' exclaimed Aben Habuz. 'What a treasure would be such a ram to keep an eye on these mountains around me, and then such a cock to crow in time of danger! Allah Achbar! how securely I might sleep in my palace with such sentinels on the top!'

'Listen, O king,' continued the astrologer gravely. 'I was present and examined this talisman, and studied its secret, and can make one of like and even of greater virtues.'

'O wise son of Abu Ayub,' cried the king, 'better were such a talisman than all the watch-towers on the hills and sentinels on the borders. Give me such a safeguard and the riches of my treasury are at thy command.'

The astrologer immediately set to work, shutting himself up in his hall. He summoned to his assistance the spirits and demons of the Nile. By his command they transported to his presence a mummy from a chamber in the centre of one of the pyramids. It was the mummy of the priest who by magic art had built it.

The astrologer opened the outer cases of the mummy and unfolded its many wrappers. On the breast of the corpse was a book written in ancient letters. He seized it with a trembling hand, then returning the mummy to its case, ordered the demons to transport it again to its dark and silent chamber in the pyramid.

This book, say the traditions, was the book of knowledge given by God to Adam after his fall. It had been handed down from generation to generation to King Solomon the Wise, and by the aid of the wonderful secrets in magic and art revealed in it, he had built the temple of Jerusalem. How it had come into the possession of the builder of the pyramids, He only knows who knows all things.

Instructed by this volume and the genii which it put at his command, the astrologer soon erected a great tower upon the top of the palace of

Aben Habuz. It was built with stones brought from Egypt, taken, it is said, from one of the pyramids. In the upper part of the tower was a circular hall with windows looking towards every point of the compass, and before each window was a table on which was arranged, as on a chess-board, a mimic army of horse and foot, with the effigy of the king who ruled in that direction, all carved of wood. To each of these tables was attached a small lance, no bigger than a bodkin, on which were engraved certain mysteri-ous characters. This hall was kept constantly closed by a gate of brass with a great lock of steel, the key of which was in the possession of the king.

On the top of the tower was a bronze figure of a Moorish horseman, fixed on a pivot, with a shield on one arm and his lance elevated perpen-dicularly. The face of the horseman was towards the city, as if keeping guard over it, but if any foe were at hand, the figure would turn in that direction and would level the lance as if for action.

When this talisman was finished, Aben Habuz was all impatient to try its virtues. His desire was soon gratified. The news was brought early one morning that the face of the brazen horseman was turned towards the pass of Lope and his lance pointed directly there.

'Let the drums and trumpets sound to arms,' said Aben Habuz.

'O king,' said the astrologer, 'let not your city be disquieted nor your warriors called to arms; we need no force to deliver you from your enemies. Dismiss your attendants and let us proceed alone to the secret hall of the tower.'

The ancient Aben Habuz mounted the staircase of the tower, leaning on the arm of the still more ancient Ibrahim Ebn Abu Ayub. They unlocked the brazen door and entered. The window that looked towards the pass of Lope was open. 'In this direction,' said the astrologer, 'lies the danger. Approach, O king, and behold the mystery of the table.'

The king approached the seeming chess-board, on which were arranged the small wooden effigies, when lo! they were all in motion. The horses pranced and curveted, the warriors brandished their weapons, and there was a sound of drums and trumpets and a clanging of arms and neighing of steeds, but all no louder nor more distinct than the hum of a bee.

'Behold, O king,' said the astrologer, 'a proof that thy enemies are even now in the field. They must be advancing through yonder mountains by the pass of Lope. Would you produce panic and confusion among them, and cause them to abandon their enterprise and retreat without loss of life, strike these effigies with the butt end of this magic lance. But would you cause bloody feud and carnage among them, strike with the point.'

A livid streak passed across the face of Aben Habuz; he seized the mimic lance with trembling eagerness and tottered towards the table; his grey beard wagged with chuckling exaltation. 'Son of Abu Ayub,' exclaimed he, 'I think we will have a little blood!'

So saying he thrust the point of the magic lance into some of the pygmy effigies, and belaboured others with the butt end. The former fell, as dead, upon the board, and the rest turned upon each other and began, pell-mell, to fight.

It was with difficulty the astrologer could stay the hand of the monarch and prevent him from absolutely exterminating his foes. At length he prevailed upon him to leave the tower and to send out scouts to the mountains by the pass of Lope.

They returned with the news that a Christian army had advanced almost within sight of Granada, when dissension broke out among them. They had turned their weapons against each other and, after much slaughter, had retreated over the border.

Aben Habuz was transported with joy on thus proving the talisman. 'At length,' said he, 'I shall lead a life of tranquillity and have all my enemies in my power. O wise son of Abu Ayub, what can I bestow on thee in reward for such a blessing?'

'The wants of an old man and a philosopher, O king, are few and simple. Grant me but the means of fitting up my cave as a suitable hermitage and I am content.'

'How noble is the moderation of the truly wise!' exclaimed Aben Habuz, secretly pleased at the cheapness of the recompense. He summoned his treasurer and bade him dispense whatever sums might be required by Ibrahim to complete and furnish his hermitage.

The astrologer now gave orders to have various chambers hewn out of the solid rock, so as to form ranges of apartments connected with his astrological hall. These he caused to be furnished with luxurious ottomans and divans, and the walls to be hung with the richest silks of Damascus. 'I am an old man,' said he, 'and can no longer rest my bones on stone couches, and these damp walls require covering.'

He also had baths constructed and provided with all kinds of perfumery and aromatic oils, 'for a bath,' said he, 'is necessary to counteract the rigidity of age and to restore freshness and suppleness to the frame withered by study.'

He caused the apartments to be hung with innumerable silver and crystal lamps, which he filled with a fragrant oil prepared according to a receipt discovered by him in Egypt. This oil was perpetual in its nature and diffused a soft radiance. 'The light of the sun,' said he, 'is too garish and violent for the eyes of an old man, and the light of the lamp more congenial to the studies of a philosopher.'

The treasurer of the king groaned at the sums daily demanded to fit up this hermitage, and he carried his complaints to the king. The royal word, however, was given – Aben Habuz shrugged his shoulders. 'We must have patience,' he said. 'All things have an end, and so will the furnishing of this cavern.'

The king was right; the hermitage was at length completed and formed a sumptuous subterranean palace. 'I am now content,' said

Ibrahim Ebn Abu Ayub to the treasurer. 'I will shut myself up in my cell and devote my time to study. I desire nothing more – nothing – except a trifling solace to amuse me at the intervals of mental labour.'

'O wise Ibrahim, ask what thou wilt; I am bound to furnish all that is necessary for thy solitude.'

'I would fain have then a few dancing women,' said the philosopher.

'Dancing women!' echoed the treasurer with surprise.

'Dancing women,' replied the sage gravely. 'A few will suffice, for I am an old man and a philosopher, of simple habits and easily satisfied. Let them, however, be young and fair to look upon, for the sight of youth and beauty is refreshing to old age.'

While the philosophic Ibrahim passed his time thus sagely in his hermitage, the peaceable Aben Habuz carried on furious campaigns in effigy in his tower. It was a glorious thing for an old man like himself, of quiet habits, to have war made easy and to amuse himself in his chamber by brushing away whole armies like so many swarms of flies. For a time he rioted in the indulgence of his humours, and even taunted and insulted his neighbours to induce them to make incursions, but by degrees they grew wary from repeated disasters until no one ventured to invade his land. For many months the bronze horseman remained with his lance elevated in the air, and the old monarch began to repine at the want of his accustomed sport and to grow peevish at his monotonous tranquillity.

At length, one day the talisman veered suddenly round and made a dead point with his lance at the mountains of Guadix. Aben Habuz hastened to his tower, but the magic table in that direction remained quiet – not a single warrior was in motion. Perplexed, he sent forth a troop of horse to scour the mountains. They returned after three days' absence. Rodovan, the captain of the troop, addressed the king. 'We have searched every mountain pass,' he said, 'but not a helm nor spear was stirring. All that we found was a Spanish damsel of surpassing beauty, sleeping at noontide beside a fountain, whom we have brought away captive.'

'A damsel of surpassing beauty!' exclaimed Aben Habuz. 'Let her be conducted into my presence.'

'Pardon me, O king,' replied Rodovan, 'but our warfare at present is scanty and yields little harvest. I had hoped that this chance find would have been allowed for my services.'

'Chance find!' cried the king. 'What – a damsel of surpassing beauty! By the head of my father, it is a choice fruit of warfare, only to be gathered into royal keeping. Let the damsel be brought hither instantly.'

The beautiful damsel was accordingly conducted into his presence. She was arrayed in the Gothic style with all the luxury of ornament that prevailed among the Gothic Spaniards at the time of the Arabian conquest. Pearls of dazzling whiteness were entwined in her raven tresses, and jewels sparkled on her forehead, rivalling the lustre of her eyes. Around her neck was a golden chain, to which was suspended a silver lyre which hung at her side.

The flashes of her dark eyes were like sparks of fire on the withered breast of Aben Habuz, and set it in flame. 'Fairest of women,' cried he with rapture, 'who and what are thou?'

'The daughter of a Gothic prince who lately ruled over this land! The armies of my father have been destroyed as if by magic among these mountains. He has been driven into exile and his daughter is a slave.'

'Be comforted, beautiful princess! Thou art no longer a slave, but a sovereign. Turn thine eyes graciously upon Aben Habuz, and reign over him and his dominions.'

'Beware, O king,' whispered Ibrahim Ebn Abu Ayub. 'This may be some spirit conjured up by the magicians of the Goths and sent for thy undoing. Or it may be one of those northern sorceresses. Methinks I read witchcraft in her eye and sorcery in every movement. Let you beware – this must be the enemy pointed out by the talisman.'

'Son of Abu Ayub,' replied the king, 'you are a wise man and a conjuror, I grant, but you are little versed in the ways of women. In knowledge of them I will yield to no man, no, not to the wise Solomon himself, notwithstanding the number of his wives. As to this damsel, I see much comfort in her for my old days.'

'Hearken, O king,' said the astrologer, suddenly changing his tone, 'I have given thee many triumphs over thine enemies, and by means of my talisman, yet thou hast never given me share of the spoils. Grant me this one stray captive to solace me in my retirement, and I am content.'

'What!' cried Aben Habuz. 'More women! Hast thou not already dancing women to solace thee – what more wouldst thou desire?'

'Dancing women I have, but I have none that sing, and music is a balm to old age. This captive, I perceive, beareth a silver lyre and must be skilled in minstrelsy. Give her to me, I pray thee.'

The ire of the monarch was kindled; he loaded the philosopher with reproaches. The latter retired indignantly to his hermitage, but before he departed he again warned the monarch to beware of his beautiful captive. Where, in fact, is the old man who will listen to counsel? Aben Habuz had felt the full power of the witchery of the eye, and the more he gazed the more he was captivated.

He resigned himself to his passion. His only study was how to render himself amiable in the eyes of the Gothic beauty. He had not youth, it is true, but then he had riches. Granada was ransacked for the most precious merchandise of the East. Silks, jewels, precious gems and exquisite perfumes, all that Asia and Africa yielded of rich and rare, were lavished upon the princess. She received all as her due and regarded them with the indifference of one accustomed to magnificence. All kinds of spectacles and festivities were devised for her entertainment: minstrelsy, dancing, tournaments, bull-fights – Granada for a time was a scene of perpetual pageant. The Gothic princess seemed to take a delight in causing expense, as if she sought to drain the treasures of the monarch. There were no bounds to her extravagance. Yet, notwithstanding all this munificence, Aben Habuz could not flatter himself that he had made any impression on her heart. She never frowned on him, it is true, but she had a singular way of baffling his advances. Whenever he began to plead, she struck her silver lyre. There was a mystic charm in the sound; on hearing it, an irresistible drowsiness seized upon the king. He fell asleep! Still the dream of love had a bewitching power over him, and he continued to dream on, while all Granada scoffed at his infatuation and groaned at treasures lavished for a song.

At length a danger burst over the head of Aben Habuz against which the talisman gave no warning. A rebellion broke out in the very heart of his capital, headed by the bold Rodovan. The king was besieged in his palace, and only with the greatest difficulty did he quell the insurrection.

He now felt himself compelled once more to ask the assistance of the astrologer. 'O wise son of Abu Ayub,' he said, 'what thou hast foretold has come to pass. The Gothic princess has brought trouble and danger upon me.'

'Is the king disposed to put her away?'

'Sooner would I part with my kingdom!'

'What then is the need of me?'

'I would fain have one more exertion of thy magic art. Devise some means by which I may be secure from internal treason as well as outward war – some safe retreat, where I may take refuge and be at peace.'

The astrologer thought for a moment. 'Thou hast heard, no doubt, O king,' said he, 'of the palace and garden of Irem, whereof mention is made in the chapter of the Koran entitled "the dawn of day". '

'I have heard of that garden – marvellous things are related of it by pilgrims who visit Mecca, but I have thought them wild fables.'

'Listen, O king, and thou shalt know the mystery of that garden. In my younger days I was in Arabia the Happy, tending my father's camels. One of them strayed away and was lost. I searched for it for several days in the desert, until weary and faint, I laid myself down and slept under a palm tree. When I awoke, I found myself at the gate of a city. I entered and beheld noble streets and squares and market-places, but all were silent and without an inhabitant. I wandered on until I came to a sumptuous palace with a garden adorned with fountains and fishponds and groves and flowers and orchards laden with delicious fruit, but still no one was to be seen. Frightened at this loneliness, I hastened to depart, and after issuing forth at the gate of the city, I turned to look on the place, but it was no longer to be seen; nothing but the silent desert extended before my eyes.

'In the neighbourhood I met with an ancient dervish and told him what had befallen me. "This," he said, "is the far-famed garden of Irem, one of the wonders of the desert. It only appears at times to some wanderer like thyself, gladdening him with the sight of towers and palaces and garden walls overhung with richly laden fruit trees, and then vanishes, leaving nothing but a lonely desert. And this is the story of it. In old times, King Sheddad, the son of Ad, the great-grandson of Noah, founded here a splendid city. His heart was puffed up with pride and arrogance, and he determined to build a royal palace with gardens that should rival all that was related in the Koran of the celestial paradise. But the curse of heaven fell upon him for his presumption. He and his subjects were swept from the earth, and his splendid city and palace and garden were laid under a perpetual spell that hides them from human sight."

'This story, O king, and the wonders I had seen ever dwell in my mind, and in after-years when I had been in Egypt and made myself master of all kinds of magic spells, I determined to return and visit the garden of Irem. I did so, and found it revealed to my instructed sight. I took possession of the palace of Sheddad, and passed several days there. The genii who watch over the place were obedient to my magic power and revealed to me the spells by which the whole garden had been made invisible. Such spells, O king, are within the scope of my art. What sayest thou? Wouldst thou have a palace and garden like those of Irem, filled with all manner of delights, but hidden from the eyes of mortals?'

'O wise son of Abu Ayub,' exclaimed Aben Habuz, trembling with eagerness, 'make for me such a paradise and ask any reward, even to the half of my kingdom.'

'Alas,' replied the other, 'thou knowest that I am an old man and a philosopher and easily satisfied. All the reward I ask is the first beast of burden, with its load, that shall enter the magic portal of the palace.'

The monarch gladly agreed to so moderate a request, and the astrologer began his work. On the top of the hill above his cave he caused a great gateway to be built, opening through the centre of a strong tower. There was an outer porch with a lofty arch and within it a door secured by massive gates. On the keystone of the door the astrologer, with his own hand, wrought the figure of a huge key, and on the keystone of the outer arch he carved a gigantic hand. These were potent talismans, over which he repeated many sentences in an unknown tongue.

When this gateway was finished, he shut himself up for two days in his astrological hall, engaged in secret incantations; on the third he ascended the hill and passed the whole day on its top. At a late hour of the night he came down and presented himself to Aben Habuz. 'At length, O king,' said he, 'my labour is accomplished. On the summit of the hill stands one of the most delectable palaces that ever the head of man devised or the heart of man desired. It contains sumptuous halls and galleries, delicious gardens, cool fountains and fragrant baths; in a word, the whole mountain is converted into a paradise. Like the garden of Irem it is protected by a mighty charm, which hides it from the view and search of mortals, excepting such as possess the secret of its talismans.'

'Enough,' cried the king joyfully. 'Tomorrow morning, bright and early, we will ascend and take possession.' He hardly slept that night. Scarcely had the rays of the sun begun to shine, when he mounted his steed and with a few chosen attendants began to climb the steep and narrow road leading up the hill. Beside him, on a white palfrey, rode the Gothic princess, her dress sparkling with jewels and round her neck her silver lyre. The astrologer walked on the other side of the king, leaning on his staff.

Aben Habuz looked to see the towers of the promised palace and the terraces of its gardens, but as yet nothing was in sight. 'That is the mystery and safeguard of the place,' said the astrologer. 'Nothing can be discerned until you have passed the spell-bound gateway and been put in possession of the palace.'

As they approached the gateway, the astrologer paused and pointed out to the king the mystic hand and key carved on the door and the arch. 'These,' he said, 'are the talismans which guard the entrance to this paradise. Until yonder hand shall reach down and take that key, neither mortal power nor magic can prevail against the lord of this mountain.'

While the king was gazing with open mouth and silent wonder at these mystic things, the palfrey of the princess proceeded on and bore her in at the portal, to the very centre of the tower.

'Behold,' cried the astrologer, 'my promised reward! the first animal with its burden that should enter the magic gateway.'

Aben Habuz smiled at what he considered a pleasant joke of the ancient man, but when he found him to be in earnest, his grey beard trembled with indignation. 'Son of Abu Ayub,' said he sternly, 'what is this? Thou knowest the meaning of my promise, the first beast of burden, with its load, that should enter this gateway. Take the best mule in my stables, load it with the most precious things in my treasury, and it is thine. But dare not raise thy thoughts to her who is the delight of my heart.'

'What need I of wealth,' cried the astrologer scornfully. 'Have I not the book of knowledge of Solomon the Wise, and through it the command of the secret treasures of the earth? The princess is mine by right; thy royal word is pledged. I claim her as my own.'

The princess sat upon her palfrey, and a light smile of scorn curled her rosy mouth at this dispute. The wrath of the king got the better of his discretion. 'Base son of the desert!' he cried. 'Thou mayest be master of many arts, but know me for thy master – and presume not to juggle with thy king.'

'My master!' echoed the astrologer, 'my king! The monarch of a mole-hill to claim sway over him who possesses the talismans of Solomon! Farewell, Aben Habuz; reign over thy petty kingdom and revel in thy paradise of fools. For me, I will laugh at thee.'

So saying, he seized the bridle of the palfrey, smote the earth with his staff, and sank with the princess through the centre of the tower. The earth closed over them and no trace remained of the opening by which they had descended. The king was struck dumb with astonishment. Recovering himself, he ordered a thousand workmen to dig with pickaxe and spade into the ground. They digged and digged but in vain; the earth filled in again as fast as they threw it out. Aben Habuz went to the cavern at the foot of the hill, leading to the underground palace of the astrologer, but it was nowhere to be found. Where once had been its entrance was now solid rock. For with the disappearance of the astrologer, the benefit of his talismans ceased. The bronze horseman remained fixed with his face to the hill and his spear pointing to where Ibrahim had disappeared. From time to time the sound of music and the tones of a female voice could be faintly heard from within the hill, and a peasant once found a split in the rock into which he had crept and, looking down, had seen a great hall where the astrologer sat on a magnificent divan slumbering to the silver lyre of the princess.

But when Aben Habuz looked for the split, it was again closed. As to the summit of the mountain, the site of the promised palace and garden, it remained a naked waste. To add to his troubles, his neighbours, finding him no longer protected by the magic spell, attacked him from all sides. The remainder of his life was miserable.

At length he died and was buried. Ages have since rolled away. The Alhambra has been built on the mountain. The gateway still exists and now forms the grand entrance to the Alhambra. Under that gate, it is still said, the old astrologer sleeps in his magic hall, lulled by the silver lyre of the princess.

NOTES AND REFERENCES

I *Joseph and Potiphar's Wife*

1. Ebied, R. Y. and M. J. L. Young (Eds and Trans.), *The Story of Joseph in Arabic Verse*, The Leeds Arabic Manuscript 347, Leiden, Bull, 1975 (Leeds University Oriental Society Annual, Supplement 3), pp. 40 ff.

The Emperor's New Clothes

1. Abridged from Hans Christian Andersen
2. Juan Manuel, Don, *Count Lucanor (El Conde Lucanor)* or *The Fifty Pleasant Stories of Patronio*, London, Pickering and Chatto, 1888, pp. 53–57. Abridged

II *Solomon and the Queen of Sheba*

1. Watson, Paul F., 'The Queen of Sheba in Christian Tradition', in Pritchard, James B. (Ed.), *Solomon and Sheba*, London, Phaidon, 1974, p. 11
2. Fraser, J. G., *Folklore in the Old Testament*, Vol. 2, London, 1918, p. 558
3. Rodwell, J. M. (Trans.), *The Koran, Sura XXVII*, London, Dent, 1909
4. Basset, R., *Mille et un contes, récits et legendes arabes*, Vol. 1, Paris, 1924. Trans. by E.L.R.
5. Watt, W. M., 'The Queen of Sheba in Islamic Tradition', in Pritchard, *op. cit.*, p. 103
6. *Ibid.*, pp. 118 ff.
7. *Ibid.*, p. 115
8. Baring-Gould, Sabine, *Curious Myths of the Middle Ages*, London, Longmans, 1914, p. 384
9. Pritchard, *op. cit.*, pp. 136–38

She Floated Upstream

1. Many modern versions of this 'tale' are still going strong. The one here is from Vance Randolph, *Hot Springs and Hell*, Hatsboro, Pa., 1965, p.

22. It is Type 1365A, with many variants East and West. Our eastern version comes from T. F. Crane (Ed.), *The Exempla of Jacques de Vitry*, London, 1890, p. 225, in which Crane gives it as the oldest version. De Vitry was Bishop of Acre and thus had opportunity for direct contact with Arab culture, but in any case this anecdote was in the float of Near Eastern folklore, which formed the common store of western folklore as well. It was attached to the Hoja Nasr al-Din among others.

III   *Alexander the Great*

1.   Tubach, Frederic C., *Index Exemplorum,* FFC, no. 204 (1969)
2.   Campbell, Joseph, *Flight of the Wild Gander*, New York, 1969, p. 218
3.   Scott, Jonathan, *Tales, Anecdotes and Letters*, Shrewsbury, 1800, p. 329
4.   Cary, George, *The Medieval Alexander*, Cambridge, 1967, p. 120
5.   Wolohojian, Albert M., *The Romance of Alexander the Great by Pseudo-Callisthenes*, New York, Columbia University Press, pp. 23–57
6.   Ross, D. J. A., 'Alexander and the Faithless Lady: A Submarine Adventure', Inaugural lecture delivered at Birkbeck College, London, 7 November 1967
7.   Michael, Ian, *Alexander's Flying Machine*, University of Southampton, 1974, pp. 14–15
8.   *Ibid.*, p. 11
9.   Settis-Frugoni, Chiara, *Historia Alexandri Elevati per Griphos ad Aerem*, Roma, Istituto Storico Italiano per il Medio Evo, Studi Storici, fasc. 80–82, 1973, p. 331
10.   *Ibid.*
11.   Mittwoch, E., 'Dhulkarnain', in *Encyclopedia of Islam*, Vol 1, Leyden, 1913, p. 962

King John and the Abbot

1.   This folktale has been the subject of a classic study by Walter Anderson, 'Kaiser und Abt', FFC, no. 42 (1923). One of Anderson's references is to 'The King and the Potter' – here used, which is from Ibn 'Abd el-Hakem, *Futuh Misr* (mid-ninth century) translated by Charles C. Torrey in 'The Egyptian Prototype of King John and the Abbot', *Journal of the American Oriental Society*, Vol. 20 (1899) pp. 212–14. Torrey comments that the *Futuh Misr* deals not only with the Muslim conquest of Egypt and Africa; but also with the conquest of Spain, and that 'it may therefore be taken as certain that it was well known, and probably extensively circulated, among the Spanish Arabs from the ninth century on'. He concludes that 'The King and the Potter' thus became widely popular in Spain and, from Spain, in Europe. Anderson's analysis deals with almost 600 versions, of which 151, including this one, are literary. He agrees with Torrey

on a Near Eastern original, possibly in Egypt, which he dates at about the seventh century, and he traces its history in sixty-three stages. For a discussion of Anderson's study see Stith Thompson, *The Folktale*, New York, Dryden, 1946, pp. 162, 430 ff.

IV *'Antar and 'Abla*

1. Clouston, W. H., *Popular Tales and Fictions*, Vol. 1, New York, 1887, p. 50
2. As in the title of Metlitski, Dorothee, *The Matter of Araby in Medieval England*, New Haven, Conn., 1977
3. Heller, B., 'Sirat 'Antar' in *Encyclopedia of Islam*, Vol. 1, 1960, p. 521
4. *Ibid.*
5. Clouston, W. H., *Arabian Poetry for English Readers*, 1881, pp. 186 ff.
6. *Sketches and Eccentricities of Col. Davy Crockett*, New York, Harper, 1883, pp. 141–45
7. *Davy Crockett's Almanack*, Vol. 1, 1837, p. 40
8. Chadwick, H. M. and N. K., *The Growth of Literature*, Vol. 1, Cambridge, 1968, p. 1
9. Clouston, W. H., *op. cit., Arabian Poetry*, p. 445
10. Cited by Schwarzbaum, Haim, in 'Petrus Alfunsus' *Disciplina Clericalis'*, *Sefarad* (XXII), 1962, pp. 43–49
11. Boase, Roger, *The Origin and Meaning of Courtly Love*, University of Manchester, 1977. This book is invaluable in analysing, separating and evaluating different theories about courtly love. I am indebted to it here
12. *The Reader's Advisor*, Vol. 2, (12th ed.) New York, Bowker, 1977, p. 312

The Taming of the Shrew

1. Brunvand, Jan H., *The Study of American Folklore*, New York, Norton, 1968, p. 308. Collected in Bond, Kentucky, in 1959. Slightly abridged
2. Juan Manuel *op. cit.*, pp. 200–205. Abridged

V *The Disciplina Clericalis*

1. Bedier, Joseph, *Les Fabliaux*, Paris, 1925, ©1893, p. 84
2. Milas, J. M., cited in Gonzales Palencia, Angel (Ed.) *Disciplina Clericalis*, Madrid, 1948, pp. ix–x
3. Chauvin, Victor, *Bibliographie des Ouvrages Arabes . . . 1810—1885*, Vol. IX, Liège, 1905, p. 44
4. Gonzales Palencia, *op. cit.*, p. xxxiii
5. Schwarzbaum, Haim, 'International Folklore Motifs in Petrus Alfunsus' *Disciplina Clericalis'*, *Sefarad* (XXI), 1961, pp. 270 ff.
6. Jones, F. N., *Boccaccio and his Imitators*, Chicago, 1910, p. 10

7. Jones, J. R. and J. E. Keller, *The Scholar's Guide*, Toronto, Pontifical Institute of Mediaeval Studies, 1969, pp. 78–80
8. *Ibid.*, p. 100
9. 'Two Versions of a Hard-Luck Story', *North Carolina Folklore*, Vol. 2, 1954, pp. 16–17
10. Scott, *op. cit.*, pp. 341–44
11. Metlitski, *op. cit.*, p. 105
12. Jones and Keller, *op. cit.*, pp. 57–58
13. Artin Pacha, S. E. Y., *Contes populaires inédits de la vallée du Nil traduits de l'Arabe parlé*, Paris, 1895, pp. 195–200
14. Baring-Gould, *op. cit.*, pp. 140–44
15. Jones and Keller, *op. cit.*, pp. 64–66
16. Boccaccio, Giovanni, *The Decamerone*, trans. by John Payne, New York, 1931, pp. 333–35
17. Jones and Keller, *op.cit.*, pp. 61–63
18. Brewer, Derek (Ed.), *Medieval Comic Tales*, Cambridge, 1972, pp. 44–48
19. This Exemplum number (XXXV) follows Schwarzbaum, *op. cit.*
20. Gonzales Palencia, *op. cit.*, pp. 230–32. Trans. by George Cardona
21. Jones and Keller, *op. cit.*, pp. 60–61
22. *Ibid.*, pp. 89–90
23. Chauvin, *op. cit.*, Vol. 3, p. 78
24. Gonzales Palencia, *op. cit.*, p. 25
25. Harris, J. C., *Uncle Remus*, New York, 1924 © 1880, no. XVI, pp. 75–9

Get Up and Bar the Door

1. Child, Francis J., *English and Scottish Popular Ballads*, New York, 1965 © 1882–98), Vol. 5, no. 275. This version is quoted from Johnson's *Museum*, IV, 376 (1792), to which it was contributed by Robert Burns
2. Beloe, William, *Miscellanies*, Vol. 3 [Oriental Apologues], London, 1795, pp. 54–56. In the unpaged preface to this volume, Beloe says this story came from his friend Dr Russell who brought a small volume from Aleppo from which he recited: 'He finally translated them and I wrote them down.' Beloe believed that this story had never before appeared in any European language

Note

Paul Brewster sums up the history of The Silence Wager as follows: the ballad texts are all alike, consisting of the setting at night, the penalty to shut the door, the pact made, the wife mistreated and the threat to the husband, the husband the first to speak. Prose versions, on the other hand, vary. The oldest is found in the Chinese *Pai-yu ching (Book of the Hundred Apologues)* fifth century A.D.; in it the quarrel is over a third pancake.

Thieves take the couple's possessions and go to take the wife, at which point she calls her husband a fool and he wins the pancake. 'In sixteen of the eighteen prose tales summarized here, the woman is the first to speak.' Brewster also remarks that this story is found in ballad form only in the British Isles and only in folktale form elsewhere. (Paul G. Brewster, 'The Silence Wager in Ballad and Tale', *East and West* (1971), New Series 21, pp. 363–76.)

VI   The Arabian Nights

1.   Lane, E. W. (Trans.), *The Thousand and One Nights*, Vol. 1, London, Charles Knight, 1889; pp. 396–404
2.   La Fontaine, Jean de, *Fables*, Vol. 7, fable 7
3.   Baker, Franklin T. and H. H. Thorndike, *Everyday Classics*, New York, 1920, pp. 35–36
4.   Lane, *op. cit.*, Vol. 2, pp. 514–15
5.   Dorson, R. in *Journal of American Folklore*, Vol. 66, 1953, p. 464
6.   Payne, John (Trans.), *The Book of the Thousand Nights and One Night*, Vol. 3, London, 1882–84, p. 45
7.   London, Jack, *When God Laughs*, New York, 1911, pp. 93–128
8.   Woolf, Henry B., *Modern Language Notes*, Vol. 66, 1951, pp. 267–69
9.   Clouston, W. H., *Popular Tales and Fictions*, Vol. 2, New York, 1887, pp. 379 ff.
10.   Lane, *op. cit.*, Vol. 3, pp. 181–82
11.   Payne, *op. cit.*, Vol. 5, pp. 8–9
12.   *Frank C. Brown Collection of North Carolina Folklore*, Vol. 1, Durham N. C., Duke University, 1952, pp. 702–703
13.   Payne, *op. cit.*, Vol. 4, Night 390
14.   *Ibid.*, pp. 230–32
15.   Mardrus, J. C., *The Arabian Nights, The Book of the Thousand Nights and One Night*, trans. by Powys Mathers, London, Routledge & Kegan Paul, pp. 136–47
16.   Randolph, Vance, *Pissing in the Snow*, University of Illinois, 1976, pp. 23–24
17.   Burton, Richard, *Supplemental Nights*, Vol. 9, pp. 341–48
18.   Payne, *op. cit.*, Vol. 5, pp. 314–15
19.   Bedier, *op. cit.*, p. 183, in a note referring to Liebrecht, *Orient und Occident*, Vol. 3, p. 378
20.   Payne, *op. cit.*, Vol. 4, pp. 265–66
21.   *Ibid.*, Vol 5, pp. 263–65
22.   From Crane, Thomas F., *Italian Popular Tales*, Boston, 1885, pp. 159–60, where the source is given as Bernoni, Giuseppe, *Tradizioni Popu-lari Veneziana*, Venice, 1875–77, Part 1, p. 11
23.   Payne, *op. cit.*, Vol. 5, pp. 270–72
24.   Basset, *op. cit.*, Vol. 2, p. 143, trans. by E.L.R.

25. Burton, *op. cit.*, Vol. 1, pp. 222–25
26. Clouston, *op. cit.*, p. 54
27. Payne, *op. cit.*, Vol. 5, pp. 306–13
28. Burton, *op. cit.*, Vol. 5, pp. 253 ff.
29. Pearson, C. H., cited in Furnival, Frederick T., *The Wright's Chaste Wife*, London, E.E.T.S., 1865, (no. 12) front page
30. Randolph, *op. cit.*, p. 20
31. Child, *op. cit.*, Vol. 1, pp. 257 ff.
32. *Ibid.*, Vol. 5, p. 100 ff., no. 276

Beth Gelert or The Grave of the Greyhound

1. The story of this ballad is traditional in a village at the foot of Snowdon, where Llewelyn the Great had a house. The greyhound, named Gelert, was given him by his father-in-law, King John, in the year 1205, and the place to this day is called Beth-Gelert, or the grave of Gelert
2. From *Poems by the Late Hon. William Spencer*, London, 1835, pp. 150–55. I have left out six stanzas unnecessary to the action
3. Edgerton, Franklin (Trans.), *The Panchatantra*, New York and London, 1965, pp. 149–50

Note

The legend about the father, the infant, and the faithful dog slain in haste is found not only in Wales but also in almost every country in Europe. With a mongoose instead of a dog, it is equally widespread in the East because of its appearance in the *Panchatantra* – from which the eastern version used here is taken. In a process we have traced before in connection with other tales, the *Panchatantra* was translated into Arabic (indirectly, through the Pahlavi) and called *Kalila wa-Dimna*. From the extremely influential *Kalila wa-Dimna* this particular anecdote passed into the *Book of Sindibad* which, as we have also seen before, was carried *in toto* into the literature of Europe as *The Seven Sages of Rome*. Edgerton summarizes the history of our story: The mongoose, an animal unknown to Arabs, became first a weasel and then a dog, the snake remained a snake; but because dogs were associated with knights the original brahman or cleric became a noble. The Welsh version of *The Seven Sages* in *The Red Book of Hergest* which dates from the fourteenth century retains the snake, but the story separately became very popular in Welsh folklore, as distinct from literature, folklore which in the late Middle Ages presumably changed the snake into a wolf as a more likely object of a dog's attack. The association of the historic prince Llewelyn and an outstanding hound of his with the tradition of the murder of a faithful dog came as late as 1793–94 when a Welsh innkeeper confused the two legends. W. R. Spencer, whose poem made the Llewelyn version famous, is known to have visited the innkeeper prior to the publication of his work in 1800. (Edgerton, *op. cit.*, pp.18–19.)

However, independent origins of the two variants, the one of Llewelyn and the one in the *Panchatantra*, are also possible. The mistake made in haste could have occurred more than once. A document account in fact exists of a mongoose killed under the same circumstances in India in about 1920. (Emenau, M. B., 'A Classical Indian Folk-Tale as Reported Modern Event', *Proceedings of the American Philosophical Society*, Vol. 83 (1940), pp. 503–13.) More than that, the oldest written analogue of our story is not in the Sanskrit *Panchatantra* but in the Greek of Pausanias (second century, older by two or three centuries). In his book on Phocis, Pausanias tells of a father who suspected a plot against his infant son. He hid him in a vessel. A wolf tried to get at him, but a snake wound around the vessel frightened him off. The father, seeing the snake, threw his javelin at it and killed both the snake and his son. Shepherds then told him that the snake was the protector of the child. He had a funeral pyre burned for both, and the city Ophitea was named after the serpent. Kittredge, in 'Arthur and Gorlagon' *(Studies in Philology and Literature*, VIII, (1903, pp. 222 ff., 269 ff.), calls attention to Pausanias and quotes Hartland to the effect that at least one version of the tale was known in Europe 'independent of the literary current through which the apologue is generally traced'. Thus the Llewelyn variant may have developed from oral tradition based either on an actual incident involving an infant, a dog and a wolf, or on a folk legend stemming from or possibly anterior to Pausanias, rather than from the literary sources traceable via *Kalila wa-Dimna* to the *Panchatantra*.

VII   *The Arabian Astrologer*

1.   Cited in Gerhardt, Mia, *The Art of Story-Telling*, Leyden, Netherlands, 1963, p. 203
2.   Campbell, Joseph (Ed.), *The Portable Arabian Nights*, New York, Viking Press, 1952, pp. 322–54

TALE TYPE AND MOTIF INDEX [1]

This is a comprehensive list of types and motifs, not only those which occur in the text but also those merely referred to. In addition, starred entries show closely related but not identical material.

[1] In accordance with A. Aarne, S. Thompson, *The Types of the Folktale*, FFC no. 184 (1964), and S. Thompson, *Motif Index of Folk Literature*, Bloomington, Ind. 1966.

[2] I have added the decimal point 1 to the number for Bride Test: Thrift.

GENERAL INDEX

273